The Ethnic Revival

Themes in the Social Sciences

Editors: Jack Goody & Geoffrey Hawthorn

The aim of this series is to publish books which will focus on topics of general and interdisciplinary interest in the social sciences. They will be concerned with non-European cultures and with developing countries, as well as with industrial societies. The emphasis will be on comparative sociology and, initially, on sociological, anthropological and demographic topics. These books are intended for undergraduate teaching, but not as basic introductions to the subjects they cover. Authors have been asked to write on central aspects of current interest which have a wide appeal to teachers and research students, as well as to undergraduates.

Other books in the series

Edmund Leach: *Culture and Communication: The logic by which symbols are connected: an introduction to the use of structuralist analysis in social anthropology*

Anthony Heath: *Rational Choice and Social Exchange: A critique of exchange theory*

P. Abrams and A. McCulloch: *Communes, Sociology and Society*

Jack Goody: *The Domestication of the Savage Mind*

Jean-Louis Flandrin: *Families in Former Times: Kinship, household and sexuality*

John Dunn: *Western Political Theory in the Face of the Future*

David Thomas: *Naturalism and Social Science: A post-empiricist philosophy of social science*

Claude Meillassoux: *Maidens, Meal and Money: Capitalism and the domestic community*

David Lane: *Leninism: A sociological interpretation*

The Ethnic Revival

ANTHONY D. SMITH

Lecturer in Sociology
London School of Economics

CAMBRIDGE UNIVERSITY PRESS

Cambridge
London   New York   New Rochelle
Melbourne   Sydney

Published by the Press Syndicate of the University of Cambridge
The Pitt Building, Trumpington Street, Cambridge CB2 1RP
32 East 57th Street, New York, NY 10022, USA
296 Beaconsfield Parade, Middle Park, Melbourne 3206, Australia

First published 1981

Printed in the United States of America

British Library Cataloguing in Publication Data
Smith, Anthony D.
The ethnic revival. – (Themes in the social
sciences)
1. Nationalism   2. Ethnology
I. Title   II. Series
320.5′4   JC311   80-42149
ISBN 0 521 23267 8 hard covers
ISBN 0 521 29885 7 paperback

To My Mother

The reason for the Alsatians' not feeling themselves as belonging to the German nation has to be sought in their memories. Their political destiny has taken its course outside the German sphere for too long; for their heroes are the heroes of French history. If the custodian of the Colmar museum wants to show you which among his treasures he cherishes most, he takes you away from Grunewald's altar to a room filled with tricolors, *pompier,* and other helmets and souvenirs of a seemingly most insignificant nature; they are from a time that to him is a heroic age.

– Max Weber

Historicism led me out of the circle of individual problems to the broad avenue of social questions that are not as deep but are more immediate.

Every generation in Israel carries within itself the remnants of worlds created and destroyed during the course of the previous history of the Jewish people. The generation, in turn, builds and destroys worlds in its form and image, but in the long run continues to weave the thread that binds all the links of the nation into the chain of generations. The spirit of each generation turns about continually in its circuit and the spirit returns again to its circuit, the point of the nation's existence. The soul of each generation (a generation is for a nation what an individual is for society) emanates from the soul of the (collective) 'body' of all the preceding generations, and what endures, namely, the strength of the accumulated past, exceeds the wreckage, the strength of the changing present.

– Simon Dubnow

Contents

Contents

Preface

At the recent exhibition of Post-Impressionist art, held at the Royal Academy in London, a room was devoted to paintings, mainly by French artists, of life in Brittany at the end of the last century. Since the mid-nineteenth century, artists and writers had been attracted by the 'picturesque' quality of Breton life and landscape, especially the archaic customs, the religion and the distinctive costumes of the peasantry, and the harsh, primitive character of their labour. Gauguin was not untypical of this reaction, when he exclaimed: 'I love Brittany; I find there the savage, the primitive. When my clogs ring out on this granite soil, I hear the dull, muted, powerful tone which I seek in my painting.'* Others responded to Brittany's pagan, Celtic heritage, with its elements of mysticism and fatalism; or to what they saw as the 'simplicity of soul, the link with past ages, the sadness and the religiosity of the Breton people', which isolated them 'from the sounds of the profane world, from the life that belongs to Satan'. Perhaps most striking is the testimony of Emile Bernard, who admitted:

I returned a devout believer . . . Brittany has made a Catholic of me, capable of fighting for the Church. I was intoxicated by the incense, the organs, the prayers, the ancient stained glass windows, the hieratic tapestries, and I travelled back across the centuries, isolating myself increasingly from my contemporaries whose preoccupations with the modern industrial world inspired in me nothing but disgust. Bit by bit, I became a man of the Middle Ages, I had no love for anything save Brittany.

By no means all the artists or writers who made the Breton pilgrimage followed Bernard all the way back to traditional faith. Each of them found in Brittany what he sought, what answered to his particular needs. Yet all of them had this in common: they all turned their

* This, and the other quotations, are taken from the articles, and entries on particular artists, by Mary Anne Stevens and John House in the exhibition catalogue, entitled *Post-Impressionism*, Royal Academy of Arts, London, Weidenfeld and Nicolson, 1979–80.

backs on the materialism of city life, on technological advance and commercialism, and on the ever-increasing complexity of a central-ised, regulated state, and sought instead some antidote far from the capital, which might restore them to themselves and express con-cretely a more 'natural' and more 'spiritual' form of existence than that which they had abandoned. And here, in this twofold move-ment, at once rejection and quest, lies the mental spring of that eth-nic renaissance which we have been witnessing for the last two cen-turies and which has re-emerged once again in its European heartlands today.

This revival, like the twofold movement that underlies it, has been a highly self-conscious and much-discussed creative process. Unlike previous revivals, this modern renaissance of ethnic solidarity and sentiment has taken its cue from a highly charged romantic nation-alism which, though often aggressive and fanatical, has tried to channel the passions and claims it unleashed into the creation of a new global political order based upon the 'nation-state'. Ethnic na-tionalism has striven to turn the ethnic group into that more abstract and politicised category, the 'nation', and then to establish the latter as the sole criterion of statehood. Its lack of success to date in secur-ing such 'national congruence' has not deterred nationalists from pursuing their ideals or from spawning new separatist movements in every continent. Though it has many powerful opponents, the ideal of the nation has been generalised to encompass a vast number of ethnic communities, large and small, and now exerts considerable pressure upon the global system of states which has been con-structed with scant reference to the aspirations of ethnic communi-ties and ethnic nationalism.

Today, ethnic nationalism proposes a radical alternative legitima-tion and rationale for the world political system to the prevailing statist framework. This new ethnic legitimation has its disadvan-tages. Among the latter, we may count: the difficulty of providing a clearcut demarcation for the entity entitled to be called a 'nation' (though such vagueness may aid particular nationalist causes), the chronic problem of controlling nationalist passions and preventing them spilling over into aggressive acts which will undermine the hopes for an 'orderly' development of the world system, and the dan-gers of ethnic closure and exclusiveness both for individual citizens and for foreign immigrants, especially where the state becomes closely identified with a single ethnic community.

On the other hand, an ethnic rationale also possesses several ad-vantages over the present *étatiste* legitimations. They include: the generalising capacity of ethnic nationalism, its mobilising popular potential, and its identity functions. These factors are closely inter-related. The modern ethnic revival, unlike its predecessors, has largely forsaken traditional solipsist attitudes. Modern ethnic nation-alisms have had to ground their aspirations in an overall critical dis-course, appealing to general principles like popular sovereignty, in-alienable rights and cultural diversity. They have had to become reflexive and make use of universal notions of 'liberty', 'spirit', 'na-ture' and 'history', which are applicable to many ethnic communities and to different strata of the population. Hence, the 'multi-class', popular, appeal of ethnic nationalism, as each class and each stratum has moulded its general precepts to fit their needs and ideals. Yet, not only can it fire and mobilise all kinds of strata, it can also minister to the special identity needs of those groups which had become es-tranged from their communities, like the disillusioned intellectuals and artists in Brittany. The ethnic renaissance has the power to heal the rift in the alienated consciousness of marginalised men and women, and to draw from them its special ideological character.

That character and consciousness is an essential aspect of the 'eth-nic' dimension of modern social life. For it is exactly the conceptual forms and content of ethnic movements that are so problematic. Re-cent research on nationalism or 'ethnoregional' movements has tended to concentrate either on their ideological formulations, largely divorced from social conditions, or on those conditions and social background alone. There has been little attempt to provide a more unified picture, or to integrate the different kinds of analysis. But a sociological approach must treat both the ideological forms and the social conditions as equally problematic. Hence it becomes nec-essary to supplement recent analyses of the social background with an investigation of the conceptual forms and content of ethnic na-tionalisms. Only in this way can we grasp the special significance of ethnic meanings and ideals, which continue to act as ideological 'switchmen' of the ethnic revival.

What follows, then, is essentially a work of interpretation. I do not intend to add to the innumerable case studies of ethnic movements, whether of nineteenth-century European nationalisms, or twentieth-century 'Third World' separatisms or European 'neo-nationalisms'; nor to the more-or-less empirical surveys of recent ethnic national-isms. Instead, I hope to fill the lacuna left by the few existing theo-retical interpretations of the causes, origins and significance of eth-nic movements in the modern world, since their predominantly economic approach fails to do justice to some important dimensions of the ethnic renaissance.

I am encouraged in the belief that such a need exists for alternative interpretations by the parallel work of Professor Walker Connor, to whose original and perceptive articles I am much indebted, even on those occasions where our views diverge. I should also like to express my gratitude to Dr Maria Hirszowicz, Dr Nicos Mouzelis and Dr John Stone, for some helpful suggestions and stimulating discussions on questions of ethnicity and nationalism. I am also very grateful to the Cambridge University Press and to Susan Allen-Mills for approaching me to write on this subject and publishing the results. Naturally, responsibility for the views expressed here, as well as for any errors and omissions, rests with the author alone.

ANTHONY D. SMITH

London School of Economics
June 1980

Introduction

The dissolution of ethnicity. The transcendence of nationalism. The internationalisation of culture. These have been the dreams, and expectations, of liberals and rationalists in practically every country, and in practically every country they have been confounded and disappointed. Although in the latter half of the twentieth century the world has become more unified, and its states more interdependent, than at any previous period of history, the hopes of cosmopolitans everywhere seem farther than ever from being realised, and ethnic ties and national loyalties have become stronger and more deep-rooted than ever. Today, the cosmopolitan ideals are in decline and rationalist expectations have withered. Today, liberals and socialists alike must work for, and with, the nation-state and its increasingly ethnic culture, or remain voices in the wilderness.

How has this state of affairs come about, and why were the liberal hopes just so many delusions? For delusions they undoubtedly were, resting as they did on a systematic underestimation of one of the fundamental trends of the last two centuries. I have called this trend the 'ethnic revival', for reasons to be explained shortly; and my main purpose in this book is to analyse the social and cultural roots of its development, and to document its worldwide importance. Such an analysis will, I hope, also reveal the underlying reasons why liberals and rationalists have consistently failed to appreciate the significance of the ethnic revival; and why it is only in recent years that some scholarly circles have begun to attach the importance to the phenomena of ethnicity and nationalism which they so obviously deserve.

Unfortunately, some of the recent scholarly treatments which do accord a central role to the ethnic revival remain bound to some of the rationalist assumptions behind the liberal and socialist arguments, and this prevents them from presenting a full picture of this major historical trend in all its deeper ramifications. In order to gain a more rounded view, we must therefore recall the main lines and assumptions of the liberal argument.

1

Liberals have generally taken the view that, as mankind moved from a primitive, tribal stage of social organisation towards large-scale industrial societies, the various primordial ties of religion, language, ethnicity and race which divided it would gradually but inexorably lose their hold and disappear. The great forces of trade and industry would bind continents together and erase internal barriers and differences. Ancient customs and traditions would become obsolete, and the myths of common ancestry would be recognised for what they were and consigned to the museum of mankind's memory. True, large-scale industry would require an effective territorial base for its markets, and for a period the 'nation-state' might provide a suitable framework.[1] But, as industrial capitalism expanded its operations, the boundaries of the nation-state would impede further economic development, and it would be necessary to organise production and trade on a regional, continental and ultimately global scale. Technological advances, after all, know no barriers. Economic booms and recessions respect no frontiers. In an age of swift development, protectionist controls are an anachronism and impede the growth of global interdependence. So are frontier controls for the movement of labour. Men, after all, will go where economic prospects are brightest; and industry, in turn, requires a high level of geographical mobility and an increasing level of technical skills.[2] Thus the rational use of skilled labour, as of scarce raw materials and other resources, must render old cultural differences and political divisions increasingly irrelevant, or positively harmful. Besides, the vast expansion of communications across the planet, the growth of mass tourism, the exposure of huge publics to interlinked mass media, must erode all cultural barriers as they diminish cultural distances, and create in their place a single, standardised mass culture with perhaps even a global lingua franca in which to purvey that culture. In such a world, what room would be left for the ancient customs of a diminishing countryside, and for the ancient cultures of ethnic minorities? Would they not become, in Engels' graphic phrase, so many 'ethnographic monuments'?[3]

This, then, was the liberal reasoning, which foresaw the imminent dissolution of ethnicity. If we examine it closely, we see that it is based on three main propositions. The first is that industry and commerce would dominate the world economy, reducing agriculture and the peasantry to a residual role; and that an industrial society requires achievement and universalist values which are incompatible with the retention of ascriptive cultural and historic divisions and identities. A second proposition maintained that worldwide communications would inevitably bring about a cultural fusion, an intermingling of all that was best in the several national cultures, as travel and education broadened men's minds and caused them to reflect on the virtues to be found in lands and communities other than their own. Besides, the mass media would create a mass public, fed on the same diet of information and entertainment, and would help to convince humanity of its global interdependence and underlying unity of thought and emotion. Finally, liberal reasonings assumed the transitional character of nation-states and nationalism. They conceded, with Mill, the right of self-determination based on popular consent and mutual sympathies;[4] but they regarded such political decisions as a transitional phase, and a natural result of the expansion of industry and communications, which created problems of personal and collective adjustment, that in time would find a more rational global solution. Perhaps, too, early industrialisation and modernisation were unable to erode cultural cleavages, and might even sometimes exacerbate them at first. In the long run, however, free trade and industrial abundance would, along with enhanced communications, render such cleavages obsolete.

It is, of course, easy to criticise the naive optimism and confidence of the liberal assumptions. Clearly, none of them has stood up well to the facts of historical development in the last century or more. The very economic and industrial trends that they assumed would undermine tribalism and nationalism, have instead tended to reinforce ethnic and national divisions and loyalties. The creation of vast factories and plants, massive urbanisation and slum conditions, fierce competition for jobs and housing, the rise of mass literacy and the impact of radio and television, have all tended to bring new insecurities, anxieties and frustrations which unscrupulous demagogues could manipulate by appealing to the comforting warmth of old ethnic bonds. To be restored to one's cultural family, to be an equal in one's own closed circle, to receive the protection of one's brethren, seems the only sure route to sanity and dignity in the computer age. Communications, too, have only accentuated ethnic antagonisms, and heightened the visibility of national differences. Far from creating a single world culture, the mass media have been ready instruments of state authorities, who have used them to mould or instil a national culture in every citizen and every household. Industrial society has been able to accommodate ascriptive bonds, and in many cases to incorporate a large rural sector with its ancient village traditions and customs, even after capitalist farming has been introduced. Travel and education can just as easily bring home to men and women their cultural differences and reinforce their national loyalties as erase them; and, all too often, this is what has happened. So that, far from being merely transitional phenomena, the nation-state and nationalism have become more firmly entrenched within the world order, even in the most advanced industrial societies. Indeed, within Europe itself, in the industrial heartlands of the West, we are witnessing a resurgence of ethnic nationalism in the wake of an era of massive economic growth.[5]

So impressed, indeed, have many observers been by today's ethnic resurgence that a new orthodoxy may soon replace the outworn expectations of liberalism. It is now becoming fashionable to argue that industrial capitalism actually generates ethnic protest, and that modernisation endows ethnic bonds with a new political salience and importance. Ethnic movements, especially the post-War European ones, should be viewed as a product of economic development and capitalist industrial expansion, and not as some regrettable deviation or culture-lag of modernisation. Nationalism is therefore an inevitable concomitant of industrial development, and its uneven diffusion, even within Europe.[6]

The main difficulty with this critique of liberalism, as I shall endeavour to show at greater length later, is that it remains firmly within the orbit of the liberal assumptions. To be sure, it reverses the causal arguments; yet it ends up with much the same kind of conclusion, although for different reasons. That is to say, ethnicity and nationalism are still viewed as 'transitional' phenomena, although perhaps a little more durable now. They will pass away, when modernisation or industrialism or capitalist expansion has been completed, and when the ethnic regions and communities that have to date been neglected hinterlands or latecomers in the race of modernisation, catch up with the more modernised central areas. When that happens, even mass communications will reinforce the unity and equality of different regions within and between states; for communications *per se* merely amplify and accentuate existing trends.

While this kind of position undoubtedly represents a great advance upon previous liberal arguments, it too places a disproportionate weight upon economic and economically oriented factors, with the result that it presents a rather one-sided picture of the ethnic revival, and reduces its long-term significance. This is in line with the current fashion of presenting many cultural and political issues in economic terms, a fashion to which many current ethnic nationalists themselves subscribe. As a result of such economic preoccupations, other important factors – cultural, psychological above all, political factors – have received less attention than they merit.

It is no part of my intention to deny the short- and long-term importance of economic factors and technological developments. Nor do I exclude such factors from the analysis presented here, part of which turns upon the role of occupational mobility. But, if we are to grasp the long-term significance of the ethnic revival, and not reduce it to the limited issue of the current upsurge of ethnicity in the West, which has provoked so much comment, then we have to take a much broader historical perspective and shift our emphasis away from immediate technological or economic issues to a consideration of the slower rhythms of political formation and cultural change. My aim, therefore, is to redress the balance of scholarly argument, by presenting an alternative which, while it does not exclude economic factors, gives more weight than is customary to other kinds of development. Hence, no attempt will be made to present some sort of 'synthesis' of existing approaches, which would be premature in this field and in the present state of research. On the contrary, the present interpretation attempts to place political, social and cultural changes at the centre of analysis, and to treat economic developments, like the economic arguments that are so much in vogue, as catalysts, triggers, and contributory factors in the process of ethnic revival. Because ethnic nationalism is ultimately a cultural theory and an ethic of politics, a central role in any explanation of the ethnic revival must be accorded to the conjuncture of culture and politics; the parallel economic developments will then be found to reinforce political and cultural trends, or to act as catalysts in particular situations.

The critique of predominantly economistic definitions and explanations of the ethnic revival goes hand in hand with a rejection of the fashionable view of that revival as a phenomenon of the later twentieth century, particularly in the West. Again, I do not wish to deny the special character of the post-War resurgence of ethnicity in the West; indeed, I devote a chapter to considering the more specific factors involved in this recent renaissance. But I also claim that that resurgence is a special variant, and extension, of a much broader trend of ethnic revival, which began in the eighteenth century, and even earlier in Western Europe. It is this broader historical definition and perspective on the ethnic revival, which forces one to reexamine the close links which much current theory assumes to exist between industrialisation and ethnicity. For the modern ethnic revival – and there have been previous revivals in history – assumes special forms and demands a distinctive political ideology, that of nationalism; and these new factors, which differentiate the modern revival from every previous ethnic revival, call for a different kind of approach and explanation.

5

It is this broad socio-historical approach which dictates the structure of my argument. The latter falls into three parts. In the first part (Chapters 1 to 3), I examine the general evidence and isolate the main forms and antecedents of the modern ethnic revival; and then go on to assess the strengths and limitations of some recent economistic and culturalist theories of that revival. In the second part (Chapters 4 to 6), I set out an alternative interpretation based upon this broad socio-historical approach. Chapter 4 discusses the main features of ethnicity and ethnic community, and suggests some factors which may account for the persistence, with cyclical fluctuations, of ethnic ties and sentiments in the pre-modern era. In Chapter 5 I examine the cultural basis of the modern ethnic revival, notably the movement of 'historicism', which attracted so many secular intellectuals, and discuss some of the reasons for their rediscovery of ethnicity after 1750. Chapter 6 turns to consider the related problems of the professional intelligentsia, whose expansion and mobility the rise of bureaucratic states has both fostered and restricted. I also discuss some of the reasons for the radicalisation of the professional intelligentsia, and for their gravitation towards the ethnic historicism of the intellectuals, in coalition with other new strata. The third part (Chapters 7 to 9) applies this scheme, with necessary historical modifications, to three main types of ethnic revival in different continents. For example, Chapter 7 looks more closely at the role of the imposed post-colonial state in Africa and Asia, and its dependent position in the world economic and political order. My aim is to identify those features of the political situation which tend to promote ethnic separatism, and to assess the special role of the 'Third World' professional intelligentsia who generally assumes leadership of such movements. I also attempt to relate these more local developments to the geopolitical situation of the superpowers and their client-systems, which both encourage ethnic movements and curb their secessionist tendencies and impulses. The next chapter takes a brief look at the rather different 'communalist' movements in America, discussing the debates about ethnic pluralism and 'symbolic ethnicity' in the United States, and the special character of non-white, notably Black, ethnic movements. Chapter 9 examines some of the reasons for the recent wave of 'autonomy' movements in Canada and Europe, laying emphasis upon the contraction of opportunities for social mobility, especially among peripheral professional elites, following the massive shift in power, prestige and economic outlets away from Europe. This geopolitical situation is also related to the vastly increased interventionist powers of the scientific state, and to the influence of 'Third World' ideologies of liberation on western minorities who have become disenchanted with the class-based parties of liberal democracies.

By way of conclusion, the final chapter attempts to assess the long-term significance of the modern ethnic revival as a broad historical and sociological phenomenon; and to show how it is related to other major trends, notably the rise of the scientific state and the demands for greater mass participation. As I hope to show, the modern ethnic revival is unlike any previous revival. The modern revival is simultaneously an ethnic transformation, whose ideal, as yet largely unrealised, is the full and genuine nation-state. The distance between reality and ideal gives one some idea of the likely course and persistence of this ethnic revival and its national transformation.

ขʋ

An 'ethnic revival'?

What do we mean, when we speak of an 'ethnic revival' in the modern world? Are we justified in using such a term to refer to certain recent trends and phenomena? And, if so, what importance should we attach to such a revival?

In this chapter I want to argue that we are fully justified in isolating a broad historical trend in the modern era, and designating it as an 'ethnic revival', but that such a 'revival' of ethnicity is also a transformation, and that it possesses a unique character, shared by no previous ethnic revival. Ethnic communities and ethnic sentiments have existed throughout recorded history, and their social and political importance has been subject to periodic fluctuations. Hence the need to use the term 'revival' of the present fortunes of ethnicity. At the same time, I hope to show, through a discussion of the forms, scope, intensity and course of the present ethnic revival, that it possesses new dimensions and characteristics, which involve a degree of self-transformation. I shall return to this theme, and develop it, in the conclusion.

PLURALISM AND ETHNIC CONFLICT

Thirty years ago most people, if asked whether ethnicity was important any longer or whether they could discern an ethnic revival, would surely have responded negatively. Looking across the globe in the aftermath of a world stricken by two major wars, they would have felt justified in thinking that the fires of tribalism, nationalism and racism had been extinguished once and for all. In Europe itself there appeared to be few signs of ethnic protest; ethnic and nationalist movements, active during the War, were now quiescent; and ethnicity as such was hardly a factor in European politics. In America, though ethnic communities persisted, their hold appeared to be weakening; and even the smouldering racial divide seemed latent and inactive. In Asia and Africa, nationalist movements were indeed making their appearance; but they seemed to be grounded on the colonial state rather than on ethnic communities and divisions, with a few exceptions in Burma and Iraq. Even the so-called communal differences of southeast Asian colonies appeared to be held in check;[1] and in Latin America, hispanicisation seemed to turn ethnicity into a modern irrelevance.

Today, thirty years later, such optimism seems naive and myopic. Today, more and more people are realising that the world is 'plural'; that is to say, the so-called 'nation-state' is rarely a true appellation, for very few states have ethnically homogeneous populations. On the contrary: most of them are composed of two or more ethnic communities, jostling for influence and power, or living in uneasy harmony within the same state borders. Large and small states alike often possess sizeable minorities, and most states have small ethnic minorities. Take first of all the states with fairly large minorities. They include: Canada, the United States, Mexico, Brazil, Peru, Trinidad, Bolivia, Guyana, Paraguay, Ecuador; Britain, France, Belgium, Switzerland, Spain, Yugoslavia, Rumania, Czechoslovakia, the Soviet Union, Cyprus; Iraq, Israel, Jordan, Syria, Lebanon, Saudi Arabia, Egypt, Turkey and Iran; Pakistan, Afghanistan, India, Burma, Sri Lanka, China, Malaysia, Indonesia, Vietnam, Laos, the Philippines, Australia and New Zealand; and in Africa: Morocco, Algeria, the Sudan, Ethiopia, Kenya, Uganda, Tanzania, Zambia, Zimbabwe, South Africa, Namibia, Angola, the Congo, the Cameroons, Nigeria, Ghana, Ivory Coast, Sierra Leone, Senegal and many other new states. If we extend this list to include states which have small minorities – like the Frisians in Holland, the Tyrolese and Friulians in Italy,[2] the Lapps in Sweden, Karelians in Finland, the Gypsies, Armenians, Turks, Pomaks, Wallachians, Karakachani, Gagauzi and others in Bulgaria,[3] the Sorbs or Wends of Lusatia in Eastern Germany,[4] the Ainu of Japan, the hill peoples of northern Thailand,[5] the Saharauis of ex-Spanish Sahara incorporated in Morocco,[6] and the Amerindian minorities in Costa Rica, Honduras, Nicaragua, El Salvador and Belize[7] – few states today can claim to be 'pure' nations, with a completely homogeneous ethnic composition. Portugal, Greece, Iceland, Malta, West Germany (despite some few North Frisians), Norway and, with the exception of the Ainu, Japan, may be ethnically homogeneous; even Denmark has Eskimo and Faroese minorities, and Austria has its Slovenes. But, the fact is that very few of the world's states are ethnically homogeneous, and many of them are distinctly polyethnic in composition. According to Walker Connor, of 132 independent states in 1971, only 12 were ethnically homogeneous, representing 9.1% of the total, while another 25 (or 18.9%) have a single ethnic community comprising over 90% of the state's population. A further 25 have a single ethnic community comprising 75–90% of the population, and 31 have an ethnic community representing 50–74% of the state's population. On the other side, in 39 states (or 29.5%), the largest ethnic group comprised less than 50% of the population; while in 53 states (40.2%), the population is divided into more than five significant groups.[8]

Clearly, the very term 'nation-state' is a misnomer. Ethnic pluralism rather than ethnic homogeneity appears still to be the norm, despite the acceptance of the principle of self-determination. Most state structures to this day take little cognisance of ethnic aspirations, although some states have made provision for safeguarding the cultural rights of their ethnic minorities. In a few cases, like Yugoslavia, federalism is enshrined in the constitution, and in some others it is to all intents practised. But most states make little provision for ethnic rights, and are even less sympathetic to ethnic aspirations for greater autonomy.

Little wonder that many poly-ethnic states are bent upon rapid 'national' integration. In their desire for social integration, the leaders of these states generally employ policies of cultural assimilation. As we shall see, the new states of Africa and Asia are particularly anxious to counter the fragility and artificiality of state borders by integrating their culturally disparate populations. Haunted by a fear of 'balkanisation', African leaders are especially keen to counter 'tribalism' and ethnic movements by turning the members of often antipathetic ethnic communities into fraternal citizens of the new 'national' state.[9] Unfortunately, the very act of integrating such divided peoples may well exacerbate ethnic antagonisms and highlight ethnic solidarities, at least in the short run. In fact, the role of state homogenisation policies in reinforcing ethnic cleavage is not confined to 'Third World' countries. Its effects can be witnessed in the West and the East, even among the most liberal and 'consociational' systems. Pluralism and integration are woven together in a complex nexus, and provide the political basis for the increasing salience of ethnic cleavage today.

For the crucial fact is that interethnic conflict has become more intense and endemic in the twentieth century than at any time in history. Few countries have been able to avoid serious ethnic conflicts. There have been ethnic riots in Malaysia, chronic ethnic antagonism between Burmese, Karen, Shan and Kachin, conflict with the Chinese, Ambonese and Achinese in Indonesia, between Tamils and Sinhalese in Sri Lanka, a war against Huk and Moro guerillas in the Philippines, ethnonational conflict between Khmers and Vietnamese, Chinese conflict with Tibetans, Japanese hostility to Burakumin, and a whole series of ethnic and linguistic conflicts in India and Pakistan, involving Baluchis, Marathis, Bengalis, Andhrans and Pathan. Western Asia, too, has witnessed a considerable amount of ethnic conflict, notably with the Kurds in Iraq and Iran, the Turkmen in Iran, the Armenians in Turkey, the Assyrians in Iraq, the Maronite–Muslim civil war in Lebanon, the Palestinian conflict, the antagonism of Wahhabis and Hijazis in Saudi Arabia, the Dhofaris in Oman, not to mention the chronic Middle East conflict itself. In Africa, the best-known conflicts have been those between Ibo and Hausa in the Nigerian civil war, the Somali–Ethiopian conflict which has clear ethnic dimensions, the related Eritrean conflict, and the various wars in the Congo, which involved the Bakongo, Baluba, Lunda and other ethnic groups. But ethnic antagonisms have surfaced in other African states. They underlie the continuing conflict in Angola, they were prominent in southern Sudan, they have appeared in Ghana and Togo in the guise of Ewe irredentism, and they played a prominent role in Uganda, Zanzibar and, of course, South Africa. Most other African states, from Rwanda and Burundi to Senegal and Chad, have been threatened by ethnic conflict or ethnic rivalry. Nor have America and Europe been spared ethnic antagonism in recent years. The Quebecois in Canada, the Indians, Chicanos, Puerto Ricans and Blacks in the United States, the Indians in Mexico and Peru and Guyana; the Ulster conflict, the Scots and Welsh, Bretons and Corsicans, Basques and Catalans, Serbs and Croats, Flemings and Walloons, the Jurassiens in Switzerland, the Tatars, Lithuanians, Slovaks and Ukrainians, are only the best-known cases of ethnic rivalry and protest in the more industrialised north. There have also been persistent ethnonational rivalries, as between Greeks and Turks, especially in and over Cyprus, between Algerians and Moroccans, between Indians and Pakistanis, and between Bulgarians and Yugoslavs; and there are important ethnic dimensions in the rivalry between the great powers.

Along with ethnic rivalry and conflict, there has been a proliferation of ethnic movements of all kinds. Few states have been immune. Europe, especially, has witnessed a remarkable flowering of such movements. In addition to those mentioned above, there have been smaller movements on behalf of the Manx, Cornish, Faroese, Shetlanders, Channel Islanders, Occitanians, Alsatians, French Basques, Galicians, Andalusians, Frisians, Val d'Aostans, Sardinians, Sicilians, Tyrolese, Slovenes, Lapps, Estonians and Latvians, and the Canary Islanders.[10] Outside Europe, too, ethnic movements have arisen among smaller communities, as well as those listed above; they include the Azoreans, Anguillans, Bahamans, the Saharauis (Polisario), Berbers, Ovambo, Chagga, Konzo, Soli, Fang, Luba, Shona, Mandingo, Copts, Azeris, Sindhis, Naga, Mizo, Kazakhs, Tadjiks, Uzbeks, Yakuts, Mongols, the Chakma of Bangladesh, the Batak, Meos, Uigurs and many others.[11] Even in Latin America, the cult of *indianismo* and *sertanismo* has made itself felt among the Indian populations of the Andean republics, Mexico and Brazil.[12]

In every continent and practically every state, ethnicity has reappeared as a vital social and political force. The plural composition of most states; their policies of cultural integration; the increasing frequency and intensity of ethnic rivalries and conflicts; and the proliferation of ethnic movements; these are the main trends and phenomena which testify to the growing role of ethnicity in the modern world.

CULTURE COMMUNITIES

To what extent, however, can we designate the communities and movements enumerated above as specifically 'ethnic', and what do we mean by this term? An attempt to give a fuller definition of 'ethnicity' must be deferred until we have examined some of the recent approaches to the subject, and will therefore be considered in Chapter 4; and even then a precise definition must elude us, given the present stage of research and the protean nature of the subject-matter. Nevertheless, some attempt to delimit the field is a prerequisite of systematic study, and the following remarks are offered for that purpose.

Let us look, firstly, at the present spate of political separatisms. They can usefully be divided into two groups, territorial and ethnic. A territorial separatist movement is based mainly on political boundaries and geography. The populations of faraway or overseas territories acquire a sense of political community, which gradually marks them off as a separate unit, both from neighbours and from their 'mother-country'. Thus, the dominant immigrant groups of the thirteen colonies of North America shared their culture and social institutions with Britain; even on the eve of independence, it was not cultural difference that constituted the basis of their claim to autonomy, but geography and political remoteness from the centres of power, exacerbated of course by economic grievances.[13] Similarly, the creoles of the Latin American provinces of the Spanish and Portuguese empires shared their culture with their Iberian rulers; yet they increasingly identified with their local habitat and began to feel a 'Latin American' identity by the beginning of the nineteenth century. Geographical distance from Spain, a different landscape, new local institutions, perhaps the vestiges of pre-Columbian cultures, all contributed to the formation of a sense of political community apart from Spain and Portugal, and unique to themselves.[14] Australia, New Zealand, Canada, even Iceland, developed in similar ways. Such movements for independence as surfaced in these dependent territories were essentially based on geographical and political distance and on the gradual evolution of local institutions; even their divergent economic interests were the result of geographical distance, and of the long-run impossibility that 'men living thousands of miles across the oceans, preoccupied with other and more pressing issues, could take decisions on the colonists' behalf'.[15]

Ethnic separatism, in contrast, is based upon cultural differences and the sense of cultural distinctiveness. Ethnic movements make their claims in virtue of an alleged 'community of culture', in which the members are both united with each other by a shared culture and differentiated from others by the possession of that culture. They are, moreover, different not only from their rulers, but also from their neighbours in one or more significant cultural dimensions. It is in virtue of this real or alleged cultural individuality that ethnic movements claim a communal solidarity and the recognition of their political demands. In these cases, political separatism is based upon the ideology of cultural diversity and the ethic of cultural self-determination.

Ethnic separatism, then, is based upon the reality or myth of unique cultural ties, which serve to demarcate a population from neighbours and rulers; and, as a result, separation became not only an end in itself, but a means of protecting the cultural identity formed by those ties. The uniqueness of each ethnic community demands political separation, so that it can run its own affairs according to inner laws of the culture community, uncontaminated and unmolested by external influences. This was the basis of the claims of nineteenth-century Central and East European ethnic nationalisms. Poles, Hungarians, Czechs, Greeks, Bulgarians and Rumanians came to see themselves as distinct communities of culture with their own myths and customs, languages and institutions, even though they were incorporated into alien empires. Of course, there was also a territorial component in most of their claims; their memories included the reality of medieval or ancient civilisations and kingdoms, and their nationalism enthused over the beauty of their landscapes, its fine rivers, wild mountains, quaint villages and historic towns. Culture and terrain were inextricably linked; yet in these cases, ter-

13

ritory and geography fed the sense of unique culture and was an integral element in that culture, as was its art, music and literature.

This selfsame distinction between cultural and political–territorial bases can be applied to social groupings as well as to movements. Communities, too, can be divided into political and cultural units. The Roman or Habsburg empires belong to the former category, so did Switzerland and the United States until recently, perhaps. Canada, Australia, possibly Yugoslavia, are essentially political–territorial communities. They have not yet succeeded in evolving a common ethnic culture, although political community, as Weber stressed, can over many generations mould a common and unique culture.[16] That, indeed, is the aim of many nationalist leaders in the new 'state-nations' of Africa and Asia today.[17]

A good example of this gradual fusion of ethnicity and political community can be found in modern Switzerland. The four linguistic groups – German, French, Italian and Romansh – and two religious confessions have retained a measure of separate identity; and yet, time and again, it has been shown that in the last century (since the religious war) a Swiss sense of identity has prevailed over the cultural and political pull of its powerful neighbours.[18] All kinds of factors can be invoked to account for this phenomenon; the fact remains that Switzerland has succeeded in evolving a special 'political culture' which takes account of its cultural pluralism, and the ethnic origins of that pluralism, but which transcends it (even in the Jura) within a community that is simultaneously cultural and political.[19]

Switzerland may be one of a few exceptions. On the whole, as we saw, most states remain obstinately plural without much compensating cultural unity. Alternatively, a monoethnic state has been created, as in Portugal, Japan and Somalia – sometimes by force. The distinction between the political and the cultural community remains, until it is eradicated by nationalism, or transcended.

The notion of a community of culture, and of cultural ties, helps us to locate in a preliminary manner the nature and scope of the ethnic revival. Essentially, we are interested only in those trends and phenomena which reflect an increase in the power and hold of specific and unique cultures and cultural identities. In fact, most of the separatist and autonomy movements that have surfaced have based their claims upon real or alleged cultural uniqueness and hence on ethnic sentiments, even when they have also mobilised other interests and affinities. The field of the 'ethnic revival' is, therefore, vast in scope, and takes several forms. It is these forms to which we turn next.

MODERN ETHNIC STRATEGIES

In pre-modern times, ethnic or culture communities have oscillated between a position of isolation and a stance of political expansion and aggression. Post-exilic Jewry in antiquity, after the return from Babylon, is an example of the defensive isolationist stance; so were most smaller ethnic communities, like the Guti or Lullubi in the Zagros mountains.[20] The Persians provide a classic instance of the aggressive, expansionist posture. Fanning out from the Iranian plateau, they succeeded within a remarkably short space of time in wresting a whole empire for themselves and their Median kinsmen.[21] So, of course, did the ancient Egyptians under the New Kingdom, the Hittites and the Carthaginians; not to mention the Han Chinese and the Arabs.

In modern times, even the smallest ethnic communities have adopted an aggressive, if not always expansionist, posture. They have not been content with submissive isolation or accommodation. Fired by an ideology which puts a premium on cultural solidarity and autonomy, they have sought to ensure that their political demands are met by the state within which historical accident has incorporated them; or, failing that, to break away and set up their own state. Moreover, they have employed a range of strategies to achieve these ends, and it may be useful to enumerate them, in order to grasp some of the variety of what I have called the 'ethnic revival'.

Broadly speaking, six main strategies are open to ethnic communities incorporated in polyethnic states. They are:

1. *Isolation.* As I said, this was the most common strategy for smaller ethnic communities in the past. The ethnic community chooses to stay aloof from society as a whole, as with the Ottoman millets, the Chinese in pre-colonial southeast Asia, the Druze, Bedouin, Parsees, Armenians, as well as the more enforced cases of the Jews in medieval Europe and the Burakumin in medieval Japan.[22]

2. *Accommodation.* Here the ethnic community aims to adjust to its host society by encouraging its members to participate in the social and political life of that society and its state. Often, individual members try to assimilate to the host society, or at least become acculturated, for individual advancement. Many second-generation members of white ethnic communities in America chose this path. They forsook the purely defensive but collective orientation of their more isolated fathers, in order to break into the wider society, but on an individual basis. They refused to accept anything resembling a 'pariah' status, believing that western, particularly American, societies

15

were fluid and open enough to accommodate them, and allow them to ascend the ladder of wealth and influence. Generally speaking, however, such individuals remain linked to their community; they live in two worlds, albeit uneasily, in the public world of work and politics and the private world of family life and culture.[23]

3. *Communalism*. In some ways this is simply a more dynamic and active form of accommodation. Yet its basically collective focus marks it off from the previous strategy. Here the aim is communal control over communal affairs in those geographical areas where the ethnic community forms a demographic majority. Again, America furnishes a classic illustration. The demand has arisen, notably among Blacks, for a greater control by the ethnic community over specifically communal matters in the urban areas where it predominates. There is the further claim that the community be recognised as a political actor on the 'national' (i.e. state-wide) level.[24] So ethnic communities begin to act as pressure groups controlling an 'ethnic vote' and trading it for political concessions. Or, as in several sub-Saharan African states, a complex 'ethnic arithmetic' is involved in allocating posts and resources between the various communities, who press their claims in the rapidly expanding African cities.[25] Either way, the overall aim is to influence the direction of state policy towards the interests of the ethnic community.

4. *Autonomism*. There are, of course, various forms and degrees of autonomy, of which the two most important are cultural and political. Cultural autonomy implies full control by representatives of the ethnic community over every aspect of its cultural life, notably education, the press and mass media, and the courts. Political autonomy or 'home rule' extends this to cover every aspect of social, political and economic life, except for foreign affairs and defence. Ideally, autonomists demand a federal state structure, and this strategy is really only open to communities with a secure regional base, such as Scots, Bretons and Catalans possess. In other words, an autonomist movement aims to secure benefits from maintaining its links with the overall state structure, while asserting the political identity of the ethnic community which it represents. In practice, there are various degrees of autonomy open to given ethnic communities on the scale from minimum cultural rights to maximum 'home rule' federalism.

5. *Separatism*. This is the classic political goal of ethnonational self-determination, as sought by most of the East European communities in the last century, and by the Bengalis in Bangladesh, the Eritreans, Kurds, Ibo, as well as by the Scottish National Party and the Parti Quebecois. In each case, the aim is to secede and form one's own sovereign state, with little or no connection with former rulers. As

we shall see, outright separatism today is rare, and the aspiration for separation is mainly confined to Africa and Asia; yet it remains an option even in a Europe of regional *ethnie*.[26] There have also been a few variant examples of ethnic separatism, which can be classified as 'diaspora' movements. Here the aim is to reunite all ethnic members, scattered across the globe, in a single historic homeland, from which they have been partly or wholly expelled, or which their ancestors felt compelled to leave, usually for economic reasons. Armenians, Greeks, Jews, Chinese and the Black pan-African movement in the United States furnish examples.

6. *Irredentism.* Here, an ethnic community, whose members are divided and fragmented in separate states, seeks reunification and recovery of the 'lost' or 'unredeemed' territories occupied by its members. In general, this is only possible where the ethnic community has its membership living in adjoining states or areas; such was the case in the Balkans and Eastern Europe, where Bulgarians, Poles and Greeks sought to recover their lost territories and members. It can also be found today among the Somali, the Ewe, the Kurds, the Pathans, the Turkmen and the BaKongo. It is also not uncommon for an ethnic community to pursue a strategy of secession from the state where most of its members live, and then carry on to an irredentist strategy in order to complete its ethnic complement. A variant of irredentism is the 'pan' movement, where several culturally similar states seek to form a large super-state, as was sought by pan-Germanists, pan-Slavists and pan-Turkists, and perhaps today by pan-Arabists. On the whole, such a strategy has been unsuccessful.[27]

The general trend of the 'ethnic revival' has been to move away from the isolationist and accommodationist strategies to those of communalism, autonomism, separatism and irredentism. Defensive, solipsist stances have been exchanged for aggressive and activist postures. Purely self-centred, inward-looking and static conceptions of ethnic community have been replaced by a much more open, dynamic and pluralist self-image. Communities have bent their efforts towards the creation of new identities, which they have then sought to impose on the rest of the world. This has on occasion led to expansionist tendencies, not unlike those witnessed in antiquity, but on a much more self-conscious level and in pursuit of a clearcut ideological vision. In other cases, notably with smaller communities, the creation of new identities has brought a violent self-assertion in its train, especially when such efforts at self-discovery have been thwarted or denied. In either case, the conscious adoption of more assertive and activist strategies has mobilised populations, and contributed immeasurably to the overall ethnic revival.

17

THE IMPACT OF NATIONALISM

Perhaps the single most potent influence on the ethnic revival has been the birth and diffusion of nationalism.

As an ideological movement, nationalism seeks to attain and maintain the autonomy, unity and identity of a social group, some of whose members conceive it to constitute an actual or potential 'nation'. The aim of nationalism is always the creation of 'nations', or their maintenance and reinforcement. A 'nation' can be created in various ways and from a variety of bases and circumstances. The two commonest bases are a territorial state or political community, and a community of culture. In the first case, that of 'territorial' nationalism, the leaders of the political community or new state aim to create a culturally homogeneous population, with a sense of unique ethnic ties. This is generally a slow and uneven process, often called 'nation-building', and it relies heavily upon the coercive and administrative apparatus of the state. It was very much the way in which some of the old West European nations, Spain, England, France and Sweden were built up, although they also had the benefit of fairly large dominant ethnic communities at their core.[28] It is this model which leaders of several new states in Africa and Asia aspire to follow, though their ethnic divisions are often deeper.

The second case, that of 'ethnic' nationalism, relies first and foremost, on the existence of an identifiable community of culture. In these cases, the nationalists come to believe that their cultural communities are, or can become, nations; many, in fact, are so recognised by one and all, while others are treated as ethnic groups which may, or may not, be eligible for the status of nations. The adoption of communalist, autonomist, separatist and irredentist strategies by the leaders of ethnic communities represents the acceptance of nationalism's postulates in their own cases, and the attempt to fashion an appropriate nationalist strategy for their community's particular situation. Even the communalist strategy has clear nationalist overtones, since it is designed for fairly scattered communities without a strong regional base, and compensates for the lack of territorial cohesion of a group held to constitute a potential nation, as with the Blacks in the United States.[29]

The revival of ethnicity, therefore, is strongly bound up with the widespread acceptance of nationalist ideologies in the modern world, and with the rise of self-conscious nationalist movements. The principles of self-determination, popular sovereignty and cultural diversity which nationalism enshrines, lend movements on behalf of ethnic communities a self-confidence and legitimacy that was

absent in the case of previous ethnic revivals. Nationalism also endows the ethnic revival with a scope and intensity which have no
parallel in previous ages. True, the Greeks and Jews of antiquity
evinced a fervent sense of ethnicity and resisted invasion and tyranny with a passionate, if intermittent, sense of solidarity.[30] True,
the völkerwanderung of the 'dark ages' witnessed a strong, if unfo-
cussed and temporary, revival of ethnicity in Europe and the Mediterranean. Yet none of these was global, as is the modern revival;
and none showed any durability or had a lasting influence. Meteoric
or isolated, they were soon dissipated or submerged by alternative
principles of social and cultural organisation; and, even in the ancient Near East, ethnic community, though often vital, possessed little consistency as a political principle.

Modern nationalism, by contrast, has given the present ethnic revival its political consistency and staying-power. As a generalising
doctrine, applicable in principle to every collective claimant, nationalism undergirds a great variety of social movements on behalf of
forgotten or neglected groups, especially if they can convince themselves and others that they possess a common culture. Moreover, nationalist movements form a chain of examples and legends. Successful movements have a catalytic effect for others, near or far; the
success of small communities, in wresting and maintaining sovereignty, has effects out of all proportion to the immediate significance.

Nationalism has also extended the scope and intensity of the current ethnic revival in two other ways. In the first place, the doctrine
of popular sovereignty, once invoked, requires that every member of
the ethnic group be a citizen, with theoretically equal rights and duties. Peasants and workers must be taught that they are Indians, Tan-
zanians or Hungarians, if they do not know it. They must be per-
suaded that they have, indeed, a stake in 'their' fatherland. Artisans
and shopkeepers must be convinced of a 'national interest', for
which they should toil; and women must be exhorted to bear children for the nation's well-being and strength. All previously excluded strata must be mobilised for the nation, and be turned into
cohorts of active, industrious citizens. In this way, nationalism
binds together elites and masses in a single ethnic nation with a single legislative will.

In the second place, nationalism extends the scope of ethnic community from purely cultural and social to economic and political
spheres: from predominantly private to public sectors. To make any
real headway in the modern world, ethnic movements must stake
their claims in political and economic terms as well as cultural ones,

and evolve economic and political programmes. They must organise themselves in the political market-place, and demand political autonomy. Even dominant ethnic groups must turn a latent, private sense of ethnicity into a public, manifest one, if only to ensure the national loyalty of their members against the claims of other groups. Today, therefore, ethnicity is a 'total' phenomenon, covering all aspects of social life; and this is largely due to the impact of all-embracing nationalist ideologies and movements.

Nationalism has endowed ethnicity with a wholly new self-consciousness and legitimacy, as well as a fighting spirit and political direction. It is these qualities that have turned ethnicity into such a politically volatile issue in the modern world, and multiplied existing tendencies to conflict and war.

LOCATING THE MODERN ETHNIC REVIVAL

When did the modern revival of ethnicity commence, and where? Many observers would date its emergence to the late 1950s, the moment when Breton, Basque, Catalan and Quebecois movements first emerged. They would go on to argue that it was only in the mid-1960s that these movements began to attract mass support, and that other ethnic autonomist movements like the Scots, Welsh, Corsicans and Jurassiens gained a large following. Other observers have pointed to the events of 1968 in Paris and Prague as the catalyst which brought into being a host of smaller ethnic movements – Occitanians, Alsatians, Frisians, Manx, Cornish, Galicians, French Basques, Faroese and others.[31] And they also point to the restiveness of ethnic minorities in Eastern Europe and Russia, notably the Croats, Slovenes, Slovaks, Transylvanians, Tatars, Ukrainians and Lithuanians.[32] Even in the Third World, the rise of new states spurred a wave of ethnic unrest. In Africa, the Ewe, BaKongo, Somali, Lunda, Yoruba, Ibo, Baganda, Eritreans and Saharauis, and in Asia, the Kurds, Palestinians, Turkmen, Pathan, Baluchis, Mizos, Nagas, Moros, Ambonese, Shan and Karen, all staked their political claims for autonomy or separation during the 1950s and 1960s. Both within the West and outside, therefore, the 'ethnic revival' seems to have taken wing in the later 1950s, and to have grown in scope and strength until today.

This is a fairly commonplace view, yet a moment's reflection will show that it suffers from several defects. By and large, this account is parochial. Though it concedes the fact of ethnic unrest in Africa and Asia, it concentrates largely on the resurgence of ethnicity in the West; and this is largely because most observers have been surprised by the phenomenon. Having just surmounted what they took to be the worst excess of 'tribalism' in modern European history, they were aghast at the spectacle of its revival only ten or fifteen years after its apparent destruction in the bunker of Berlin. As we saw, they were also shocked to find that the liberal theory of modernisation failed to predict such a resurgence, and could not account for it. Hence, their understandable preoccupation with the European and Western segment of the global 'ethnic revival', to the relative neglect of other segments.

There is another, more positive, reason for this preoccupation with the western ethnic resurgence. It is only since the late 1950s or early 1960s that many ethnic movements have succeeded in galvanising wider strata and a 'mass' following, although one should add that many ethnic movements on behalf of small communities have been confined to a minority of activists and their sympathisers. (It is also difficult to gain a clear idea of the degree of support enjoyed by pre-War, or nineteenth-century, ethnic nationalisms.) [33] But, clearly, there has been a broadening of support for some of the larger movements, notably in Scotland, Brittany and Quebec, and a proliferation of ethnic organisations everywhere. As we shall see, this is not simply a function of increased populations or expanded communications networks, though both factors are important.

In other words, the resurgence of ethnicity in the West calls for a specific explanation over and above any general theory of the global ethnic revival in the modern era. Because the western ethnic movements show some distinctive features, and enjoy wider support, they deserve special attention; and so we shall be devoting Chapter 9 to western 'neo-nationalisms'.

On the other hand, I hope also to show that even this recent resurgence of ethnicity in the West owes a good deal to the example and influence of 'Third World' ethnic movements, as well as to earlier ethnic nationalism in Europe itself. The western resurgence of ethnicity is really only a continuation, in a special form, of an earlier tradition, and is best regarded as a variant of the wider and deeper ethnic revival. The most obvious aspect of this continuity lies in the antecedents of many current ethnic movements in the West. Most of them were founded, as specifically political movements, before the Second World War or even earlier. The Parti National Breton, for example, was created shortly after the First World War, along with an ethnic newspaper, *Breiz Atao* ('Brittany for ever'). Even before 1914, there had been a Breton political organisation, the Federation Regionaliste de Bretagne, with its paper, *Breiz Dishual* ('Free Brittany'); and that in turn was the successor of a more cultural organisation, the Union Regionaliste Bretonne, founded in 1898. In Wales, too, the Plaid Cymru party, founded in 1925, was preceded by a political organisation, Cymru Fydd, which was founded in 1886.[34] The Scottish National Party was, admittedly, a latecomer; it was founded in 1934 through an amalgamation of members of the Scottish Party with the National Party of Scotland, founded in 1928. But, as a political issue, Scottish nationalism reached farther back. The Young Scots Society was formed in 1900 on the following platform: 'To stir interest in progressive politics, to encourage the study of history, social and industrial science, to promote Liberal principles; to further the interests of Scotland and to secure for Scotland the right of self-government'.[35] Even earlier, a mainly Liberal organisation, the Scottish Home Rule Association, had been formed in 1886, preceded in 1853 by the shortlived National Association for the Vindication of Scottish Rights.[36] Catalan and Basque nationalism, too, can be traced back to the late nineteenth century. The Catalan Lliga Regionalista, which dominated Catalan politics until 1923 under Francesc Cambo, was founded in 1901; but the earliest Catalan political organisation, the Catalanist Congress, had been founded by Valenti Almirall in 1881, and the first Catalan daily newspaper, *El Diari Catala*, had appeared in the same year. The chief Basque party, the Partido Nacionalista Vasco, had also emerged in the 1890s, embodying the ideology of the founder of Basque nationalism, Sabino de Arana y Goiri.[37] As for the Corsicans, they could claim an even older political ancestry going back to Paoli's revolt of the 1750s against the Genoese and later the French.[38]

Outside Europe, too, several ethnic movements could claim an early-twentieth-century, or even nineteenth-century, political pedigree. In America, the Blacks had formed political organisations like Garvey's Universal Negro Improvement Association as far back as 1916, not to mention the first pan-African Congress of 1900.[39] Though the Kurdish revolt under Mustafa Barzani broke out in Iraq in 1961, it was really only heir to a long series of revolts in Turkey, Iraq and Iran, aiming to secure the autonomous Kurdistan envisaged in the still-born Treaty of Sevres of 1920. Moreover, Kurdish political activity had begun with the Young Turk revolt of 1908, with the first Kurdish political club and newspaper.[40] Bagandan ethnic movements in Uganda had emerged in the 1920s and 1930s, with the founding of the Bataka Party and the Sons of Kintu; while Kikuyu ethnic sentiment was crystallised in 1928, with the founding of the Kikuyu Central Association.[41] Similarly, Tatar resistance to Moscow dates back to the end of the Tsarist regime, with political organisations being established in Tatary and Central Asia after 1905.[42]

So far I have confined my remarks to strictly political organisations. If we include cultural societies and cultural activities, then the origins of the ethnic revival go back even further. In most cases, it can be shown that political organisations were preceded by, and grew out of, pre-existing cultural organisations, or were formed around journals and newspapers. The earliest manifestations of Welsh ethnic sentiment go back to the late eighteenth century, with the formation of literary societies after 1750, and the revival of the Eisteddfod in 1789 and the invention of the Gorsedd with its Druid ceremonies in 1792.[43] Breton cultural and linguistic movements appeared in the early nineteenth century; and the same was true in Catalonia, Flanders, Kurdistan, Armenia, the Ukraine, Tatary, and among the Arabs, Iranians and Jews, to name but a few examples. In some cases, there is quite a long gap between the first cultural manifestations of ethnic sentiment, and the emergence of political demands and organisations. In others, the two types of ethnic organisation and sentiment are almost contemporaneous, although in most cases cultural manifestations appear earlier than political ones. But, if we take the broad view, we find that the 'ethnic revival' as a whole is a far more durable and global phenomenon than many recent commentators would concede.

The truth is that this revival is closely bound up with the rise of nationalism, constituting the most numerous and significant branch of such nationalisms. As we saw, it was nationalism that energised and legitimated the discontents of ethnic communities, large and small. And nationalism itself, as an ideological movement, first emerged into political prominence in the late eighteenth century, or more precisely, at the beginning of the French Revolution. One can argue that ethnic sentiments had begun to crystallise earlier, that, in Holland and England, they came to the fore in the seventeenth century; and that the formation of 'national' states in Western Europe itself evoked an incipient national sentiment. There is, undoubtedly, much truth in this argument, although historians still debate the extent of such national sentiments in the early modern period.[44] The fact remains, however, that it was really only with the French Revolution that what was until then an isolated and reversible phenomenon came to be an almost irresistible and worldwide trend; and for the reason that we have given, namely, the impact and example of nationalism in one of the world's leading states. It was the French example that helped to spur ethnic nationalisms elsewhere, notably in the lands conquered by Napoleon; and it was the success of the French fusion of popular sovereignty, national unity and ethnic fraternity or identity that made it possible for other subordinated

23

communities to entertain similar aspirations. This is not to say that their ethnic revival is simply a matter of diffusion and imitation or reaction; the reasons for the ethnic revival all over the world lie deeper than any mere contemplation of nationalism's success, or a desire to imitate a new formula. On the other hand, the new doctrines of nationalism furnished a universal language in which to convey and legitimate ethnic aspirations, once they began to emerge; and their success in one area of the globe simply enhanced their appeal and potency in the eyes of new claimants.

We see, then, that the 'ethnic revival' is not only a global phenomenon, but a major trend stretching back, at least in Europe, for two centuries or more. It began in the late eighteenth century, erupted in the French Revolution, and spread quickly to Central and Eastern Europe. There, the doctrines of nationalism fired and sanctioned the budding ethnic sentiments and movements of Poles, Hungarians, Greeks, Serbs, Czechs, Italians and others. By the late nineteenth century, the Middle East had been caught up in this revival, with Armenians, Egyptians, Arabs, Kurds and others staking their ethnic claims. In India, too, a sense of Hindu ethnicity soon made itself felt; and, by the early twentieth century, ethnic communities in southeast Asia and even West Africa were giving political expression to their ethnic grievances. The recent manifestations of ethnic nationalism, both inside and outside Europe, are, therefore, really only further episodes in this overall historical trend, a new wave engulfing communities that were peripheral or only partly involved in the earlier phases of the same revival.

If this is the case, then it means that the ethnic revival is a far more durable and powerful phenomenon than is usually depicted; and that it draws on far deeper historical roots and sociological conditions than many would allow. To concentrate exclusively on the latest European phase of this trend is to miss this significance, and hence to overlook these deeper roots and conditions. It is also to miss the continuity with classic nineteenth-century nationalism.

For what we are really dealing with is the transformation of passive, often isolated and politically excluded communities into potential or actual 'nations', active, participant and self-conscious in their historic identities. The modern ethnic revival, unlike previous ones, involves the elevation of ethnicity into the corner-stone of social and political organisation, at least in theory. A whole new way of thinking and feeling is involved in this revival, which justifies us in looking upon it as a metamorphosis of social and cultural relations.

Hence, our task is a dual one: to analyse the causes of this modern ethnic revival, and to demonstrate throughout the novel elements in that revival, which justify us in regarding it simultaneously as a transformation. The particular theme of transformation will be taken up in the concluding chapter; for the present we shall concentrate on the aspect of revival, and try to establish a continuity with the pre-modern era. Herein lies perhaps the true significance of the ethnic revival; it is at one and the same time an attempt to preserve the past, and to transform it into something new, to create a new type upon ancient foundations, to create a new man and society through the revival of old identities and the preservation of the 'links in the chain' of generations.

2

Uneven development

The tendency to define and explain ethnic nationalism and the ethnic revival in preponderantly economic terms, has a long history. On the one side, it can be traced back to the fragmentary writings of Marx and Engels on the subjects of nations and classes; on the other, to a more recent 'industrialisation' theory which in turn harks back to its liberal laissez-faire economic origins, and its debate with later nineteenth-century protectionists. Of the two currents, the marxist has proved much more significant for recent economic theories of ethnic change; and hence requires some preliminary consideration.

The basic contention of the marxist position is the functional equivalence of nation and class in certain situations. Marx's theory of capitalist development posits the polarisation of class interests between the owners of the means of production and the exploited wage labourers, a polarisation which will produce a revolutionary struggle and the overthrow of the capitalist class. In various articles and pamphlets, Marx and Engels developed the idea that nations can be divided into 'progressive' and 'reactionary' forces, along the lines of their equivalent classes.[1] Germans, French, English, Poles and Hungarians were designated 'progressive', and, where they were being oppressed by 'reactionary' nations like the Russian, their national struggle was to be supported by communists in the same way that they were committed to the struggle of the proletariat against the bourgeoisie. Other nations were depicted as reactionary, either because they were feudal (or bourgeois) oppressors, like Russia or Ottoman Turkey, or because they were too small and backward to accommodate the economic forces of history, i.e. capitalism and socialism. This was the case with several of the small ethnic nations of Eastern Europe.[2]

In other words, ethnic nations were assimilated to the roles and positions of social classes; and their national discontents and demands for autonomy were treated as so many forms, disguises and masks for real material discontents and aspirations. However both Marx and Lenin recognised that, as an ideology, nationalism was capable of being utilised by self-interested strata, and that it was particularly well suited to the interests of the bourgeoisie, who could appeal to the ill-defined concept of a 'national interest' to contain and conceal horizontal class divisions. Indirectly, therefore, the early marxists did concede the force of national sentiments and ideals, while attempting to channel them to their own ends.[3]

There were two further aspects of the marxist legacy which are relevant today. The first is the essentially linguistic definition of the nation. For Marx and Engels, national boundaries are determined by 'language and sympathies', and Karl Kautsky felt that language was the most important component of nationality.[4] The second and more influential aspect concerns the impact of capitalism in the overseas colonies of the western powers. For Marx, capitalist expansion was both painful and beneficial; in a country like India the British were eroding traditional, feudal structures through the introduction of capitalist exploitation, and this was inevitable.[5] Hence, colonialism was a necessary stage in the global generalisation of capitalism; it was a necessary, if brutal, instrument of dialectical historical forces, part and parcel of the cunning of reason, which liberates mankind by intensifying his alienation. In line with this view, Lenin affirmed that, brutal and exploitative though it may be, imperialism, as the 'highest stage' of capitalism, unites the world and breaks the power of feudal structures and bonds, thus paving the way for the inevitable proletarian revolution of the exploited masses.[6]

REGIONAL DEPRIVATION

To this marxist legacy, recent economic theories of ethnic change have added two other elements. The first is the economic role of intrastate regions. Typically, that role is viewed as dependent, even parasitic, and the region itself backward and lagging behind the rest of the economy on all indicators. This concern with regions is, of course, partly a product of ethnic protests themselves, but it is also a reaction to overcentralisation of political control over the economy. The ethnic nationalists themselves make much of this argument, claiming that many of their community's economic ills are the product of this centralised control. But even spokesmen of the dominant elites, untouched by nationalism, are well aware of the economic disparities between geographical areas within their states, and of the disadvantages of excessive centralisation. In their desire for 'devolution', the 'region' has emerged as the natural unit for the exercise of a genuine, if circumscribed, 'rational' authority.[7]

The second element, which appears in only shadowy fashion in

Marx, is a shift from absolute to relative deprivation. The basic idea here is that social groups, and their members, only compare their position and fate with a limited range of other groups or individuals, usually those a little higher in the social scale. Although the position, material and social, of the group may have (or be) improved in absolute terms, what matters for their perceptions and action is their progress relative to that of other similar groups. Social movements and political action are the outcome of perceived frustrations on the part of individuals or groups, who feel disadvantaged and deprived relative to others and handicapped in the race for wealth, status, services and power.[8]

According to this perspective, ethnic protest and ethnic nationalism are the outcome of regional relative deprivations. Since ethnic communities are generally located within specific regions, and the latter are typically backward, with growth rates lower than those of their neighbours or of the core area, it is small wonder that regional ethnic groups become discontented and frustrated, and turn to political movements which promise a reversal of their situation. It is hardly surprising if they come to share the view of the nationalists who argue for a total break with a political system which is responsible for their economic and social plight. In other words, the perception of a situation of relative backwardness on the part of the inhabitants of the affected region will bring about ethnic protest and ethnic movements for separation. Like the deprived lower classes of marxist theory, ethnic regions seek to redress their disadvantaged situation through political movements and revolutionary action.

This approach has much to commend it, but it is clearly inadequate as an explanation of the ethnic revival. The theory sounds plausible, but its central concept is ambiguous in nature and effects. There are, first, several kinds of relative deprivation: economic (wealth, income, employment), services (health, education, housing, amenities), political and social (mainly status concerns). It is by no means clear that the peoples of a region suffer from all these kinds of deprivation, or that their effect on political behaviour is uniform. Indeed, existing data suggest that political and status deprivations are more closely related to political action than economic or services wants. Nationalists may nowadays frame their appeals in economic terms; but the core of that appeal remains psychological and political rather than economic. If anything, economic arguments tend to run counter to nationalism's political appeal.[9]

Moreover, there is a fairly large gap between a sense of being deprived relative to others, and engaging in political action to rectify the situation. Not only do we have to presuppose a political climate and regime which tolerates protest action, which would tend to limit the theory's applicability largely to the West; we must also assume that those who feel deprived share a common perception that there is a single cause of their plight, and that they possess the organisational means to overcome it. This in turn presupposes the existence of a social movement which can coordinate and organise their efforts effectively, and of a body of convinced nationalists with a well-thought-out ideology. Clearly, the notion of relative deprivation, even when it is properly specified, can never provide a full explanation of ethnic nationalism or the ethnic revival, but can only function as a partial mechanism within a broader perspective.

Empirical data would appear to confirm this view. We would expect, on this theory, to find ethnic movements only in relatively backward peripheral regions. But this is not the case. In Spain, the Basque provinces and Catalonia have enjoyed greater economic prosperity and higher living standards than the core areas, Castile and Aragon. Speaking of Catalonia, Stanley Payne says: 'The region dominated Spain's domestic and international trade and was the main focus of industrial development, in this respect being rivalled only by the growth of heavy industry in the Basque country and Asturias.'[10] Both the Basque and the Catalan economies were protected by the Spanish tariff and some regional tax privileges, and Basque economic elites had close links with Madrid and were readier to adapt to large-scale industrial capitalism.[11] Yet, despite their economic progress relative to the backward core areas, both Catalonia and the Basque country have witnessed strong ethnic movements since the end of the last century, and have retained a widespread sense of cultural distinctiveness.

In Yugoslavia, too, regional economic disparities do not follow the predictions of relative deprivation theory, at least in its economic forms. Thus Slovenia and Croatia enjoy higher living standards than a preponderantly agricultural, and rather backward, Serb core area. And yet, Slovene and especially Croat discontent and desire for greater autonomy, even in federal Yugoslavia, remain powerful political forces.[12] Ethnic groups in economically advantaged regions, like the Lunda in Shaba province (former Katanga), are just as susceptible to violent ethnic protest movements as those which inhabit backward areas, like Ireland in the last century.[13]

'INTERNAL COLONIALISM'

Similar theoretical and empirical problems beset a popular recent variant of relative deprivation theory, namely, the model of an 'internal colonialism'. This model derives in part from the studies made by Andre Gunder Frank and his followers of the unequal relationship between the economies of Latin America and the West. The former are characterised as 'peripheral' and 'structurally underdeveloped'; and their stagnant, dependent character is attributed to the exploitative needs of the metropolitan western economies, whose dynamic expansion was fed by the extracted resources and exploited labour of the peripheral territories.[14] Thus western capitalist development, so explosive and all-embracing since the sixteenth century, has been achieved at the cost of the necessary and permanent 'underdevelopment' (rather than un-development) of the Latin American (and other) colonies.[15]

The notion of 'peripheral regions' characterised by a stagnant, dependent economy has obvious attractions for economic theories of ethnic change. As we saw, most ethnic groups are concentrated in particular regions within the state's territory, and their situation is therefore inextricably bound up with the economic progress, or otherwise, of their region. This means, of course, that disparities between regions must be reflected in inequalities between the ethnic groups in a plural state; and this fact is independent of any overt discrimination that may be practised by the dominant ethnic group, or its elites, towards minorities within that state.

From this standpoint, it is but a small step to treating these ethnic regions as so many 'internal colonies' of the metropolitan 'nation-state', a charge, incidentally, which a good many ethnic nationalisms are now making against their rulers. In its more scholarly formulation, the thesis holds that the major western states annexed, not only overseas colonies, but also 'internal' ones within their heartlands, in their search for larger markets and cheaper labour. The chief proponent of this view is Michael Hechter, whose thorough historical study of British national development sets out to explain the background to the emergence of Irish, Scottish and Welsh nationalism today. Hechter claims that overseas colonial development 'produces a cultural division of labour: a system of stratification where objective cultural distinctions are superimposed upon class lines. High status occupations tend to be reserved for those of metropolitan culture; while those of indigenous culture cluster at the bottom of the stratification system'.[16] He goes on to characterise some of the consequences of the territorial expansion of Western European states within Europe, the quest for what Fernand Braudel called 'internal Americas', in terms very similar to descriptions of overseas colonialism, notably by Georges Balandier.[17] Thus:

Commerce and trade among members of the periphery tend to be monopolised by members of the core. Credit is similarly monopolised. When commercial prospects emerge, bankers, managers, and entrepreneurs tend to be
recruited from the core. The peripheral economy is forced into complemen-
tary development to the core, and thus becomes dependent on external markets. Generally, this economy rests on a single primary export, either agricultural or mineral. The movement of peripheral labour is determined largely
by forces exogenous to the periphery. Typically there is great migration and
mobility of peripheral workers in response to price fluctuations of exported
primary products. Economic dependency is reinforced through juridical, political, and military measures. There is a relative lack of services, lower
standard of living and higher level of frustration, measured by such indicators as alcoholism, among members of the peripheral group. There is national
discrimination on the basis of language, religion or other cultural forms.
Thus the aggregate economic differences between core and periphery are
causally linked to their cultural differences.[18]

Hechter claims, further, that if core groups did not permit the acculturation of peripheral ones in the past, then 'at a later time' the
peripheral group may come to desire independence from a situation
'increasingly regarded as oppressive', and that this accounts for current nationalistic cultural 'rebirths'. 'It is not that these groups actually uncover evidence of their ancient cultural past as an independent people; most often such culture is created contemporaneously
to legitimate demands for the present-day goal of independence, or
the achievement of economic equality.'[19] Because the 'uneven wave
of industrialisation over territorial space' creates relatively advanced
and less advanced groups, with different interests, the more advanced 'core' groups try to maintain the inequitable distribution of
wealth and power, by allocating high status roles solely to members
of their own group, thus creating a 'cultural division of labour' in
which individuals are assigned to social roles 'on the basis of objective cultural distinctions'.[20]

This is what, according to Hechter, has happened in the British
Isles since the sixteenth century. British state unification, and British
capitalism, have turned the peripheral regions of Ireland, Wales and
Scotland into 'internal colonies', with dependent, stagnant economies and a cultural division of labour which assigned low-status
roles in the hierarchy to Irish, Welsh and Scots. Industrialisation, by
increasing economic and cultural contact, has only accentuated this
dependence; it has ensured the persistence of cultural inequalities,
or 'peripheral sectionalism'. But there have been differences between
Ireland, and Scotland and Wales, during the last century. Ireland has

a rather small industrial enclave, concentrated largely in the north, which therefore did not impede her cultural unity nor mute her ethnic nationalism. In early-twentieth-century Scotland and Wales, however, industrialism was more pronounced and tended to split these regions into dynamic industrial areas and agricultural hinterlands, and therefore 'interfered with the development of a single regional political identity in Wales and Scotland'.[21] Nevertheless, both Wales and Scotland suffered economic stagnation, which sapped people's faith in the all-British class-based parties, so that today 'Nationalism has re-emerged in the Celtic periphery largely as a reaction to this failure of regional development.'[22] Ethnic nationalism in Ireland, Wales and Scotland is really a reaction to an exploitative industrialism and its associated hierarchical cultural division of labour; and, since the bureaucratic state is responsible for this failure of regional development and this hierarchy, 'The most recent crystallisation of Celtic nationalism may ultimately be understood as a trenchant critique of the principle of bureaucratic centralism.'[23]

This is a persuasive argument. It clearly grasps the plural nature of most modern states and their origins in conquest of neighbouring areas. It also graphically portrays the neglect, and often outright exploitation, of several of these outlying areas for the benefit of central elites and it illuminates the many ways in which political domination has utilised economic policy to perpetuate the subordination and sometimes impoverishment of peripheral populations.

Yet, as a general model of economic control designed to explain ethnoregional movements, and the ethnic revival as a whole, the thesis of 'internal colonialism' presents several problems. Theoretically, there is the difficulty, which Hechter recognises, of specifying the number and degree of variables of dependence which must be present, in order to designate a particular area an 'internal colony'.[24] Must the region suffer from a 'relative lack of services' and depend on a single primary resource, agricultural or mineral? If so, a 'region' like Scotland hardly fits the model on either count; and Hechter has recently recognised the need to amend the model to take account of an alternative mode of cultural division of labour, namely the *segmental* type, in which 'members interact wholly within the boundaries of their own group', and as a result 'group members monopolise certain niches in the occupational structure'.[25] It is in regions, like Scotland, with 'considerable institutional autonomy', that the prospects for 'interactive ethnic group formation are maximised'. Hence, for Hechter, Scotland is not to be viewed as a proletarian nation, as Hobsbawm has contended; though both would agree that exploitation of that region has been minimal.[26]

32

The introduction of this alternative cultural division of labour undoubtedly marks an advance on the earlier monolithic model; yet it fails to explain the case of Catalonia and the Basque country, which is deemed to result from the 'peculiar character of Spanish national development', or for that matter the instances of Croatia and Slovenia. Moreover, it suggests that the cultural division of labour can be analytically separated from the 'core-periphery' spatial relationships postulated by Hechter's model; and this has important consequences, because it opens up the possibility of analysing the effects of a cultural division of labour *within* regions such as Quebec or Wales, divisions which may be as important in fanning separatist sentiment as any purely economic and spatial relationships *between* different regions.[27]

Even with this important amendment, certain problems remain. There is, first, the problem of timing. The model of internal colonialism, at least in the British case, spanned four centuries, yet it is really only toward the end of the last century that Celtic nationalism assumed political form, and only after the Second World War that it became a popular movement. But, even if we take industrialisation as the efficient cause, why did Welsh and Scottish nationalism gain wide political support in the 1960s, and not before or after the First World War? In his earlier explanation, Hechter utilised a theory of relative deprivation to bridge this gap; but, as we saw, the latter is ambiguous, and more recently Hechter has singled out state policies as the basic determinant of the *timing* of separatism, thus modifying the economic thesis in favour of political factors.[28]

Second, the model of an 'internal colonialism' is necessarily of limited applicability. Its focus is on ethnic regions in 'metropolitan' states, that is, those which constitute the core of modern industrial capitalism. Accordingly, it possesses little relevance for most non-western areas, where, despite some western commercial penetration, there was little capitalism or industry at the moment when ethnic nationalism emerged. In the Middle East or Africa, for example, nationalism made its appearance in the late nineteenth and early twentieth centuries, at a time when western capitalist industrialism had had little chance to turn these regions into economic colonies or enforce a cultural division of labour, with a few exceptions; and similarly in southeast Asia, with the partial exception of India. Moreover, in some regions there was rapid economic development and educational expansion – the Ibo, Baganda and Karen are examples – yet, in these regions, ethnic nationalism emerged as forcibly as in more depressed and backward areas.

Finally, it is not at all clear why, according to the model of 'internal colonialism', social discontent in depressed and dependent regions need assume ethnic form and content. If the original thesis is valid, it ought also to hold for depressed regions in ethnically homogeneous states, like the northeast of England, or, for ethnically heterogeneous and backward regions within a plural state, like the south of Italy. But, in neither case, has there been much sign of *ethnic* protest, or separatism (with the possible exception of Sicily), despite enduring social and economic discontent. The latter, in fact, is either channelled into the state-wide political parties, or erupts sporadically in marches and street violence. Only where a region (backward or not) is populated mainly by a distinctive ethnic community, does the discontent take the form of a movement for political autonomy.[29]

In other words, economic development appears to cut across ethnic boundaries, while the ethnic factor operates, in many cases, independently of economic differentials. Till recently, it had been assumed that economic progress would diminish ethnic antagonisms and bring about cultural assimilation; yet, as the experience of Turkic-speaking Muslim peoples – Tatars, Uzbeks and Tadjiks – in the Soviet Union suggests, rapid economic progress does not diminish ethnic aspirations, and, similarly, ethnic communities like the Catalans, Croats and Slovenes which have enjoyed higher living standards than their neighbours have not abated their ethnic demands. In all these cases, peripheral identities have been reinforced by real economic progress or, for that matter, by a more-or-less stable difference in economic position between an advantaged peripheral community and a poorer core. In yet other cases, as Hechter and others vividly demonstrate, economic decline has exacerbated ethnic differences and fuelled ethnonational demands.

Perhaps, then, it is not the fact of economic progress or decline that is relevant for the ethnic revival, but simply economic change *per se*. Most change, today, is painful and uprooting. Given the growing interdependence of economies all over the world, we should expect ethnic groups to feel the effects of international economic changes and fluctuations. And yet, the fact is that for many such groups, the economic position is fairly stagnant. Such ethnic communities as the Naga and Mizo, the Ewe and BaKongo, the Shan and Pathans, all of which are demanding greater political autonomy, have experienced no major economic change in the last few decades, beyond a very partial influence of the western commercial system. Their economic standing relative to other neighbouring groups, has not radically altered, despite greater political incorporation from the centre of the new nation-states.

This discussion has taken us some way from the 'internal colonialism' model itself, but, since the latter is a recent variant of more general economic theories of ethnic change, it was necessary to deal with the broader economic arguments. For, if economic factors operate independently of ethnic ones, and ethnic protest can emerge independently of economic changes, then the central failure of the 'internal colonialism' model to explain why social discontent is focussed upon ethnic identities becomes apparent. The 'ethnic nature' of political movements for autonomy cannot be accounted for in largely economic terms; it requires consideration of other, more relevant factors. The plausibility of Hechter's model derives from the fact that many ethnic groups populate a single, readily identifiable territory, and hence suffer the disadvantages (or enjoy the benefits) of that terrain, with its soil and climate, distance from trade routes, possession of valuable minerals, strategic importance, communications networks and the like. Hence the importance of the 'land' for nationalists. But, equally, such a 'territorial reductionism' fails to do justice to that other crucial variable, history, with all its cultural attributes. Nor is it only the economic potential and situation of the land which must be taken into account. Territory is linked with history in many subtle ways, which become part of the group's cultural heritage and outlook. Moreover, ethnic groups are not necessarily coextensive with an economically defined 'region', as we shall see. They may share it with other ethnic groups, as in the Russian Pale of Settlement, or be scattered across several regions. Yet, even in these cases, ethnic communities like the Blacks in America, the Armenians, the Jews and the Gypsies, have experienced an ethnic revival, and formed movements of ethnic nationalism.

If we return to the empirical applications of the 'internal colonialism' model, we find, as one might expect, that its relevance varies from case to case. The original formulation is most clearly applicable in depressed areas like Ireland and Brittany, although even here it is doubtful whether capitalist industrialism has been more relevant than political and cultural discrimination in maintaining the sense of historic grievance and ethnic identity.[30] In the case of Belgium, the model, which might have illuminated communal relationships in the last century, seems increasingly irrelevant today, when, despite their demographic and economic ascendancy, the Flemish community continues to retain ethnic aspirations which, nevertheless, fall short of outright independence. Here the contrast has been between an upwardly mobile and economically preponderant community, the Flemish, and a culturally and politically advantaged Walloon community, a situation that is found in some Asian countries.[31] Nor can it be said that Flanders retained the degree of institutional autonomy enjoyed by Scotland, and hence a segmental cultural division of labour. On the contrary: the main spur to Flemish resentment of the Walloon position has been the superiority enjoyed by Francophones.

Nor does the model help to explain the rather different concerns of recent ethnic movements. Thus, as Nairn has observed, the Welsh movement (like some others) is still strongly attached to language issues, and is perhaps more romantic in its approach than its Scottish counterpart, where since 1945 the SNP has been at pains to frame its appeal in hard-headed economic terms, taking for granted its cultural base.[32] Even this contrast does not take into account the Quebec example of an ethnic nationalism which is practical and strongly oriented to economic issues, yet fervently linguistic in its aspirations. Nor, again, does the 'internal colonialism' model throw much light on the *religious* dimension to the ethnic conflict in Northern Ireland.[33]

There is also the related problem of the *intensity* of ethnic movements. It is interesting that here Hechter and Levi focus upon political determinants, suggesting that 'ethnoregionalism is likely to exist to the extent that the central state tolerates cultural and political diversity'.[34] Yet, neither in Ireland nor in Brittany did the British and French states show much tolerance for 'cultural and political diversity', to put it mildly, and it is precisely in these communities that strong cultural associations have been formed and ethnic movements have flourished.

Finally, the 'internal colonialism' model does not do justice to the effect of national sentiment among dominant ethnic communities like the French, Serbs, Afrikaners and Malays today. The nationalisms of these strategic or dominant ethnic communities have in the past helped to stir the reactive nationalisms of the 'peripheral' ethnic communities, which in turn have further crystallised the exclusive sentiments of the dominant group. This kind of discrimination, which may be more or less overt, and is often a political factor independent of the economic framework, has played a considerable part in the rise of several ethnic movements today.

For these reasons, an 'internal colonialism' model, while it illuminates economic relationships today and in the past, must remain of limited relevance in accounting for the ethnic revival as a whole, and even of the recent ethnic wave. Because of its rather static quality and the instrumental role it assigns to cultural differences, it leaves many puzzling features unexplained, and fails to give enough weight to the historical basis and ethnic forms of political nationalism. And because it tends to equate the ethnic community with the territory in which it resides, and concentrate mainly on the latter's economic features, it overlooks other attributes of ethnic groups, and so obscures the independent causal force of ethnicity despite rapid economic change.

IMPERIALISM AND UNDERDEVELOPMENT

An attempt to do more justice to the ethnic quality of modern nationalisms, while retaining a basic economic framework, can be found in the recent analyses of Britain's ethnic problems by Tom Nairn. He argues that the latter can only be understood within the general framework of European nationalism as a whole from about 1800, and that Europe's nationalisms in turn can only be understood in the context of the grossly uneven economic development of Europe (and the world). Nairn equates this uneven tide of development with the 'advancing capitalism of the more bourgeois societies', which after the French and Industrial Revolutions 'bore down upon the societies surrounding them – societies which predominantly appear until the 1790s as buried in feudal and absolutist slumber'.[35] The trouble was that development came to them in the form of a new domination; a French empire and the 'tyranny of the English "City" over the European "Country". In short, there was a sort of imperialism built into "development". And it had become a prime necessity to resist *this* aspect of development' (italics in original).[36] Of course, says Nairn, nationalities and ethnic disputes have existed long before the eighteenth century. National*ism*, on the other hand, is a novel, and universal, phenomenon, an intrinsic feature of the modern world, whose uneven processes of development 'made use of the "raw materials" provided by Europe's particularly rich variety of ethnic, cultural and linguistic contrasts. But – precisely – it also altered their meaning, and gave them a qualitatively distinct function, an altogether new dynamism for both good and evil.'[37] Capitalism's uneven development is necessarily 'nationalism-producing', because development always comes to the less advanced peoples within the 'fetters' of the more advanced nations and their bourgeoisies, especially those of England and France. These bourgeoisies are the original motor of nationalism; but resistance to their impact only turns into 'nationalism', when the dilemma of underdevelopment 'is (so to speak) refracted into a given society, perceived in a certain way, and then acted upon. And the medium through which this occurs is invariably, in the first place, an intelligentsia – functioning, of course, as the most conscious and awakened part of the middle classes.' But how were the relatively poor middle classes and intelligentsias of the less advanced countries to resist the domination of foreign, richer bourgeoisies? Only by mobilising their one asset, the people. 'People is all they have got: this is the essence of the underdevelopment dilemma itself.'[38] Hence the new middle-class intelligentsia of nationalism had to 'invite the masses into history', and hence nationalism, while not necessarily democratic, is invariably populist. It has to form 'a militant, inter-class community rendered strongly (if mythically) aware of its own separate identity vis-à-vis the outside forces of domination'.[39] And that, in turn, means taking cultural diversity seriously, because popular and peasant life is divided by folk dialects, myths, customs, skin-colour and the like, all those cultural differentiae which an irrational but inter-class cultural mode like romanticism, with its subjectivist idealism, seizes upon and exaggerates. If the intellectuals are not united through a romantic ideology, then there can be no 'national culture' and no nationalist revolt, as there was none in nineteenth-century Scotland.[40] The intellectuals must be able to perform their task of depicting the 'prehistoric' quality and 'archaic' naturalness of popular culture, so as to mobilise the masses. Hence 'the true nerve of political nationalism . . . is constituted by a distinctive relationship between the intelligentsia (acting for its class) and the people'.[41]

To this general theory of nationalism, Nairn adds a more specific thesis about recent West European 'neo-nationalisms'.[42] The latter have arisen in the ' "original" nation-states which fostered modern capitalism' and its developmental imperialism, and are the product of capitalist expansion in the 1950s and the European Economic Community depriving these traditional 'state-nations' of their power and status. Multinationals and superpowers have reduced these old states to quite second-rate powers, and in Britain the main parties have been unable to halt its decay. Despite the higher base of their development, therefore, the peripheral regions within the old 'State-nations' suffer from a 'relative deprivation' to the centres of these states; so that today: 'The impact of the oil industry on Scotland and of the US multi-nationals on the French Midi is provoking a new Scottish and Occitanian separatism; but, to a greater extent than is realised, this is a *sui generis* phenomenon which should not be assimilated to classical European or Third World "nationalism" at all.'[43] Nevertheless, Nairn also considers this 'neo-nationalism' to be a nationalist resurgence, and as a 'second round' of bourgeois nationalisms, despite their much higher developmental stage. The new nationalism has, besides, inherited much of the ideology of the old; and the question is whether it too will lead to what Nairn considers the logical culmination of a non-rational and ambivalent nationalism, namely, fascism.

I have concentrated above on the general schema presented by Nairn, rather than on its specific applications to Scotland, England, Wales and Ulster, because Nairn himself emphasises a comparative and historical approach, and because such an approach is a prerequisite for an understanding of the general problem of the 'ethnic revival', even in its modern phase. The great virtue of this approach, namely its dynamic historicity, is shown in the recognition of the close relationship between nationalism and war. Development, for Nairn, is not just uneven (an idea which he has drawn from Gellner, to whom he refers several times), it is a brutal process, engendering war and hate. Kant was wrong; commerce is perfectly compatible with war, indeed it resuscitates the 'atavistic urges' and throws up national barriers.[44] Whether the causal links are exactly of this kind, we shall consider later; but Nairn is surely right to suggest this jagged connection between war and nations. Also interesting is the emphasis upon the intelligentsia and their relationship with the culture of the 'folk', so that, in a sense, they face two ways: inwards to the 'people' and its untapped energies, and outwards to the bourgeoisies of the advanced metropolitan states. This is the sociological counterpart of their cultural ambivalence, and it well captures the 'two-worlds' situation in which they find themselves.

Even more significant is Nairn's emphasis upon the importance of the state as the mediator of capitalist development. (Indeed, by tracing the peculiarities of the 'transitional' British state form both to its historical location as the first example of development, and to its peculiar basis in the patrician class of commercial landlords, he is able to cast much light on its present problems.) The weakness of marxist analysis of nationalism derives largely from its failure to analyse political structures, especially the 'bourgeois-democratic state'.[45]

And yet, just here, the theory turns back to its marxist roots; nationalism is a product, not of Stalin's 'early capitalism' or Hilferding's 'mature finance-capitalism', but of 'uneven development', that is, 'the unforeseeable, antagonistic reality of capitalism's growth into the world'.[46] The state becomes, once again, an instrument, a useful framework, for the 'sordid material interests' of the English and French bourgeois classes, which took the cultural form of Anglicisation, Frenchification, and, later, Americanisation. The new state forms and military powers are not really just associated, for Nairn, with the new dynamic forces of production; they are the latter's vehicle and form, but no more.

But, if the state is no more than a vehicle of capitalist development, how do we arrive at the ethnic content, the nationalist aspiration, of anti-imperialist response? Why should the unevenness of capitalist

advance correspond to cultural divisions? Unless, of course, the English and French (and other western) bourgeoisies were already
themselves in the grip of the nationalist malady, and hence to their
'sordid material interests' were added other ethnic ones? But that
assumes the independence, and historical priority, of ethnic nationalism from the uneven development of capitalism.

And this, actually, makes better historical sense. For the doctrine,
even the movement, of nationalism was born in the core areas themselves, and so was not simply a 'peripheric' response to the 'imperialism' of the capitalist bourgeoisies. On the side of pure 'doctrine',
the first nationalist formulations are those of Bolingbroke, Burke,
Rousseau, Siéyès, Zimmerman, Jefferson, Moser, Herder, and Alfieri.[47] Nationalism as a 'movement' is also as much metropolitan as
peripheric: there was a strong national revival in England at the end
of the eighteenth century, and of course a full-scale nationalism
erupted in France just before and during the Great Revolution, in-
spiring others all over Europe.[48] In America, too, the Independence
War soon produced a strong nationalist current, which led to a federal Constitution. If England alone did not manifest an explicit nationalist movement, this has more to do with the prior gestation of
its national sentiment, and its state form and development, than
with its early capitalism.

It is, of course, true that the development of nationalism in the
early nineteenth century coincided with the development of capitalism in the western half of that continent. Yet, depending of course
on how strictly we define 'capitalism', it is difficult to demonstrate in
detail a causal connection between the importation of capitalism and
the emergence of nationalism in a particular ethnic group. Quite
often, the timing will not fit: Greek, Serb and Polish nationalisms,
for example, clearly antedate the 'uneven development' of capitalism. The great 'tidal wave' of capitalism (let alone industrialism) was
not much in evidence in late-eighteenth-century Corsica or Switzerland when their nationalism began to emerge; even in Germany and
Italy it was more a distant menace than a present trend. Even in
France itself, though there were plenty of entrepreneurs and finan-
ciers, their link with an emergent French nationalism is far from
clear.[49]

This is not to doubt the importance of growing commerce as a
background and indirect factor in the rise of nationalism; or the role
of merchants (not usually commodity capitalists in the modern,
western (Marxist or Weberian) sense) in the genesis of some nationalist movements. Serbian pig-dealers and Greek merchants clearly
were, inter alia, influential in promoting the ethnic cause.[50] But this

is not really the same thing as the jagged 'uneven development' implying foreign domination that Nairn presupposes (the foreign domination of the Ottomans had, after all, lasted three centuries).

These examples must also make us wary of characterising all ethnic nationalism as 'populist'. True, to be effective in the face of strong rulers, nationalist intelligentsias need to appeal to other strata. But to *whom* they will appeal, depends on both the group's situation and its social composition. The Greek intelligentsias who tried to enlist klephtic support were, in a sense, rebuffed; they were fighting the same enemy, but different battles.[51] Early Indian and West African nationalists were chary of 'mass mobilisation'; they realised it would alienate 'middle-class' support. Today's 'neo-nationalisms' tend, as we shall see, to prefer a middle-class constituency, in contrast to the marxist nationalisms which *are* genuinely populist, in the sense of appealing to the peasants and trying to incorporate their grievances into the nationalist platform. Nor is it so certain that every nationalism is equally romantic; some like the Polish and Irish were, others like the present-day Scots and Quebecois are less so. Nairn is right to say that there is a strong subjective element in all nationalisms, and to link them with a general romanticism. But, equally, many nationalists can be hard-headed and realistic; and, in today's world, nationhood is very much part of the 'objective' political landscape.

Perhaps the source of these overgeneralisations lies in the oversharp opposition Nairn draws between 'objective' and 'subjective' factors, and between a 'materialist' and an 'idealist' conception of nationalism's role in history. The 'subjective–objective' distinction is not really very helpful, when it comes to defining the concepts of ethnic community, nation and nationalism, though it may help in classifying theories of nationalism (and that only to some extent). In like manner, Weber utilised the terms 'ideal' and 'material' only as poles of a continuum; to oppose them too drastically, to opt for the logical and substantive priority of one at the expense of the other, when it comes to providing a theory of ethnic nationalism (as opposed to defining the problem and its concepts), creates more problems than it solves.

But this is exactly what Nairn has done. In his own words: 'the most notoriously subjective and ideal of historical phenomena is in fact a by product of the most brutally and hopelessly material side of the history of the last two centuries'.[52] This most subjective and ideal of historical phenomena is, of course, nationalism itself, whose 'real origins' are located 'in the machinery of world political economy', the material fact of uneven development. Nairn justifies this opposition on methodological grounds:

It is a fact that while idealist explanations of the phenomenon in terms of consciousness or Zeitgeist (however acute their observations may be, notably in German writers like Meinecke) never account for the material dynamic incorporated in the situation, a materialist explanation can perfectly well account for all the most 'ideal' and cultural or ideological symptoms of nationalism (even at their most berserk). Start from the premise of capitalism's uneven development and its real class articulation, and one can come to grasp the point even of chauvinist lunacy, the 'irrational' elements which have played a significant role in nationalism's unfolding from the outset to the end. Start from the lunacy itself and one will end there, after a number of gyrations – . . .[53]

One may well agree with the last point, yet it remains extremely doubtful whether a materialist conception can really encompass the cultural and ethnic elements in nationalism's rise and development, particularly if, having bridged the gulf between capitalism's uneven development and ethnic nationalism (through the state and its forms), the theory then fails to develop this all-important dimension. Besides, the arguments advanced against relative deprivation and internal colonialism models, apply also here. Capitalism, like industrialism, often creates cleavages which cross-cut ethnic ones, and ethnic nationalism can emerge (and is still doing so in the 'Third World') in areas which at the time were hardly touched by capitalist development. Thus nationalism is a force that varies independently of capitalism; indeed, the well-known failures of historical-materialist analysis of fascism and Nazism (surely rather different phenomena from classic nationalism),[54] should warn us of its more general weaknesses in the sociology of culture, ideology and even politics.

Perhaps the root of the trouble lies in the very terms of the marxist methodology employed: 'material' and 'ideal' are very schematic categories, abstract and distant from complex historical realities, and the actual factors involved in any convincing account of ethnic phenomena necessarily partake of elements falling towards both ends of the continuum. As first approximations, these categories can help to correct exaggerations and reveal monocausal accounts; but they are too crude to illuminate or untie the tangled skein of history. Such a dichotomous schema can only suggest the need for research into the (two-way?) historical relationships between capitalism and nationalism at different times and places; just as the assertion that intelligentsias acting for their bourgeoisies appeal to the 'people' requires more empirical investigation of the social composition of nationalism. The rest is dogma.

UNEVEN DEVELOPMENT

Since one of the chief impulses of Nairn's and other recent economic theories of ethnic movements has been the notion, advanced by Ernest Gellner, of 'uneven development', we need to examine this pregnant idea by way of conclusion.

For Gellner, it is industralisation or modernisation (the social concomitants of industrialisation) that is 'uneven'.[55] It is not capitalism. Moreover, for Gellner, modernisation erodes social structure and replaces it by culture as the binding cement of modern society. That is its first, and major, function. Its second consequence is the creation of an intelligentsia, a stratum of 'clerks' who can run a state-wide educational system in a given language, and become one of the two prongs of national secession movements (the other is the proletariat). A third consequence is the creation, by an uneven industrialisation's tidal wave, of a new urban stratification system; but this is not the usual marxist one of bourgeoisies versus workers, but a cleavage within the proletariat itself. For what Gellner is referring to is the jagged process of urbanisation in which newly uprooted arrivals from the countryside are kept down or excluded by the entrenched city-dwellers, even though neither are members of the 'bourgeoisie'. This was a familiar process and conflict both in Eastern Europe in the last century, and in the Middle East and North Africa, during this century; and Gellner is quite explicit about the way in which this tidal wave of industrialisation-cum-urbanisation may divide ethnically homogeneous societies like Italy. Only when cultural differences are superimposed on the urban intraproletarian cleavages, do the new arrivals, as a result of cultural discrimination, retort by trying to found their own ethnic state, in conjunction with their culturally similar intelligentsias.

It follows from this that for Gellner the importance of 'uneven development' lies largely in its potential for cultural cleavage. Of course, industrialisation is globally uneven, hitting different areas at different times and rates and intensities. But that, in itself, is not so interesting; the critical case for ethnic nationalism is when it activates cultural discrimination, in a world where culture has become so much more important. This shift in emphasis is vital; by neglecting the cultural context in which 'uneven development' has significance, the economistic approach, however historically minded, cuts itself off from the so-called 'ideal' factors and perpetuates an ultimately unbridgeable methodological chasm.

One could also go further. If modernisation is relevant for ethnic nationalism mainly as an activator and elevator of culture to its present critical social role, then we could characterise economic factors in general as catalysts and exacerbators of ethnic movements. That is, of course, just what 'neo-nationalists' (indeed, most nationalists) do; they accuse the ruling foreigner of economic oppression, interference or neglect. On the other hand, they still remain intent on independence, or economic autonomy, even when they realise that the living standards of their compatriots may fall; and tend to oppose any large-scale immigration of foreigners, even when this raises their living standards, as is the case with many of Russia's nationalities, or with Swiss opposition to foreign, mainly Italian, workers. In all these cases, ethnic passion outweighs economic interests, in the final analysis. Economic deprivation, economic exploitation, economic growth, are all grist to the nationalist mill; but in themselves they do not generate ethnic sentiments or nationalist movements. The uneven development of industralisation, which roughly coincided with the development of nationalism, has undoubtedly sharpened ethnic tensions and contributed a new store of national grievances; but the cleavages and antagonisms, so accentuated, together with the aspirations and ideals based upon them, have their roots and inspiration elsewhere.

vwv

Language and community

One of nationalism's abiding myths is the identification of national-ity with language. This myth has its origins in the seminal ideas of Herder, although even earlier there had already been a tendency in France and Germany to emphasise the vernacular (at the expense of Latin) and to insist on its national educational uses.[1] Herder, how-ever, originated the identification of language groups with nations, and nationalism with a linguistic movement, which has played so important a part in European nationalisms, to this day.[2] This equa-tion was in turn a consequence of Herder's doctrine of language, which he developed from the ideas of his teacher, Hamann. Hamann had seen in language the only means of understanding groups and individuals, and their literary products; Herder went further, assert-ing that language was the primary social bond, the sole means of communication and association between men, and so a natural growth. Though communities are the product of various factors, bi-ological, geographical and psychological, they are held together by human communication. We think and act through language; hence language is the chief vehicle and cement of social action, and of com-munity as such. 'Language', says Herder, 'expresses the collective experience of the group'; and 'every nation has its own inner centre of happiness, as every sphere has its own centre of gravity.'[3]

Now, as the last sentence tells us, what really interested Herder was cultural diversity and incommensurability. But his cultural populism, which proved so influential, was much broader than his German (and other) followers allowed. For Fichte and his fellow-Romantics, language was basically verbal communication, and na-tions were 'pure' language groups. For Herder, communication was the central concept, and he included all kinds of thinking and acting under this heading, such as dress, architecture, hunting, music, art, eating habits and history. Verbal communication was perhaps the most important and accessible mode of communication, but it was only one way of being at home, of belonging. Similarly, the origi-nality and authenticity, in which he so passionately believed, was much broader than that of Fichte and his followers. When he urged peoples to 'find themselves' and 'learn not to think in other people's thoughts', when he denounced 'idle cosmopolitans' and praised rude savages for their genuine feelings and ways of life, he was thinking less of language purity than of group belonging and of decentralised communities, in which men can truly communicate.

CULTURE MARKERS

Herder's 'communications' approach, and his cultural view of nationality, has had many followers. In Eastern Europe, especially, nationalists and students of nationalism have tended to single out language as the basic ingredient of nations, and the main issue fuelling nationalist movements. Some recent scholarly treatments, too, have followed German romanticism in concentrating on the linguistic criterion, notably those of Znaniecki and Kedourie.[4] Like the historians of nationalism, Carlton Hayes, Hans Kohn and Louis Snyder, they have adopted a fundamentally 'cultural' approach to ethnicity and nationalism; unlike these historians, they have elevated one element of culture, namely language, into the main pillar of nationhood.

To this school of thought belongs the recent analysis of Ernest Gellner, which constitutes an original attempt to root this cultural concern within a broader social context. As we saw in the previous chapter, Gellner regards linguistic education as the main precondition of citizenship today, because culture has become the fundamental social bond in an industrial world, and culture must be conveyed and taught through the medium of language. Hence, too, the importance of 'clerks', a secular intelligentsia, which has superseded its clerical forbear.

To his earlier account, Gellner has now added a theory of educational mobility and its diversifying effects. Modernisation and industry, he argues, require a vast expansion of mobility, both social and geographical; and this in turn means that men must have an all-round, general education at the primary level, and a specialist education thereafter, that is, an education on and for the job. Specialist education presupposes the acquisition of basic skills of literacy and numeracy, which the general education on a nationwide basis provides. But, because the modern division of labour demands frequent changes of job, or their personnel, the education system 'cannot train them specifically. It can only give them a kind of generic training, leaving the specific job training to a much later stage'.[5] It is this generic training which today fits men for citizenship, as well as for all the specialised and changing jobs in the peculiar modern division of labour. General education is a necessary, if not a sufficient, condition of almost any job in a modern society; and general education can only be inculcated by a complex, but specialised, set of institutions – the 'educational system'.

A general education, then, is the vital precondition of mobility in a modern society; and such mobility tends to destroy or at any rate erode every intermediate kin and social unit. But there is a limit to mobility; and that limit is set by the range 'of the language and/or the culture, which happen to be the media of the educational system which formed the man in question'. And Gellner continues: 'It is these culturally imposed limits of mobility which are decisive, and which thereby generate the limits of loyalty and the concepts in terms of which effective loyalty can be felt'.[6] It is language and/or culture which divides men, perpetually, in the modern world; and which, equally, constitutes the chief bond between men today.

Nationalism, for Gellner, is closely tied up with this new role of language and culture. For nationalism is basically a movement 'which conceives the natural object of human loyalty to be a fairly large anonymous unit defined by shared language or culture'. Hence there is always a tendency to aspire to cultural and linguistic homogeneity in the modern world, and to define pretty sharply the boundaries of the new cultural/linguistic units, or 'nations'.

But here we encounter a problem. Traditional societies tended to be divided into 'deep, permanent human and moral chasms between their members, or rather classes of members', and because of their complexity and multiplicity, as well as the stability of a traditional society, these chasms did not constitute a major source of friction and conflict. But today they do. Widespread mobility makes these chasms unacceptable, since it destroys the stability and routine of life and society. It also blurs the cultural differences which accompanied these chasms, the elite culture of a feudal aristocracy, or the traditions of the Brahmins. On the whole, men can 'pass' today, at least in three generations.[7]

Yet, some cultural differences refuse to be blurred. Gellner cites the case of pigmentation, where passing is rendered impossible, and which then reinforces the cultural differences. Religion is another difference, which may be 'irrevocable' at times. 'It is at these boundaries', concludes Gellner, 'that new nationalisms are born.' And he summarises his argument as follows:

Thus the natural limit of the political unit, if not bedevilled by the chasms, is the limit of the validity of its educational certificates. But where their limits do not correspond to the deep chasms, and the old inequalities that cannot be obscured, there is the basis for an irredentism, a nationalist movement on behalf of either a unit which does not exist yet, or at least on behalf of radical re-drawing of existing boundaries.[8]

So we have two situations: a normal one, in which 'language and/or culture' determines national boundaries and loyalties, and an 'irredentist' or separatist one, in which the population is divided into deep chasms with irremovable cultural markers, which modern mobility cannot blur or erode, and which form the basis of two nations and two nationalisms. As Gellner puts it: 'If the frontier [of the chasm] is not marked by anything insuperable, mobility in both directions results, and the erstwhile deep difference is obscured. If, on the other hand, the old frontier is marked by irremovable markers, then *two* new nationalisms are born' (italics in original).[9]

Essentially, Gellner's theory is an attempt to show that nationalism and ethnic separatism are part and parcel of the modern, industrial world. Prior to industrialisation and modernisation, men owed allegiances to a variety of groups, some smaller, some larger, than the nation-state; today their primary allegiance is to the anonymous, large-scale, co-cultural nation. And the main reason for this shift in loyalties is the emergence of a linguistic culture as the chief bond between human beings. It is this type of culture that binds populations into 'nations'; and, where it cannot do so, where mobility cannot erode other cultural cleavages, then the trend towards cultural homogeneity creates two new nations along the line of this cleavage. This means that Gellner views the role of language as fundamentally integrative, although it also sets the boundaries of political units; and, conversely, the role of the other cultural markers is fundamentally divisive, although they can also act as a rallying-point for excluded populations. It also means that, for Gellner, language is the cradle and matrix of the 'classic' nations; whereas, the other cultural markers like colour or religion seem responsible for separatism. The rise of language and the growth of larger units go hand in hand; whereas the other cultural markers tend to break up this trend towards increased scale. So, in many ways, Gellner sees the role of 'language' as antithetical to that of other cultural markers.

Unfortunately, language today can be as disruptive a force as any other cultural marker. Of course, the very fact of integrating citizens into a culturally homogeneous nation-state entails exclusion of those who do not speak the language and are not accounted citizens; and language may, therefore, disrupt the political map. But today language-cum-culture has become one of the main planks of movements for secession, which can only lead to the dismemberment of the most developed, large 'nation-states'. In Brittany and Wales, Occitania and the Basque country, Quebec and Kurdistan, among the Shan, the Ewe and the BaKongo, language has become a divisive, disintegrative force, creating fissure and the spectre of a world of mini-states, in flat contradiction to that trend towards modernisation and enlarged scale, that spacious homogeneity which so many have envisaged.

In fact, it may well be the case that the Herderian legacy has exaggerated the part played by language and communications in generating the desire to become a 'nation'. Language by itself only rarely performs the task which that legacy attributed to it, that of providing the social cement for populations. The difficulties of pan-Arabism, in this respect, are illuminating. Arabs share a common speech and literary heritage, a common Arabic-medium education, and a Koran written in Arabic; yet, while these factors have stimulated the urge for unity among an intelligentsia, they have been unable to overcome the many obstacles to greater social and political unity.[10] Undoubtedly, common language enhances communication and creates a more intimate understanding between its speakers; at the same time, it has failed to excite a fully fledged mass sentiment towards Arab unity among such dispersed and historically separated populations. Not only do the several Arab states enjoy different political regimes and states of economic development; they have been nurtured under separate colonial auspices and, in some cases, possess histories of great antiquity, which separate them more than they unite. For language to generate a deeper, more widespread feeling of national unity, it must be accompanied by a coextensive history, which the language then expresses, transmits and symbolises.

Besides, increased social communication and language are relatively neutral *vis-à-vis* the generation of nationalist movements and consciousness. That is to say, they may increase ethnic cohesion and the desire for national autonomy in a population; but, equally, they may divide that population and exacerbate conflicts. Social communications tend to amplify pre-existing trends and situations rather than generate them in the first place. By tracing the lines of communication (including language), we can show how and where the diffusion of national ideals has taken place. But this tells us very little about the origins and reception of those ideals.

Moreover, by inflating the role of language, we are prevented from grasping the problems peculiar to 'linguistic' as opposed to other, say, 'colour' or 'religious' nationalisms. Language nationalisms have particular problems of identity and self-understanding, over and above those common to all nationalisms. And ethnic communities defined primarily in linguistic terms have special problems, not shared by others defined in terms of another cleavage or 'problem-area'. The point is that the cleavages pose certain problems for individual and group identity, and express the history of the community most intimately. They point to powerful but often ambiguous crucibles of communal identity, in and through which the deeper issues of solidarity, regeneration, uniqueness and dignity are expressed and worked out. Hence they are more than boundary markers for the participants, and they are not so clearcut and unambiguous as is often supposed. They embody a tension and inner conflict which goes some way towards explaining why they can unleash such powerful emotions.

But this means, too, that we can no longer view such cultural cleavages as the markers of some pre-existing social chasms. In fact, the old social divides, the castes, estates, and millets, have on the whole proved divisive for the new ethnic and cultural cleavages fostered by nationalism. The latter crosscut the social chasms, with the exception perhaps of the Ottoman millets; the new ethnic cleavages are, on the whole, 'vertical', while the old social chasms were, on the whole, 'horizontal'. Besides, we cannot predict ethnic cleavages, much less political separatisms, on the basis of the presence of some 'irremoveable' marker like colour or religion, since the effects of such cultural differences have proved extremely variable.

Some examples may help. Colour has, indeed, often proved a powerful cultural and social barrier, most obviously in the United States and South Africa, but also elsewhere. Yet there are countries, like Brazil or Mexico, where colour has proved less divisive. There is some prejudice against Afro-Brazilians in the Sao Paolo area, where industrialism has taken most hold, but it has not crystallised into a full-scale colour-based ethnic cleavage or generated a separate ethnic community, perhaps because of the extensive miscegenation practised throughout the period of Portuguese rule, as a result of which the ensuing colour gradations proved to be too fine and complex to allow ethnic origins to become a caste-like basis for separate ethnic communities.[11] In Mexico, miscegenation and hispanicisation went even further, and, although about a quarter of the population is of Indian descent, this cleavage plays almost no part in the political life of the country.[12] Even in countries where colour has helped to congeal populations into separate historic communities, such as the United States and South Africa, it has not necessarily bred ethnic separatism. In South Africa, especially, 'ethnic origin' may subdivide 'racial' categorisation among both whites and blacks, and possess a force of its own, irrespective of colour categories.[13]

Religion, too, has operated in various ways. Sometimes it is associated with a strong national tradition, even a fervent nationalism; Poland, Ireland, even the Serbs and Croats, to this day, preserve this religio-national identification.[14] Under the Ottomans and Romanovs, religion played an active role, as both discriminatory badge and fomentor of separatism, in the case of Greeks, Armenians, Jews and Tatars.[15] Even today, religion remains a potent source of separatism – among the Eritreans, and Moros in the Philippines, and in Ulster.[16] But it has not always proved so irremovable, nor so divisive. Religion plays an important ethnic role in the United States, but its edges are fairly frayed. Switzerland has managed to live with its two denominations, despite a civil war over the issue in the last century; and so has Germany. In both cases, language took precedence over religion; and, in Germany, religious divisions, though important, failed to stem the tide towards ethnic unity based upon common language and sense of medieval political unity.[17]

What these examples illustrate is not only the variability of effects that identical cultural factors may produce, but the need to examine them in relation to the sense of historical unity (or lack of it) among a given population, and the particular historical configuration of that community. This does not mean that we cannot engage in a comparative historical sociology of various kinds of ethnic nationalism; it does mean that we have to recognise that religion, language, colour and the like take their meaning from particular historical situations, even when they have an independent, often variable, effect on that situation. Thus communities which are focussed around a religious identity have rather different features and dilemmas than those in which colour, or territory, or language, is the principal focus; but even then, 'religion-shaped' peoples may differ in the precise contents and effects of their religion for the rise of ethnic aspirations; and such effects require prolonged investigation.

The problem, as always, lies in striking the right balance between the obvious modernity of nationalism and the often premodern historical dimensions of ethnicity. Nationalism has indeed often brought nations into being where none existed before, above all in areas where ethnic groups were submerged and obscured by other historical forces. To that extent, its dynamic, creative role needs to be underlined. But the forces that impel nationalists to emerge and demand autonomy for 'their' communities cannot be derived exclusively from the processes of 'modernisation', since, as we saw, there is nothing inherent in modernisation, however we define the term, which demands the creation of nations or nation-states. None of the trends usually associated with modernisation can, singly or together, account for the well-nigh-universal appeal of nationalism, nor the ubiquitous revival of ethnicity.

It is, rather, the *impact* of these processes of modernisation upon historic communities and categories, and upon the 'mass sentiments' often associated with them, that can alone help to account for the rise and diffusion of ethnic nationalism in the last two centuries. Nations may not be natural, but neither are they purely artificial constructs utilising pre-existing cultural markers. Rather we may view the nation as an attempt, often unsuccessful, to adapt latent, historic ties of culture to certain aspects of modern change. Thus, though they have considerable latitude in their methods and strategies, the nationalists must nevertheless operate within the constraints of the specific sentiments and histories of the area.

THE LOSS OF COMMUNITY

One of Gellner's central arguments is that the tremendously increased mobility of modern societies actually promotes the rise of new cultural ties, since language and culture must now perform the integrative tasks previously accomplished by the complex role structure of a traditional society. Of course, from a nationalist standpoint, this argument is rather suspect. Nationalists tend to view geographical mobility, at any rate, as a threat to the nation. Since they purport to be able to find the 'nation', its lineaments and true character, beneath the tangled structures thrown up by historical accidents, their concern is to husband its strength; and that means safeguarding its demographic and political character. So that, just as they resist colonisation by 'alien' settlers within the demarcated 'homeland', so they equally oppose the enforced ethnic emigration of skills and talent, which strengthens the centre and the dominant group at the expense of subordinate and peripheral ones. Mobility and emigration, for a nationalist, diminish the number of actual or potential language-speakers and the ethnic reservoir; and that is too high a price to pay for the defection of a few ethnic intellectuals from the dominant culture. Mobility really only serves to strengthen the language and culture of the assimilating centre.

In a sense, then, nationalists tend to accept Karl Deutsch's early thesis about the correlation between mobilisation and cultural assimilation.[18] But, whereas Deutsch thought that such a correlation was part and parcel of the process of modernisation, the nationalists and their sympathisers tend to lay the blame at the door of the over-centralised state. In this, they are merely updating Herder's cultural populism and his opposition to political regimentation. They lament the depopulation of the countryside and the overcrowding of the great cities, along with the threat to a dying language or way of life; but their real concern is with the loss of community which the economic planning and controls of the modern 'Jacobin' state entail.

This notion of the loss of community is at the heart of Patricia Mayo's recent analysis of some contemporary European ethnic movements. Mayo views the rise of Basque, Breton and Welsh ethnic nationalisms as part of a broader and 'fundamental political and social malaise' in European society.[19] She argues that man is a social animal and therefore requires a communal identity. Today that identity is threatened by the twin forces of overspecialisation and uniformity. Man's natural 'communities' are being engulfed and eroded by an anonymous 'society', dominated by the modern 'Jacobin' state, with its nineteenth-century coercive apparatus and its lack of sensitivity to the needs of its citizens. The centralised 'Jacobin' state tends to plan regional welfare and development from the top downwards and according to an administrative grid, with the result that the historic balance between region and region, town and country, and man and his natural environment, is upset. It is against the ensuing imbalance that current autonomist movements are striving. They are trying not only to preserve dying languages and revive depressed regions, but, more important, creating the conditions in which local institutions can emerge which can truly express a spontaneous and 'natural' identity. Therefore, the roots of today's ethnic revival stem from the twin pressures of centralising administration and non-participatory government.[20]

Political parties, too, have, according to Mayo, failed to mitigate the growing alienation and malaise in European society. Neither Conservatives nor Gaullists can be expected to show much sympathy for movements which challenge the integrity and unity of the existing nation-states; similarly, the parties of the Left, with a few exceptions, have generally favoured centralisation and state control, especially when in office. Thus:

In the United Kingdom and France, but less so in Federal West Germany, Left-wing governments have been inspired by a philosophy which has been heavily uniformist and centralist, in which they have had strong support from their respective Civil Service departments: their conception of society as a mass of unorganised individuals who should be ruled from above by uniform methods of administration, combined with a refusal to allow for the existence of the natural and informal group at the base or for the diversity essential to all true forms of growth. Inspired by this philosophy the Jacobins in France suppressed provincial assemblies, independent universities and other bodies which had acted as a buffer between the individual and central government.[21]

The political remedy for this 'volcanic' situation is a European federalism such as was envisaged by Jean Monnet, with a directly elected European Parliament, and a much greater degree of local political participation, such as one can find in federal Germany and Switzerland. Only then can man be restored to his natural social environment, the spontaneous social group or community, in which conflict 'could be channelled and used to become a true source of growth'; for, 'to be happy and balanced, man must have his roots in a living social group'.[22] In Wales and Brittany, however, and in the Basque country, especially the French part, the living social group is being drained of its best spirits. The ablest youth emigrate; unable to find employment, they cannot return to areas and communities which central government insists on treating as mere provinces. The protest movements of today, therefore, are the cries of dying communities which are being slowly strangled by bureaucratic penetration and overcentralisation.[23]

Many of Mayo's arguments echo those of moderate ethnic nationalists in Europe today; and in one sense her book is a skilful plea for the restoration of these ancient communities in a federalised continent. But how far is her programmatic or 'operational' account also an 'analytic' theory? How far, that is, does it help to *explain* the origins and growth of the ethnic revival today and the autonomist movements, as well as *prescribing* a federal Europe composed of 'natural' and diverse social groups, as many of the moderate autonomists propose?[24]

In fact, it is possible to extract an 'analytic' theory from Mayo's account, and one which may be conveniently labelled 'ecological'. The core of this theory is the assertion that ethnic communities constitute a species of 'natural social group' with its peculiar niche in the environment, which is now being disturbed and threatened by a mechanical and standardising bureaucratic state, with the result that men are losing their communal identity, and are trying to stem the ensuing tide of alienation through protest movements.

This is an important and widely accepted explanation; but, in its generally perceived form, it suffers from a number of defects. These fall under three headings: the nature and role of the 'natural' social groups, the character and impact of the centralised state, and, finally, the applicability of the theory to a wide range of cases. On the first point, the nature of the social groups, it is not at all clear which the 'natural' groups are, and why they should be more 'natural' than others. Mayo contends that they are informal and diverse; and certainly, in comparison with the 'Jacobin state', they are. But they are not informal in the same sense as a family or a gang, nor so diverse as to be incommensurable (as nationalists would have us believe). Mayo also appears to think they must be relatively small; but, again, it depends upon the standard of comparison. In fact, ethnic groups tend to be quite large compared to previous units, but at the same time they vary greatly in both size and scale (compare the 40 million Ukrainians with the 212,000 Icelanders). This common assumption appears to be very much part of the current 'small is beautiful' ecological outlook.[25] As to the 'natural' quality of ethnic communities, this is, in large part, a function of changing attitudes. Of course, such communities have existed for several millennia, and have often been remarked upon; the Bible, for example, does appear to regard the distinctions between peoples as divinely ordained and hence 'natural'. Yet, not every age or civilisation has regarded ethnic groups as either natural or important; and it is only fairly recently that people have generally come to accept ethnicity as something natural and appertaining to the character of mankind. Without going so far as those theorists who claim that ethnic groups and nations are 'unnatural', we may say that the naturalness attributed to ethnicity has fluctuated in line with the social importance of ethnic groups, and that both have received a very considerable boost in the last two centuries. Hence to claim that such groups are 'natural' begs the question.

It also tends to deflect attention from the divisions and conflicts within ethnic groups, and the changes which they have undergone, even before the impact of the modern state. What this amounts to saying is that ethnic communities are historical rather than natural formations; they are the product of historical events and forces, not of some law of global evolutionary growth. The question then becomes one of the extent to which such communities can, and are, providing a true collective identity, or at any rate, a more adequate and satisfying one than other social and political formations. Simply to assume that they can, and must, do so (given the right conditions) and the bureaucratic state cannot, is to accept the neo-romantic premises of much current social thought, including that of the nationalists themselves, and to side-step the difficult questions about the role and potential of these very ethnic communities today.

A second set of difficulties arises from the character and role which Mayo attributes to the centralised state. Now, the opposition between a 'Jacobin state' and a 'living community' or 'natural social group' is illuminating as an ideal-typical construct, since it draws attention to the very different principles involved in the two kinds of sociopolitical organisation. Historically, however, the content of this 'Jacobin state' has varied considerably. Curiously, the original Jacobin revolutionaries whom Mayo berates, were also ardent exponents of a fervent French ethnic nationalism and glorified the French culture and language, which men like the Abbé Gregoire and Barrère wished to strengthen at the expense of the regional languages.[26] Moreover, the Jacobin penchant for state centralism was largely a product of the war emergency and of the state apparatus which they had inherited from the French monarchs. It was the rather less fervently patriotic Napoleon who carried through the administrative programme of *départements* and prefects which incurs so much hostility from ethnic nationalists in France today.[27] This is really only one of several examples which makes us aware of the different levels at which the concept of ethnicity may operate simultaneously; a Welsh and a British, an Occitanian and a French, a Catalan and a Spanish ethnic identity. An ideal-typical opposition between Welsh ethnic identity and British statehood, between a Breton ethnic identity and French statehood, overlooks the historical formation of, and attachment to, a British and French circle of allegiance and identity. Exactly this dual allegiance gives today's ethnic situation in Europe its peculiarly complex and ambiguous character.

Now this is not to say that there has not been an important shift in the relationships between the state supported by the dominant ethnic community and the minority or subordinate ethnic communities. A change has clearly taken place, and one of its symptoms is the growth of disillusionment with the centralised state. But such a disillusionment is not confined to members of the ethnic minorities; nor have all members of those minorities come to regard the state as somehow illegitimate. This suggests that we need to specify, far more closely than the ecological thesis has done, the exact nature of the mechanisms linking the bureaucratic state with different sections of the ethnic minorities. We need to know why the young (and which of the youth, in particular) feel unable to identify with the traditional nation-state; and why there has been a reaction against the sort of bureaucratic nationalism or étatisme which upholds the equation of the state and society. While Mayo touches on some of the reasons at different points in her account of the Welsh, Breton and Basque movements, they remain unintegrated with her ecological thesis. While the role of bureaucracy is fundamental, it needs to be related to cultural changes and the rise of new strata, if we are to arrive at a more adequate general framework.

This leads to the third difficulty, that of trying to apply the ecological theory outside the context of Western Europe today. Mayo, in fact, restricts herself to providing an account of post-War developments in this one area; but she recognises the need to go back into the distant past of the three communities, if we are to understand the present rediscovery of, and interest in, their distinctive character. In doing so, she draws attention to the historical antecedents of the present ethnic resurgence, and the earlier waves of nationalism in the nineteenth and early twentieth centuries, which form the matrix of the movements. What the ecological thesis fails to explain is the timing and intensity of the present resurgence, or of the earlier waves, because it assumes a universal need for roots and does not specify the extent to which such roots have been penetrated and disturbed by the bureaucratic state, and the periods when this occurred in its most acute forms. In many ways, the present movements for autonomy in the West resemble the earlier waves of nationalism in Europe more than they differ from them; and the ecological thesis needs considerable modification to take account of this historical continuity.

What of its applications outside Europe? In a note, Patricia Mayo mentions autonomous movements in Quebec, Biafra and Bangladesh, only to restrict the geographical range of her thesis to Europe.[28] This is perhaps wise, insofar as the 'social and political malaise' she has in mind is largely European. But, again, because the similarities between the European and nonEuropean autonomous movements are as great, if not greater, than their differences, we may ask whether a thesis so clearly modelled on West European experience can say anything useful about ethnic movements in Kurdistan, Bangladesh, Eritrea and Eastern Nigeria. In some areas, like subSaharan Africa, the thesis may, in fact, be more applicable than in Europe, because, although it does not yet possess the power to penetrate the hinterland which its European counterparts possess, the African state is a more artificial imposition, and much less closely related to its ethnic populations. It does not have the historical resonance of, say, the French or Spanish state. There is a very real dichotomy between state and society in Africa and Asia, since the former was an alien creation, an instrument and framework of mobilisation and regimentation, which often ignored the ethnic composition and sentiments of the population which it incorporated.[29]

The other part of her thesis, on the other hand, concerning the nature and reactions of 'natural' social groups, is even less applicable than in Europe. The ethnic sentiments of many (though not all) Asian and African groups have been shaped even more directly by European penetration in the modern era than their counterparts in Europe. Moreover, Africans and Asians have lived in a variety of large and small social groups, which can be called 'natural' only in the sense of being pre-colonial and indigenous. The 'tribe' is often claimed to be the typical African grouping; but tribes are composed of smaller kin groups, their size and characteristics vary considerably, and only some of them claim the status of 'ethnic groups' like their European counterparts, and are so recognised.[30] Besides, it was not 'tribal' nationalism that won political independence for the African. African intelligentsias were attracted rather by the 'territorial' nationalism of the colonial states recently carved out by the European invaders, and the two kinds of nationalism have coexisted uneasily where they have not openly clashed.[31] If African leaders hope to create new political nations out of their culturally heterogeneous populations, after the Swiss model, they are equally haunted by the European experience of 'balkanisation', as they see it. They would hardly endorse a characterisation of their 'state-nations' as purely 'artificial' or term the nationalism of their ethnic communities 'natural'. In fact, such an ideological opposition misses some of the complexities of relations between political units and ethnicity, and underestimates the influence of the state in moulding ethnic communities.[32]

ETHNONATIONALISM

In fact, most cultural approaches to the problems of the ethnic revival fail to treat this question of the systematic links between states and ethnic communities. For such treatments, we have to go to the work of the political scientists. Unfortunately, though they have provided us with some admirably detailed studies of these links, their focus has been usually narrowly contemporary and has lacked historical depth. They are, moreover, generally preoccupied with the consequences and management of current ethnic conflicts, rather than with their origins and causes. Much of their efforts have been directed towards the elucidation and application of the 'consociational' theory or model of ethnic politics, developed by Lijphart and others.[33] But this model is problematic, and is only marginally relevant to the problems of the ethnic revival.

One political scientist has, however, concentrated on the historical matrix of the ethnic revival, and attempted to bridge the gap between the cultural and political dimensions. In a series of interesting and arresting articles, Walker Connor has argued the case for a modernisation theory of ethnic separatism. His starting-point is the simple, but significant, fact that most modern states are 'plural'. For Connor, the very term 'nation-state' is a misnomer: only 12 (9.1%)

states out of a total of 132 in 1971 were ethnically homogeneous; 53 states (40.2%) even had a population divided into five or more important ethnic communities.[34] Hence the many opportunities for ethnic conflict today.

But why are such conflicts and movements specifically ethnic, and why should we be witnessing an ethnic resurgence today? To the first question, Connor answers that 'Since 1789, the dogma that "alien rule is illegitimate rule" has been infecting ethnically aware peoples in an ever-broadening pattern. Indeed, as far as Europe is concerned, the region's subsequent history has been largely a tale of national liberation movements.'[35] The French Revolution has linked the abstract idea of popular sovereignty with the popular notion of a 'particular, ethnically defined people', with the result that popular sentiment against alien rule has 'proved a potent challenger to the legitimacy of multinational structures'.[36] The national idea itself has remained substantially unchanged since its first proclamation in the Declaration of the Rights of Man and of the Citizen; but it has come to inspire an ever-increasing number of ethnically aware communities in every part of the globe, so that the latest phase of 'ethnonationalism', as Connor terms the phenomenon, is merely an extension of 'the force field of nationalism'.[37] In other words, nationalism is likened to an evolutionary and self-propelling growth, feeding on unsatisfied ethnic aspirations, and the present surge of ethnonationalism among Basques, Scots and Bretons 'reflects a quite natural and perhaps even predictable stage in a process that has been underway for approximately two centuries'.[38]

But this ideological process has received a powerful impetus from external sources, notably in the realm of communications. These catalysts include the demonstration effect of other successful nationalisms; the influence of small peoples achieving independence and so undermining accepted notions of 'viability'; the impact of decolonisation on Europe's minorities in revealing the weakness of the classic European states; above all, the quantum leap in mass education and communications since World War II, which has transformed a difference of degree into a difference of kind.

This last factor is crucial for Connor. 'Modernisation' is the real catalyst of the diffusion of nationalism (though not of its origins and content); and 'modernisation' for Connor means largely mass communications. Prior to World War II, there were few roads and vehicles, radio was mainly local, education was minimal and thinly spread, and income levels were low. The result was that people were largely immobile and ethnic communities were insulated from changes. Even Europe's small ethnic groups occupied a 'pre-industrial' niche within fast industrialising states. But, by the end of World War II, the gradual growth of contacts through education and travel, easier transport, the growth of mass media, higher income levels induced a 'qualitative change'; and 'the cumulative impact of the quantitative increases in the intensity of intergroup contacts now constituted a threat to the ethnicity' of a significant number of people. And this 'represented, in political terms, a qualitative transformation'.[39] Gradual and cumulative, the processes of modernisation eventually broke through the dams of ethnic self-containment and drew these self-aware communities into conflict. The 'railroads' had indeed resulted in national hatred.[40]

It is at this point that Connor takes issue with the conventional Deutschian thesis. Though Karl Deutsch himself had noted that the process of social mobilisation, the uprooting and activation of villagers and small townsmen, might be so rapid that there was no time for a nation-wide cultural assimilation, he had nevertheless lent his authority to the more usual view that social mobilisation would automatically result in cultural assimilation of smaller ethnic groups.[41] For Connor, the reverse is true. The immense rapidity and spread of communications must lead to cultural conflict, for it sets the uprooted and incorporated ethnic communities at each others' threats. Ethnic conflict is the inevitable result of modernisation; and so it will increase with the further spread of communications and education. This is because communications now penetrate to the remotest hinterlands, bringing the message of national self-determination and the example of successful nationalisms in their train. *Force majeure* and diplomacy may contain ethnic demands for a time; but the dominant trend towards fissure and ethnic 'balkanisation' which spread to the Third World, has now once again been brought back by the tide of intensive communications into the most peripheral areas of Europe.

Hence, for Connor as for many others, the twin processes of modernisation and nationalism run *pari passu*, and reinforce each other. Although he disagrees with the conventional view that nationalism will abate with the progress of modernisation, arguing indeed that the contrary is true, Connor nevertheless ties the ethnic revival very closely to the processes of modernisation. And both modernisation and ethnonationalism are viewed as cumulative, self-generating and unfolding processes.

But the fact that we are witnessing a powerful resurgence of ethnonationalism in Europe today, many decades after the Industrial Revolution and the communications revolution of the turn of the century, must prompt the question of the extent to which the two processes are interwoven and cumulatively interdependent. Should we indeed tie nationalism so closely to the processes of modernisation, as the prevailing orthodoxy holds? It is not simply that a good many 'traditionalistic' regimes and states have utilised ethnonationalism when it suited their interests; Wilhelmine Germany and Tsarist Russia are obvious cases, but Gaullism was equally uncommitted to modernisation. Nor is it simply a case of ethnic nationalism furnishing as useful a rationale for conservative interests and social order as for radical change; ideologies do, after all, contain many potentialities, and none more so than nationalism.

The real difficulty with the modernisation theory of nationalism is its vagueness and untestability. The term 'modernisation' is usually so all-encompassing as to include practically any and every kind of social change in the last two centuries, and so to make the link true and necessary by definition. If, on the other hand, the term *is* pared down to one of its constituent processes, say communications, then, until we can specify their extent and density, we remain unable to relate them to the growth and spread of ethnonationalism. Besides, ethnic conflict and sentiments have flourished in periods prior to the modern; and, while they clearly required some degree of intergroup contact, some clash of cultures, such minimal communication hardly deserves to be called 'modernisation', and is rarely so termed.[42]

Of course, Connor's own claim for modernisation is more modest; he sees it as a catalyst and amplifier rather than a major cause of ethnonationalism. But this means that ethnonationalism contains within itself the potential and 'drive' for its own diffusion. If we ask why this should be so, and why this particular ideology should have exercised so great an appeal, we are thrown back on Connor's phrase about 'ethnically aware peoples'. But this only pushes the question a stage further back; how do ethnic groups become self-aware, become, in fact, nations? For Connor holds that 'The definitions of state and nation quoted above make clear that what we have thus far been calling self-differentiating ethnic groups are in fact nations. Loyalty to the ethnic group, therefore, should logically be called nationalism.'[43] It is this subjective state that really differentiates ethnic groups from nations. As Connor puts it, 'A prerequisite of nationhood is a popularly held awareness or belief that one's own group is unique in a most vital sense. In the absence of such a popularly held conviction, there is only an ethnic group.'[44] Cultural signs may well contribute to this sense of uniqueness, but they are only symbols of national identity or issues by which nations may differentiate themselves. The essence of nationhood lies not in these signs and symbols, but in the sense of group uniqueness itself.[45]

But how, then, does this vital sense of uniqueness arise? What transforms an unselfconscious ethnic group into a self-aware nation? And must there not be some minimal correspondence between the sense of uniqueness and one or more 'objective' differentiating cultural factors? Does it really make sense to relegate the latter to the status of mere signs or symbols?

It is these questions that I shall try to answer in the next chapters. Connor's historical analysis provides the only sound framework and point of departure for an understanding of the ethnic revival; but it stops short of providing an account of the transition from ethnicity to nationhood which forms the core of that revival. In setting the present ethnic resurgence firmly within the context of a much broader and more enduring growth of ethnonationalism, Connor has invested it with the importance and centrality it merits in the modern world.[46] But, by linking it to processes of communications and treating ethnonationalism as an autonomous, self-propelling force, he bypasses the sociological questions of its appeal to various strata and its institutional settings and causes. The spread of communications and the ideas of ethnonationalism cannot, in themselves, explain why ethnic ties, having lain dormant for several centuries, should become once again socially significant to the point of requiring explicit political expression and recognition as perhaps the major principle of global organisation today.

4

Ethnic consciousness in pre-modern eras

One of the main difficulties in constructing a convincing account of the ethnic revival has been the common tendency to confuse ethnic communities and regions, and ethnic sentiment with regionalism. The tendency is understandable, because ethnic communities usually 'possess' a recognised territory, with which they are habitually associated. Ethnic groups also often display a jealous and deep-rooted attachment to particular areas or regions within one or more plural states. And, as we know, nationalism as an ideology and movement is very much concerned with the practical and symbolic uses of land; a nation without its 'homeland' is almost unthinkable.

The result of this conflation of essentially different, if closely linked, categories, is twofold. Theoretically, it has led to an underestimation of the dynamic character, and historical depth, of ethnic ties; with the result that theorists have looked elsewhere, usually to superimposed economic disparities, for the motor forces of the ethnic revival, with all the ensuing problems which I have discussed. In practical terms, the tendency to identify ethnic groups with regions, and to equate the sentiments of these two quite different categories, has led statesmen and civil servants to substitute administrative solutions for deeper cultural understanding and political action.

For these reasons, it becomes necessary to distinguish the two categories as sharply as possible. This will allow us to grasp the particular role of ethnicity in history, prior to the eighteenth century, as well as the empirical links between ethnic communities and their territorial habitats. It also serves to remind us of the antiquity, and near-ubiquity, of ethnic formations, which go back to the first recorded cultural divisions in the ancient Near East. Through a better understanding of the mechanisms that sustained ethnic groups in most parts of the globe throughout recorded history, we will be able to gauge the extent and depth of the modern ethnic revival, and discover how and why pre-existing ethnic ties should once again become socially significant and politically important.

ETHNIE AND REGIONS

By 'region' we generally understand a more-or-less-compact geographical area possessing a distinctive economic and ecological profile, which marks it off from neighbouring areas. The mountainous regions of Kurdistan or Eritrea are as much 'regions' in this sense as the south of Italy or the northeast of England. One can treat Brittany and Wales as 'regions' like the Ruhr or the 'eastern region' of Nigeria. But, of course, such categorisations are as much political and administrative as ecological. The designated area lies usually within a state's territorial jursidiction, and its administrative elites generally find it convenient to divide the territory into administrative zones enjoying an official status and some devolved powers. For all that, the central government will tend to justify its selection of administrative units on economic and ecological grounds; in many cases, objective considerations will support the selection.

Now, in some cases, these administrative and ecological zones will correspond to what may be termed 'historic areas', that is, more-or-less-compact areas which at some earlier period of history enjoyed a separate and independent status, before being incorporated into the existing state. Perhaps, too, the area's inhabitants will share a common language, and the historic area will also be a distinctive 'language area' (in some cases, the old historic boundaries may not quite correspond to the present language-area boundaries). Further, the area's inhabitants may possess distinctive cultural characteristics, a unique religion, distinctive customs and institutions, different pigmentation, special myths, above all, a unique history. This is the case in Brittany, the Basque country, Kurdistan and Nagaland. Yet, for the central government, this coincidence of a culturally distinctive group and a designated region is largely irrelevant, an accident of history. For the central bureaucracy, regions are administrative and ecological divisions of state, to be accorded the privileges of other similar divisions and treated as equal parts of the territorial state, each of which makes its own contribution to the overall economy, and hence to the prosperity and stability of the state. It follows that the plight of a region's inhabitants is the product of the area's lack of material resources and its dependent role in the statewide economy. Poor regions like the south of Italy, Brittany and Andalusia must have similar problems of underdevelopment and unemployment, which are quite different from those of well-developed regions like Catalonia or Croatia. That many of these regions or zones also contain culturally distinctive groups and coincide with historic and/or language areas, is beside the point; and the fact that most of the latter are the seats of collective protests points solely to a failure of devolution. The rest is of mere ethnographic interest.[1]

An ethnic group, on the other hand, involves just those cultural dimensions that central governments habitually ignore or underrate, and just those psychological features which they are unable to grasp. For, whereas a 'region' refers to a category rather than a community, with an ethnic group it is the other way round. Ethnicity refers not just to classifiable populations, though, as we shall see, it is possible to locate 'ethnic categories'. For the most part, an 'ethnic group' is a type of community, with a specific sense of solidarity and honour, and a set of shared symbols and values.[2]

Now the important point about an ethnic, as opposed to other kinds of social, grouping, is the rationale that sustains the sense of group belonging and group uniqueness, and which links successive generations of its members. That rationale is to be found in the specific history of the group, and, above all, in its myths of group origins and group liberation. The more striking and well-known these myths of group formation and group deliverance, the greater the chances for the ethnic group to survive and endure; and, conversely, the more shadowy and obscure its myths, the less vivid its sense of uniqueness and the greater the likelihood of its dissolution.

In certain circumstances, however, external factors may supply the group with the myths it may have lacked near the outset of its career. The group may then develop common cultural features which mark it off from outsiders, or invest clear marks of differentiation with a cultural meaning. The Blacks in America, for example, had, at least until recently, some difficulty in locating their myth of origins and deliverance; hence they turned to their differentiating mark, the feature which symbolised their 'similarity–dissimilarity' pattern, as Akzin terms it, and invested it with positive cultural meanings, so buttressing and clarifying a history that was in danger, through its obscurity, of becoming lost.[3] In other cases, the ethnic group simply accentuates its historic sense of apartness, and evolves further marks of differentiation, a unique religion or language, or special customs and institutions. Hence, the group's sense of individuality is enhanced and expanded by a whole range of cultural dimensions, or by the elaboration and deepening of one major cultural attribute.

Nevertheless, in the last resort, it is the belief in the common and unique origins of the community, and in its liberation from all ills, past and present, that justifies and sustains the other cultural dimensions or 'signs' of individuality, and indeed the very sense of group uniqueness itself. Thus we cannot limit, as Walker Connor has recommended, the definition of the ethnic group (let alone the nation) to the sense of group uniqueness alone.[4] An ethnic group cannot shed all its cultural dimensions or 'signs' and retain this sense of identity intact. For signs and identity alike spring from the selfsame source, the belief in common and distinctive group origins and liberation, from a sense of unique history. Without such beliefs, without some knowledge of that history, the signs are of purely academic interest and the sense of identity has neither anchor nor content. That which, in the end, defines an ethnic group is its unique history and its unique response to that history, and from these flow its other cultural marks of individuality and its sense of collective uniqueness.

ETHNIC COMMUNITIES AND ETHNIC CATEGORIES

An ethnic group, then, is distinguished by four features: the sense of unique group origins, the knowledge of a unique group history and belief in its destiny, one or more dimensions of collective cultural individuality, and finally a sense of unique collective solidarity. For short, we may define the *'ethnie'* or ethnic community as a social group whose members share a sense of common origins, claim a common and distinctive history and destiny, possess one or more distinctive characteristics, and feel a sense of collective uniqueness and solidarity.

To some extent, this is a 'primordialist' definition.[5] That is to say, it assumes that for an ethnic group to emerge, there must be some 'primordial' ties around which to build a sense of community.[6] Of Shils' primordial ties, the key ones for the creation of ethnicity are a distinctive history and one or more of the other cultural dimensions – religion, language, colour, customs.[7] These cultural givens are regarded by the primordialists as 'natural' attachments in the same sense as kinship, and so constitute foundation blocks for the edifice of the ethnic community and even nationality.[8] We need not go so far; it suffices to claim that without such cultural similarities, we cannot begin to locate ethnic categories, and without such cultural ties, we cannot talk of ethnic communities. Nor need we assert that common descent must form the basis of ethnic attachments, for the number of genuine kinship relationships must be too small to be of any political significance. Rather, it is the myth of a common and unique origin in time and place that is essential for the sense of ethnic community, since it marks the foundation point of the group's history, and hence its individuality.[9]

Of course, the nature and intensity of the cultural dimensions and the sense of group origins and history will vary between ethnic groups. There is an important difference between groups which have a rich culture and many cultural differentiating dimensions, as well as a firm belief in and knowledge of their origins and history, and those that have a very recent and shallow culture and a shadowy sense of their history. It also makes an important difference whether the secondary differentiating dimensions are those of language or religion or colour or something else, or a combination of two or more of these dimensions. One of the great drawbacks of the opposing 'instrumentalist' viewpoint, of which the economic theories are typical cases, is that it ignores or underplays the dynamic effect of particular cultural dimensions. The fact, for example, that it was religion that 'preserved' the ethnic identity of Greeks and Jews through the ages, whereas it was language that was so important in uniting Czechs and Germans, is not merely of intrinsic interest, but is one factor in the explanation of the different trajectories of the two types of ethnic communities.[10] To treat language and religion as merely 'functional equivalents' is to miss the significance, and hence effects, of the differences between religious and language systems. And the same can be said of the role of colour, or customs and institutions.

And yet, these cultural dimensions remain secondary (though still of great importance) to the sense of common origins and history of the group. This constitutes the core of the group's identity, and of its sense of uniqueness. For a community to be said to exist, there must be a set of shared sentiments among the members, a fairly widespread sense of belonging, and a recognition of otherness, on the part of both members and outsiders. For an *ethnic* community to exist, there must be some common and distinctive cultural attributes and ties, traceable ultimately to the fact of a separate group history and origins. The cultural ties may be more lively than the sense of the history at a given point in time, and much of the history will have to be rediscovered, even 'invented'; but without some real historical foundation and without a sense of those common origins and history, however garbled and 'mythical', no ethnic community can subsist.

To this, it may be objected that outsiders, usually western scholars, have sometimes 'invented' ethnic groups by rediscovering ethnic ties and ethnic history. Thus German Protestant evangelists helped to form an Ewe sense of ethnic identity in the early twentieth century, by inventing an Ewe script and grammar, and promoting an Ewe literature.[11] In the case of the Slovaks and Ukrainians, too, it was the literary and historical labours of a few of their intellectuals which laid the cultural basis for a Slovak and Ukrainian sense of ethnic identity, and hence community.[12] Prior to the nineteenth century, an observer might have been able to distinguish peasant populations which spoke dialects and worshipped in ways distinguishable from those of their immediate neighbours; but he could hardly have described these populations as a 'community', since these populations possessed no *sense* of group uniqueness and belonging, or of their common origins and history. It took the labours of the intellectuals to discover this common history and, through it, to help endow their respective populations with a sense of unique identity. How and why the intellectuals did so, will be considered in the next chapter.

In the process of such historical and literary discovery, there was, of course, a good deal of plain invention, and, even more, of interested selection. There remained, however, a core of historical fact, in some cases not very well attested, and pretty minimal. But this modicum sufficed to form the stem around which the other cultural dimensions might blossom, and provide a rationale and a framework for the growing sense of group identity. In other words, recent history may provide the spur to the formation of an ethnic identity, where little or none exists in a population; but ancient history provides its organising principle and legitimation, its *raison d'être*.

But what of those units of population which lacked any sense of identity or community, and yet were distinguishable from their neighbours by the foreign or indeed native observer? They do not form communities, since they lack any shared attachments or common sentiments. They are a bit like the French peasants which Marx described in the *Eighteenth Brumaire of Louis Bonaparte,* an aggregate of individuals in a common situation, but lacking all sense of community and all ties and organisations which might unite them. The Ewe tribesmen or the Slovak peasants constituted an aggregate of families (and clans) possessing some common attributes – some common history, common dialects, perhaps common religious customs – but with little sense of community *vis-à-vis* outsiders or lively memories of a common fate in the past, or sense of liberation from their plight as a community; and lacking also any unifying agencies or organisation. Such a unit of population could best be termed an 'ethnic category', rather than an 'ethnic community'.

Of course, there is no clearcut distinction between ethnic communities and categories. It is partly a question of the degree to which common sentiments and institutions have evolved in a given unit of population, and this, I believe, is correlated with the richness or otherwise of its history, and the liveliness of its sense of that history. Even in clear cases of ethnic communities, by no means all the members evince these sentiments or are even aware of these ties; in practice, it suffices that the upper and middle strata are strongly aware, with perhaps some sense of group distinctiveness permeating the peasantry, who otherwise hold to their customs, religion and language without much self-awareness. The xenophobia that is traditionally ascribed to the peasants, and the 'mass sentiments' that are sometimes attributed to them, are usually quite localised; the sentiment of the villager, or perhaps of the local district, only more rarely of the ethnic group as a whole.[13] Where an ethnic category has been transformed into an ethnic community, this is the product of quite specific circumstances.

Ethnic categories usually lack large upper and middle strata, and, in a pre-industrial society, they are therefore mostly composed of scattered peasants and a few priests and headmen. Hence, at the beginning of the nationalist era, and the rise of commercial capitalism and the modern state, these units stand in a different position to well-developed ethnic communities. This need not constitute a barrier to the quest for national status and autonomy but it is clearly a handicap. It will take longer to produce the social strata and economic classes which can press the claim for national recognition; and it will take longer to convince the outside world of the cogency of the national claim, if a clearcut and ancient history supporting a vivid sense of collective identity cannot be easily presented. But, then, even well-established ethnic communities encounter barriers in their quest for national status. They may be able to present a united community and a centuries-long history; but the institutions which are the result of the very length and depth of that history may block the transformation of an ethnic community into a 'nation', and hold back the acquisition of a national status. Peoples shaped by ancient religions like the Chinese, Hindu Indians, Arabs and Jews are especially prone to this difficulty.[14]

So, of course, are peoples who lack a territorial base. One of the characteristics that distinguish ethnic categories or communities from nations is precisely the territorial dimension: a nation, by definition, requires a 'homeland', a recognised space and ecological base, if only to ensure cohesion and autonomy and the rights of citizenship, whereas an ethnic community, let alone category, can maintain its sense of belonging or its distinctive cultural characteristics without such a territorial base. The obvious case is that of the Jews; but American Blacks, Armenians, Greeks and Gypsies have constituted diaspora ethnic communities even though they lacked a territorial base. True, they did have ancestral memories of a homeland, a land associated with the formative events of the group or the category, but the memories were sometimes hazy, and the sense of community rested essentially upon foundation myths, and, above all, on a sense of common origins and a separate history of suffering and exile. The 'land' for which they might yearn, now had a primarily symbolic meaning, until, that is, the dawning of the age of nationalism.[15]

AGRARIAN MORES AND 'MASS SENTIMENTS'

The notion of an ethnic 'revival' implies, as I have said, the pre-existence of ethnic ties, and fluctuations in their social and political importance at different periods in history, and in different areas of the world. As I have also argued, however, the present ethnic revival does differ, not merely in degree but also in kind, from earlier periods when ethnicity was a significant factor in society and politics. The present revival is also a transformation, and not just a restoration of the previous role of ethnic community in social and political affairs. To clarify this transformation, it will be helpful, therefore, to outline briefly the factors that have helped to maintain ethnic ties throughout recorded history while varying their social and political importance at different periods. Since my main task is to analyse the modern ethnic revival, the description that follows in this chapter can only be cursory and schematic.

Clear-cut ethnic formations are first found with the growth of sedentary farming communities after the Neolithic Revolution in the Near East.[16] Out of the mists of the al-Ubaid and Gerzean cultures in lower Mesopotamia and the Nile district there appear the first attested ethnic communities, the Sumerians and ancient Egyptians, closely followed by the Elamites, Akkadians and others in the third millennium B.C.[17] Whether and how far there was a separate Akkadian people, i.e. ethnic community, which scholars have inferred from the existence of a separate Akkadian language, is an open question; perhaps Akkadian-speakers constituted an ethnic category, and never achieved a sense of ethnic community distinct from that of the much-better-developed community of the neighbouring Sumerians. In this, they may resemble several ethnic formations of the ancient Near East, notably the Arameans, whose language became a sort of lingua franca in the first millennium B.C., although the 'Aramean tribes' never seem to have achieved a deep and politically effective sense of ethnic community.[18]

This may be due to the fact that wandering communities like the Arameans or even the pre-Islamic Arabs, could not, in the very nature of things, achieve a clearcut sense of community because their continual population shifts precluded a definitive history or sense of origins. If this is the case (and it may well vary with particular examples), then it would suggest that one of the preconditions of ethnic formation and stability is the rise of sedentary units of population tied to the soil and having long and close dealings with each other in practical affairs. Sedentarisation, following closely on the heels of migration, seems to be of crucial importance in the formation of ethnic communities, since a period of drama, later viewed as part of the foundation myth and perhaps associated with a liberation myth, followed by a much longer period of sedentary occupation of a given territory, impresses the social consciousness of the migrants and their children with a sense of group history and unity. Coulborn has certainly argued this in the case of the Sumerians, although archaeologists and historians remain divided over the question of Sumerian 'origins'.[19] The pattern is clearly exemplified by the Israelite coalition which migrated from Egypt and Sinai to the land of Canaan;[20] and by the Hellenic myths of the 'Dorian' invasions of Greece slightly later.[21] Indeed, as Weber noted, migration myths play a particularly important role in processes of ethnic formation.[22]

But, there is also another dimension of sedentarisation. The migrants generally exchanged nomadic for agricultural habits and lifestyles. They adapted to certain 'rhythms of association' dictated in the main by the climate, soil and terrain, and by the round of the seasons. Their patterns of settlement, their mode of production, the nature of their habitats, all helped to crystallise a certain way of life. The agrarian rhythms, in turn, provided the grounds for the development of countryside mores and customs; the daily round of peasant life was broken up by festivals and enlivened by legends and myths, which gave meaning to the unending struggle with nature, and personalised unintelligible forces beyond human control. Soon there arose the myth of the golden age, when nature was bountiful and life untroubled, when man lived in harmony with his environment, before city life began to corrupt him, immediately after the creation and liberation of the community. At any rate, that is how later generations of city-dwellers came to view the distant past and thereby to extol the simple mores of the countryside.

Even from the outset, it is difficult to disentangle the popular beliefs and mores of the countryside from the civic religion, and its interpretations of those mores by city-dwelling priests and scribes. In ancient Greece, a popular religion did persist alongside the civic religions of the city-states, but there was no clearcut separation; the god of the artisans, Hephaistos, was worshipped equally alongside Athena, as patron deities of Athens and Attica.[23] In ancient Mesopotamia, the dependence of town on country in an irrigation civilisation was even more acute; the high point of the city-state, and, later, imperial, religions was the annual New Year festivals, in which kings and priests sought to intercede with the divine pantheon to ensure a plentiful harvest, and above all to avert the catastrophe of flooding by the swollen Tigris and Eurphrates.[24] In both cases, as in others, a locally fragmented peasantry were made dimly aware of their interdependence, and of the shared myths and rites which bound them to the cities, and hence to a wider ethnic community.

So one pillar of ethnic community and its survival down the ages has been the creation and preservation of agrarian rites and mores following the sedentarisation of nomadic tribes. The persistence of agrarian rhythms, and its associated mores, was largely a function of the poor state of communications prior to industrialisation and of the subsistence nature of the rural economy. The village remained the dominant unit for the mass of the population, and each district evolved its local variety of customs and beliefs, even though they were early related to the state religions of the city. And this persistence of agrarian mores down the ages meant that the peasantry became a repository of cultural distinctiveness, folk traditions, local colour, individuality of beliefs and customs, and the like. It also meant that here was a reservoir of 'mass sentiments' and attachments for later intellectuals to tap, because the countryside contained ready-made, if highly localised, communities with long and distinctive cultural traditions which could be worked up by urban intellectuals into a broader ethnic culture, when the need arose, an approach that has been successfully adopted by a number of nationalisms, and latterly by marxist nationalisms looking to the peasantry for the base of their national revolutions.[25]

We have to be careful, however, about the notions of 'mass sentiments' and folk mores that some of the nationalist marxists employ.[26] The rootedness, and xenophobia, commonly attributed to the peasantry is often so localised that it prevents any possibility of building a wider community or nation on this basis. Of course, when invading aliens terrorise the countryside and seek to conscript or otherwise oppress the peasants, as happened in northern China when the Japanese invaded in 1937, 'xenophobic' resistance is likely and it becomes possible to channel it into communist organisations and ideological frameworks.[27] Even then, it takes considerable time and effort to organise the peasantry, as it did in the Oriente province of Cuba, when Castro began his campaign against Batista.[28] In peacetime, there is little likelihood of forging any sense of community among often widely scattered villages in the countryside, and local customs and dialects will often vary considerably between valleys or regions in the same general area. There is very little 'mass sentiment' to be found in the countryside, except perhaps in times of severe distress or war; a sense of ethnic community is therefore minimal, if it exists at all. Peasants often learn that they are Poles or Slovaks only when they are informed by travelling intellectuals, or latterly through the mass media; even in so well-developed and centralised a state as France, it took many decades to turn 'peasants into Frenchmen'.[29]

If rural communities do not generally evince much ethnic sense of belonging between themselves, they tend to be even more isolated from the upper strata in the towns, despite the links provided by the priesthood. The degree of the links between strata has, of course, varied considerably down the ages. It may have been closer in the city-states of antiquity owing to their smaller scale, and only became attenuated with the growth of bureaucratic empires based on the court in a capital city. In many cases, we shall never know how far peasants in ancient empires could identify with urban and upper strata and so feel a loyalty to a wider community in their areas; in this respect, the Jews and Greeks may well have been exceptional in the relative proximity of those links. In the Middle Ages, despite some cultural penetration from the towns, feudal conditions, and a level of communications that was often much worse than had existed in ancient or classical empires, greatly increased the separation of rural villages from the state and its urban centres. The position of the Rumanian peasants, and the attitudes of the Rumanian nobles and clergy to their villagers up to the nineteenth century, was fairly common: these peasants simply did not belong to the Rumanian 'nation' when, in the eighteenth century, the concept of a Rumanian national community began to emerge among educated upper strata.[30]

The persistence of agrarian mores and beliefs did not, therefore, generate 'mass sentiments' on the part of the peasant communities, nor a sense of wider ethnic community; not, at any rate, in and of themselves. What the persistence of these mores did ensure was, first, that there was some 'cultural material' to hand for intellectuals in search of a unique community, and, second, that by virtue of their history of isolation and, often, oppression, peasant communities could on occasion be drawn together in opposition both to aliens and to alien-seeming – because remote – landowning gentry classes, even if they spoke similar tongues or worshipped the same god or gods. So that, if circumstances were propitious, 'mass sentiments' could be excited and linked up to a set of myths and symbols which united urban and rural traditions in one great 'ethnic history'. This again, as we shall see, was the supreme achievement of romantic intellectuals.

WAR AND ETHNIC CONSCIOUSNESS

If agrarian mores tended to disperse and fragment any sense of ethnic community, war tended to crystallise and unify it. Indeed, of all the factors that have gone into creating and sustaining ethnic identities, war has been the most potent and perhaps the most neglected.

Many historians and others have, of course, long noted the connection between war and patriotism or ethnic sentiment; but they have usually suggested that a pre-existing ethnic or national sentiment was decisive in triggering wars, and that wars then reinforced that sentiment. This assumes that 'wars' in the past were ethnic or national wars; that is to say, wars were always or mainly fought between ethnic communities as the outcome of a history of communal antagonism. But ethnic communities are by no means the only or even the most frequent 'subjects' of warfare; clans, villages, city-states, empires and kingdoms have often engaged in protracted wars, just as there have been slave, peasant and sectarian revolts. This is not to deny the frequency of 'tribal' or ethnic warfare in some parts of the world, and at certain periods. My purpose is only to put this type of warfare in perspective, as one among several kinds of wars in both antiquity and the Middle Ages.[31]

The greater number of wars in the historical record have been 'interstate' wars. They have been fought between the military machines of two or more states, which may have contained one or more ethnic communities or categories or, as in ancient Greece, parts of a wider ethnic community. Prior to the French Revolution, many interstate wars were dynastic; even in the case of tribal wars, they tended to be fought by what Malinowski termed centralised 'tribe-states'.[32] Individual wars are best seen as the product of the institutionalisation of warfare between a network of city-, feudal, dynastic or tribal states, one arm of whose administrative apparatus is devoted exclusively to the defence of the state and the prosecution of warfare; and the interests which the military arm was designed to protect were those of the state itself, and of its elites, rather than of the subject population as a whole, with very rare exceptions.

This did not mean that ethnic communities were irrelevant to pre-industrial warfare. Quite the contrary; ethnicity was often seen as a valuable resource by political and military elites engaged in interstate hostilities. By appealing to shared beliefs and symbols, these elites found that they could mobilise much larger populations without relying so heavily on coercive methods. Even more important, the circumstances of invasion in antiquity and the medieval era, with its ensuing destruction of crops and pillaging of villages in the countryside, tended to push a sullen and fragmented peasantry into the arms of any rulers who could effectively defend them against such depredations. The longer such hostilities lasted, and the more visible and menacing the enemy, the more the gentry and burghers required the services of their peasantries, and conversely the more the latter needed the protection of the military machine of state manned by the upper strata.

Historically, protracted wars have been the crucible in which ethnic consciousness has been crystallised. The prolonged wars between Egypt and Assyria, between Israelites and Philistines, between Greeks and Persia, Khmers and Vietnamese, and England and France in the Hundred Years' War, fought between tribal or dynastic states, are only the best-known examples of pre-industrial interstate warfare crystallising and mobilising a diffuse ethnic consciousness which embraces even some of the peasantry. Simmel remarked that war articulates the 'latent relationship and unity'; it rarely actually originates ethnic cleavages.[33] There must be some cultural divisions, some 'ethnic categories', to afford a base for common sentiments. But wars are often closely associated with the foundation and liberation myths of many ethnic communities, which suggests that political action and military organisation have been decisive in the development of ethnic community. Weber, at least, was explicit about the political origins of ethnic community: 'It is primarily the political community', he stated, 'no matter how artificially organised, that inspires the belief in common ethnicity.'[34]

In fact, Weber may have exaggerated the role of politics. It is true that the centralised state today is the single most potent factor in the creation of ethnic communities, though even here its effects are sometimes paradoxical. In pre-industrial societies, the state machine, even where it did not succumb to continual warfare, as in twelfth-century Byzantium, was rarely strong enough to obliterate the belief in common ethnicity, wherever that belief had existed in any force over a long time span. Even highly centralised and efficient state machines like those of ancient Persia or Rome, which had succeeded in subjugating vast territories with heterogeneous populations, found it difficult to create a real 'political community' out of the diverse cultures and communities in their far-flung empires, much less a common ethnicity.

Nevertheless, despite the relative fragility of many pre-industrial empires, the wars which they and other states conducted were often decisive in shaping, not only the ethnic sense of their own dominant community, but also that of their enemies and even of third parties caught in the cross-fire. The classic cases are those of the Israelites caught between the armies of ancient Egypt and Assyria;[35] and of the Swiss defending their cantons against Habsburg or Burgundian incursions.[36] In both cases, a rather shadowy sense of difference, evidenced in local beliefs, customs and dialects, was transformed into a full-fledged belief in their unique communities under the impact of their situation at a crossroads of war and trade, and of the specific military events which repeatedly threatened their very existence. In both cases, mobilisation of men and resources and propagation of favourable self-images by means of myths and heroes, the two immediate effects of prolonged warfare, gradually crystallised, through a series of dramatic leaps, a high degree of ethnic self-consciousness and identity.

The stress which I place on interstate wars for the growth and crystallisation of ethnic communities, including affected 'third party' communities, is very much in line with the recent critique of two common views of 'politics' offered by Gianfranco Poggi.[37] The two views in question are David Easton's understanding of political life as the allocation of values by command within a collectivity, and Carl Schmitt's view that, in a dangerous and menacing world, politics is concerned with distinguishing friends from foes and with protecting the boundaries and cultural identities of collectivities from outside threats.[38] Poggi's critique of Schmitt's 'demoniac or fascist' outlook, which culminates in continual preparedness for a war of annihilation of foes, is highly pertinent to my argument that it is more often the 'state' or political community which crystallises the sense of common ethnicity than vice-versa, and that interstate warfare is one of the chief agencies through which a pluralistic world of collectivities (of Us and the Others) is created and sustained. As Poggi argues:

His (Schmitt's) chief error is to take the collectivity of reference (Us) as a datum, from which he goes on to stress how fragile, threatened and conditional that datum is. But to *constitute* the collectivity, to impart to it the distinctiveness or sense of common destiny that politics, as Schmitt understands it, is designed to safeguard – all this, surely, is political business of the highest order. The collectivity is not a datum. It is itself the product of politics, which must first create it and can only then defend it. And in creating the collectivity in the first place, politics can hardly do without precisely those symbolic public processes that Easton emphasizes and Schmitt disdains.[39] (italics in original)

To attain a distinctive identity, a collectivity must be moulded by certain political processes, such as the framing of binding decisions, the legal patterning of interaction and the maintenance of internal order. For, 'how can a collectivity discriminate between friend and foe if not by referring to a conception of what makes Us into Us; and how can such a conception be generated except by ordering in some distinctive fashion the internal life of the collectivity?'[40] And that ordering is the business of rule, the realm of the state.

Poggi, like Weber, may have overstated the case for the primacy of politics over culture in generating a sense of ethnic collectivity. The world is rich in cultural differentiae and 'ethnic categories'. We cannot know today whether all, or most, of these differences were generated by political action; some, at least, owed much to the accidents of geography or the content of religious movements or the ecological forces behind mass migrations.

But if 'politics', properly understood, played a secondary role in the genesis of the 'raw' cultural materials out of which peoples, or ethnic communities, could be constructed, its impact on the *formation* of those communities themselves and of their accompanying sense of collective identity, has been enormous. In all ages, the fundamental institution shaping the *sense* of common ethnic identity has been, as Cynthia Enloe has vividly demonstrated, the state and its bureaucratic machine, and, more especially, its military arm, the state at war. Even when they have not increased the social cohesion of ethnic communities, interstate wars have always heightened an incipient sense of common ethnicity, and prolonged wars have often generated the sense of community itself.[41]

There are four ways in which interstate warfare helps to generate a sense of distinctive collectivity and ethnic identity, of Us against Them. The first, most obviously, is through mobilisation of men and resources for actual armed conflict; and, more especially, the training of infantry in the cooperative and interdependent tasks of war in battle formations. The sense of unity induced by the momentary victory at Marathon was really a consequence of the much longer period of Greek hoplite formation training in the preceding century. Conversely, the calling together of vassals on horseback with their retainers, in which individual cavalry prowess counted for everything, could not evoke any sense of collective unity and identity; feudal battles were fought for individual honour and specific lords, including the king. The more infantry-based and interdependent the fighting formations which are mobilised, the more likely it is that the 'heat of battle' will rouse in the participants a sense of the common good and of the community.[42]

Second, there is the impact of war propaganda. An essential element in any struggle between collective entities, in this case militarised states, is the portrayal of one party in favourable, and the other party in unfavourable, terms. Inevitably, the search for positive and negative stereotypes fastens on those features of the population which both unite them and simultaneously distinguish them from the population of the enemy state. Thus the ancient Greek city-states contrasted their civic 'liberties' with the servitude and luxury of the Persian Great King and his subject peoples, who were in Greek eyes equally 'barbarian'. This ideal simplification was a direct effect of the wars between them, and it greatly assisted in convincing the individual (and often divided) city-states of their common Hellenic heritage and identity.[43] Similarly, in the modern world, inter-state conflicts have generated further ethnic stereotypes in a concerted effort to sustain civilian morale and strengthen the sense of national identity.[44]

Third, interstate wars are usually fought for the acquisition or defence of territory. They are therefore concerned with the definition of the unit's boundaries. This has the effect of drawing the population's attention to the issue of boundaries, of 'territorialising' public consciousness, and of identifying a given population with a particular extent and shape of territory. Soon, clear ideas about the 'correct' boundaries and extent of the territorial state, whether of the Roman or Chinese empires, or the Israelite confederacy, or the Greek or medieval Italian city-states, became widely publicised and upheld, creating in this way an association between a given population and a certain land. Equally, this territorialism of the state searches for a legitimation in the lack of any important differences in the population within the state's territorial jurisdiction. More positively, it seeks out features that mark off a homogeneous population with which the state's territory can be made congruent. In other words, the more interstate wars thrust the problem of borders and territory to the fore, the more they require the state to find in the cultural homogeneity of the population a rationale for those boundaries. The two processes reinforce each other, to create a sense of bounded community based on the perception of otherness.[45]

Finally, the centralisation required to carry on interstate wars in turn demands the institutionalisation of an internal order with its set of rules and customs peculiar to that state and its population. Prolonged warfare cannot tolerate multiple centres of command within a given militarised state, nor the interruption of the chain of command by rival power bases. Prolonged warfare must therefore strengthen, if it does not destroy, the concentration of the facilities of physical coercion at the centre, that is, in the hands of the state agencies. To maintain the territorial integrity of the state requires a distinctive internal ordering of its population, thus turning it into a community with a sense of its historic identity.

THE PERIODISATION OF ETHNICITY

Mobilisation, propaganda, territorialisation and centralisation of command constitute the mechanisms by which interstate wars help to create ethnic communities and a sense of collective identity. It follows that we should expect the importance of ethnicity in social and political affairs to rise and decline with the prevalence and institutionalisation of such wars. The more frequent and prolonged the wars between states or tribe-states become, the more likelihood that ethnic ties will be forged and a strong sense of common cultural identity will take root. Conversely, where wars are fought between other entities – villages, clans, feudal demesnes or sects – or in eras of relative stability and peace between states, or within large empires, the ethnic factor tends to decline as a political force, though it may retain some resilience at the social and cultural levels. Ethnic communities, once formed in eras of pronounced interstate wars, may well persist as modes of cultural and social organisation even in conditions of imperial stability, or feudal fragmentation, to be revived as a political force in succeeding periods of greater interstate warfare.

The degree to which ethnic community has become a major social or political force has varied greatly, not only in time, but also in different continents or culture areas, in the pre-modern era. Tribal organisation has played a major role in many areas for long periods – in Polynesia, subSaharan Africa and Siberia, for example. But it is difficult to be sure of the extent and depth of any truly ethnic identity or sense of common ethnicity among these often loose conglomerations of 'tribes'. In better documented cases, such as the tribal confederacy of the Israelites or the Medes and Persians, we know that it took several centuries of interstate wars to endow the separate clans and tribes with anything like a common sense of ethnicity. Essential to that development, has been the creation of the 'tribe-state'; and we find similar developments in Africa, for example among the Zulu in the nineteenth century, or the Yoruba somewhat earlier.

Broadly speaking, ethnic organisation and sentiment played a major role in the ancient Near East and the Mediterranean before Roman imperial expansion put an end to interstate warfare in the area. It was not merely among the Persians, Jews and ancient Greeks that we find a strong ethnic sentiment; ancient Egyptians, Sumerians, Hittites, Phoenicians, Urartians, Elamites, Assyrians, Carthaginians and others, displayed a well-developed sense of ethnic identity. Each of these groups constituted cultural communities organised as independent kingdoms or city-states, and all possessed their myth of origins, their common history and separate cultural traits, usually a distinctive pantheon of gods, a unique language and peculiar customs. In most cases, too, these communities, or their better-educated strata, were animated by a clear sense of their cultural superiority; they were convinced that 'their' community was the centre of their world, and that its values and mores were the natural and proper ones for men to follow. Without any self-consciousness, they believed that what was 'mine' was also 'right'; and their conviction that 'history' – the history of their community – coincided with 'value' – the ideals of their community – was the source of their traditional ethnocentrism.[46]

We can trace the emergence of this ethnocentrism and sense of common ethnicity to the 'neo-Sumerian' epoch at the end of the third millennium B.C. It was during this period of renewed wars between the Sumerian city-states, after the collapse of the Akkadian empire, when Ur emerged as the temporary victor, that we can find a sense of 'Sumerian-ness', in the very attempt to recreate a vanished past prior to the Akkadian empire.[47] It was also a time of growing involvement with tribe-states and kingdoms further afield – notably the Amorites, Assyrians and Elamites. The irruption of Indo-European tribal confederacies into Iran and northern Mesopotamia towards the middle of the second millennium – of Hurrians, Kassites, Hittites and others – and the expansion of the Egyptian New Kingdom, sharpened the sense of ethnic community and endowed it with greater political significance.[48] Various inscriptions and hymns, especially from Egypt, indicate the new importance of cultural characteristics in differentiating social groups which formed political entities. This coincided with prolonged conflicts between ethnically based states – the Hittites, Egyptians, Kassites and Mitanni – and with the emergence, for the first time in history, of what may loosely be termed an interstate system of diplomacy. It was in the immediate aftermath of the gradual break-up of this interstate network in the late second millennium that three new communities were forged in the crucible of interstate warfare – the Medes and Persians, the Assyrians and the Israelite confederacy. In the succeeding era of empires – Chaldaean, Persian, Hellenistic and Roman – most of the ancient Near Eastern *ethnie* were submerged some time after the dissolution of their political communities. Perhaps the most striking case was the Assyrian: built through war, the Assyrian state succumbed to its political rivals in 612 B.C., and the Assyrians are hardly heard of again.[49]

The periodisation of ethnicity

If the period between the early part of the second millennium and the mid-first millennium B.C. witnessed the zenith of interstate warfare between sedentarised 'tribe-states' and empires, the succeeding centuries saw a gradual decline in the role of ethnicity in political life. In the second and early first millennium B.C., no single state had managed to dominate the civilised areas of the Near East and eastern Mediterranean, with some brief exceptions, notably the Egyptian New Kingdom and the Sargonid period of Assyria in its third empire (745–612 B.C.). Even these attempts at domination were hotly contested. But, with the destruction of the neo-Babylonian empire by Cyrus, the way was opened to a much longer and more stable period of imperial Persian rule in this area. And despite the break-up of Alexander's empire which followed, the *pax romana* soon reestablished the multiethnic empire of the Persians, though further west, with its domination by the victorious Roman state. Until the 'barbarian invasions' of the fourth and fifth centuries A.D., ethnic community as a political force was relegated to the margins.

There were, of course, exceptions to this generalisation. During the protracted wars of the Seleucids and Ptolemies, a certain Egyptian sentiment surfaced and found expression in an attempt to resuscitate the Pharaonic past.[50] The long wars between Rome and Carthage did much to sharpen ethnic sentiment and sense of community on both sides; so, too, did the Jewish wars fought against Seleucid and Roman domination.[51] There was also plenty of ethnic prejudice in imperial Rome. Its manifestations, however, tended to be cultural and social rather than political.[52] Spaniards, Gauls or Greeks could rise to high position at Rome; and under the empire, with its long peace and relative stability, there was a wide, though by no means universal, acceptance of alien customs and religions.[53] So that, with each fresh Roman conquest, the subject peoples' sense of common ethnicity became socially weaker and politically irrelevant.

In the following period, that of the *Völkerwanderung*, this trend towards ethnic decline was sharply reversed, as successive waves of migrant tribes contributed to the collapse of the imperial structure. Indeed, some scholars wish to place the dawn of 'national sentiment' in this 'dark age', when Christian missionaries in Gallic, British, German and Balkan lands helped to endow inchoate groups of culturally distinctive wandering tribes with a sense of their common ethnic past and unique culture, by providing them with scripts and the nucleus of a subsequent literature.[54] But in many areas, especially in Eastern Europe, the migrations did not cease until the tenth century; lack of any clearcut association between tribal groups and particular territories made it difficult to instil a distinctive ethnic, let alone national, sentiment among such wanderers. Resistance to Saracens, and, later, Mongols and Turks, helped to sharpen the ethnic sense of populations (French, Catalans, Hungarians, Russians, Poles) included within victorious states. But the consolidation of such polities was delayed both by trans-territorial ties to Christendom as a whole, and by intraterritorial loyalties to particular lords or vassals; attempts to reconstitute the Holy Roman Empire further impeded the growth of territorial states, at least until the fourteenth century.[55] So that the inability to develop strong political units during the 'feudal' era meant that the chances of a sustained ethnic revival contained in the 'barbarian irruptions', and the break-up of the western Roman empire, could not be realised until a much later period.

Such a bare sketch of the 'ethnic factor' and its salience in western history does little justice to important regional variations. But, at least, it justifies the contention that, from one point of view, the present ethnic phase constitutes a revival and revitalisation of pre-existing ethnic ties, which had become latent and submerged, and is not a totally new departure. (As we shall see, the present ethnic revival *also* involves an ethnic transformation.) In fact, we can chart a cyclical oscillation between periods of ascendancy and submergence of ethnic ties in the history of the Near East and Europe. Ethnic organisation and sentiment emerge in the third millennium B.C. in the ancient Near East, and rise to a long period of ascendancy in the second and first half of the first millennium. They then decline in an era of imperial expansion, first in the Middle East, then in the Mediterranean lands. New ethnic organisations and sentiments are forged in the middle of the first millennium A.D., with the setting up of 'barbarian' kingdoms in Italy, France, Spain, England and Germany. But these prove to be short-lived. First, Charlemagne's empire, then the burgeoning of feudal principalities within an embattled Christendom, at a time when Byzantium and the Caliphate tend to suppress ethnic tendencies in the Near East and eastern Mediterranean, dissipate and submerge once again any incipient sense of ethnicity and its political expressions, with some temporary exceptions in Eastern Europe. It is not until the fifteenth century or later, in Western Europe and some areas of Northern and Eastern Europe (Sweden, Poland, Russia, Hungary), that ethnic ties once again gradually become socially significant and politically relevant.[56]

THE EUROPEAN MOSAIC

The preceding account has concentrated first on the Middle East, and thereafter on Europe, for the simple reason that the next ethnic revival, which was also a radical transformation, started in Europe and spread thence to the Middle East and Asia, before engulfing other parts of the world. The European transformation became, moreover, the first global revival; and the transformation of ethnic ties which that revival affected was profoundly marked by its European imprint. It is worthwhile, therefore, looking more closely at the 'state of ethnicity' in Europe on the eve of that transformation.

In the later Middle Ages, when the modern state began its long development in the West, ethnic ties and sentiments were in a state of some disarray. Paradoxically, they were more salient in the eastern half of the continent than the western – in Bulgaria, Bohemia and Serbia, and to some extent in the Poland of Casimir the Great. The rise of the Habsburg empire, followed by the Ottoman conquests, however, tended to stifle the expression of ethnic ties in much of Eastern Europe, as the expansion of the Russian empire was to do in later centuries. Similarly, the successive invasions of Italy and the consequences of the Thirty Years War prolonged the political divisions of Italy and the German-speaking lands, while Cossack and other incursions weakened the Polish state, preventing it developing the absolutist forms of the West. In all these areas, ethnic consciousness declined and in many cases became submerged in local, semi-feudal or religious loyalties.[57]

In the West, on the other hand, the forms of the 'modern state' evolved in fits and starts, as the ruler gradually succeeded in curbing the powers of feudal aristocracy. The beginnings of this long development can be traced back to the thirteenth century in England and France; but it was not until the Hundred Years' War that some consciousness of ethnic community was generated on both sides of the Channel, and even that was patchy.[58] It was really only with the transition to the absolutist state, after the decline of the estates as a political force, that a wider consciousness of ethnic identity and unity began to develop.[59] In England, the early movement towards centralisation after the Wars of the Roses, followed by the rejection of Papal authority and the claims of imperial Spain, brought to the surface, in the period from Shakespeare to Milton, a new 'national' sentiment in which English identity was blended with Puritan fervour during the Commonwealth.[60] In Spain, an early drive towards centralised authority during the sixteenth century was halted and ossified, until the later eighteenth century. In France, on the other hand, the ending of the Religious Wars weakened the authority of the nobles, while the policies of Richelieu and Mazarin strengthened the powers of the Crown. And yet, not even the absolutism of Louis XIV could entirely break the lingering rights of the aristocracy and clergy, or their regional 'liberties'. But, by turning the energies and institutions of the centralised state outwards, by seeking expansion on land and markets and territories overseas, the absolutist monarchs were able to level down many intermediate bodies and to weld culturally diverse populations with purely local loyalties into a 'national' territory-wide public. By developing standing armies and navies, and by imposing uniform bodies of public law on wider sections of the population (despite many immunities), the Court and the bureaucracy began to instil a sense of community in their subjects, which looked to the centre and its institutions as the legitimate framework and rationale of political autonomy. Not the town, nor the estate, nor the local region, but the territorial state became the legitimate sovereign.

In many ways this was a new process. Even in antiquity, the sense of ethnic community had never been tied so firmly both to a politically defined territory, set in vertical relationships with other such polities, and to an inclusive and sovereign state, membership of which conferred specific legal rights and obligations. Moreover, for perhaps the first time, the state as such was shaping not just the sense of common ethnic ties through public law and interstate wars; it was also constructing a common cultural identity for populations with often diverse traditions. It was not simply crystallising that identity and self-image, as the state had done in previous eras; its rulers were also creating identity and self-image out of several local heritages, incorporating those of outlying areas into that of the centre, the cradle of the state – a process attempted much more self-consciously in several African and Asian states today.[61]

A major characteristic of this 'nation-constructing' process was the rise of a new European state system. It was in the course of increasing rivalries and warfare between competing state units that 'national sentiment', as we know it, was generated – first in the western states, and then in Sweden, Prussia and Russia, though not always with long-lasting results. In other cases, interstate rivalries allowed strong imperial units to expand at the expense of weaker states or unorganised tribal populations, especially in Eastern Europe. The resulting ethnic pattern in Europe came to resemble a mosaic of more- and less-developed ethnic polities, ethnic communities and ethnic categories, with a very uneven distribution of national or ethnic sentiment. This 'European mosaic' of ethnic ties and national sentiment, with its network of diplomatic and cultural relations which came to link all parts of the continent together, was of fundamental importance to the rise and transformation of ethnicity in the eighteenth and nineteenth centuries.[62]

THE 'NATURALNESS' OF ETHNICITY

The modern generation of scholars in the field generally start out from the premiss that nations and nationalism are peculiarly modern phenomena, and that there is nothing 'natural' or inborn about national loyalties and characteristics.[63] In making these assertions, they are often reacting against not only the claims of nationalists themselves, but of earlier generations of observers who took the 'naturalness' of nationalism for granted.

Philosophically, the 'unnaturalist' theories may be on firm ground; but, historically, their case is less sure, unless they can find clear criteria for distinguishing between ethnic communities and nations, and between ethnic sentiment and nationalism. As we shall see, such criteria are often slippery and ambiguous. Nations are closely related to ethnic communities, often 'growing out' of the latter, or being 'constructed' from ethnic materials. Nationalism, too, has much in common with ethnic sentiment, despite its far greater elaboration. Important differences, both of kind and of degree, *can* be discerned between ethnic and national phenomena; but there is also considerable overlap between them, which is reflected in the lack of clarity surrounding the concepts themselves.

Now, if a clearcut distinction between ethnicity and nationality and between ethnic sentiment and nationalism cannot be established, then there is more continuity between nationalism and its ethnic forbears than many modern scholars admit. Nationalism, though still an eighteenth- or nineteenth-century ideology and movement, has deeper and firmer roots in the distant past; and nations are not simply the inventions of a modern breed of intellectual. National loyalty and national character may not be inborn, and they are certainly historical phenomena; but their modernity, their embeddedness in a specifically recent history, is anchored in an antiquity, a prehistory, of ethnic ties and sentiments, going back to the Sumerians and ancient Egyptians. And, while that antiquity does not allow us to treat nationalism, or ethnicity, as something 'natural', it does compel us to frame our enquiry differently, to understand nations as a recent type of political formation utilising an ethnic base and transforming the style and content of much older, and often dormant, ethnic ties.

That, in turn, means that the recent ethnic resurgence must be set, not merely in the context of a broader ethnic revival, which, under the banner of national self-determination, has been developing since the later eighteenth century, as we argued before; but also that this broader revival can only be grasped as a development and transformation of pre-existing, if submerged, ethnic ties and as the recent phase of a long historical cycle of ethnic emergence and decline, which has been going on since the dawn of recorded history.

Thus, on the eve of this latest ethnic revival, Europe exhibited a variety of states of ethnic consciousness and community, many of them subtly interwoven with each other and with aligned or cross-cutting polities. In the West, and in a few areas in Northern and Eastern Europe, a slow but definite transformation was taking place and gathering momentum by the eighteenth century: the transition from a latent cultural sense of ethnicity to an overt political and territorial consciousness of nationality. Elsewhere, Europe was divided into political units which incorporated or divided ethnic communities and ethnic categories of population, most of which had little social significance or political relevance. It was this 'unfinished' development, this patchwork of ethnic sentiments and memories, that the historicist revolution of the eighteenth century helped to galvanise and transform.

vwvwvwvwvwvwvwvwvwvwvwvwvwvwvwvwvwvwvwvwvwvwvwvwvwvwvwvwvwvwvwvwvwvwvwvwvwvwvwvwvw

Historicism

In the last chapter I argued that ethnic bonds and ethnic consciousness have always constituted important elements in human existence
since the dawn of recorded history, but that their social significance
and political relevance have varied in cyclical fashion with the incidence of sustained warfare between roughly equivalent political
units or states. In Europe, the modern ethnic revival built upon a
long tradition of such ethnic sentiment, although the latter has varied greatly in intensity and salience in different areas of the continent at different periods. In the early modern period, between the
late fifteenth and eighteenth centuries, a truly national sentiment began to emerge in some parts of Western and Northern Europe, while
in other parts of the continent, the ethnic sentiments, that had been
aroused in earlier periods, were now in disarray or largely submerged.

In this chapter I shall examine the revolutionary contribution of
the new stratum of secular intellectuals to the modern ethnic revival
from the mid-eighteenth century to the present day. My argument
here is that, within Europe's evolving interstate system (soon to be
replicated in other areas), the new historical outlook pioneered by
the intellectuals was an essential precondition of the ethnic revival,
and that this 'historicist' revolution helped not only to revive submerged ethnic ties and sentiments, but also to transform their role
and meaning. Unlike previous revivals, the modern one has pro-
ceeded under the aegis of a new ideological movement, that of nationalism; and nationalism, along with recent movements for ethnic
autonomy or separatism, can be regarded as political offshoots and
expressions of this new historical vision, which I shall term 'historicism'.

'HISTORICISM'

The origins of the modern ethnic revival can be fairly accurately
placed in the third quarter of the eighteenth century, forming part of

the early romantic movement which first appeared in England and France, and then spread to Germany, Italy and Scandinavia. This early romanticism with its characteristic cults of nature, the antique and the medieval, gave a powerful impetus to the rise of an evolutionary mode of explanation and an historical consciousness, both of which had emerged in the early eighteenth century. From that moment on, evolutionism and historicism became the cultural framework and basis of nationalism and the ethnic revival, both within Europe and outside; every other characteristic concern, and every cultural marker common to ethnic nationalisms, has been predicated upon this new historical vision.

Although the term 'historicism' has. been used in a number of ways, the central feature to which it refers is a predilection for interpreting individual and social phenomena as the product of sequences of events which unfold the identity and laws of growth of those phenomena. Historicism in this sense is neither a species of disinterested empirical research, nor again the quest for global 'laws of history', although it may have recourse to the latter. Its aim is rather to establish, through detailed historical investigations, the origins, growth and purpose of particular entities, or classes of entity.[1] In doing so, the historicist attempts to reconstruct, as accurately and vividly as he can, the ways of life, attitudes and actions of the participants in a given period and area. That was the ideal, and often the practice, of the early-nineteenth-century German historicists, as it was of succeeding generations of historians in other lands.[2]

This passion for archaeological accuracy and historical verisimilitude arose in the mid-eighteenth century. It manifested itself not only in the many historical works proper which began to appear in the early part of the century and soon covered most periods and countries, but also in the related fields of language and literature, music and the visual arts, and of religion and philosophy. The standard histories of the classical world by Rollin and Gibbon were soon followed by 'national' histories of France by the Abbé Velley, Villaret and Garnier, and of Britain by Hume, Rapin and Stuart.[3] By the early nineteenth century, most ethnic communities' histories were being written up by their historicist intellectuals. The eighteenth century also witnessed developments in philology and the rediscovery of 'archaic' poets like Homer and Aeschylus, Dante, the Old Testament writers and Ossian. The vogue for Macpherson's Ossianic epics was quite remarkable, outstripping even the fashions for the Scandinavian *Edda* and the recently discovered *Nibelungenlied*.[4] In such 'archaic' poems, the contemporary passion for rude origins and primitive peoples was excited by the dark colours of their imagery and the dim, mysterious atmosphere they evoked, without too much concern for the modern tendency to distinguish sharply between fact and legend in such literature.

An identical proto-romantic enthusiasm for all things archaic and mysterious pervaded the arts. Whether the aim was to portray antique virtues and heroism, or the piety and simple religiosity of the Dark or Middle Ages, artists of the later eighteenth century evinced a similar passion for historical fidelity and detailed archaeological reconstructions.[5] 'History painters' like Benjamin West, Heinrich Füssli and Nicolas Brenet utilised antique sources culled from the recent excavations of Pompeii and Herculaneum and from Greek vases, as well as the flowing linear motifs of Gothic tombs and miniatures.[6] In the spare 'neo-classical' style of David, Flaxman and Ingres, artists were able to convey not only the 'feel' of the classical and medieval eras, but also the simple heroism and stark purity of their historical ideals. In architecture, too, the designs of a Laugier, Ledoux or Soane emphasised the primitive geometrical units out of which buildings could be constructed, taking their cue from ideal antique models.[7] The movement towards a purifying simplicity found its way into music; in the manifestoes of Gluck, and the terse thematic drama of Haydn and Mozart, the same revolt against ornate polyphony in favour of the dramatic development of musical ideas heralded a more emotional and historically oriented musical content, especially in the field of opera.[8]

Even such fields as aesthetics, religion and philosophy, fields in which absolute and ideal standards were taken for granted, were not immune to the historicist virus. Taking their cue from the Earl of Shaftesbury's *Gefühlsphilosophie* and the rise of the 'sentimental' novel, Burke, Winckelmann and Lessing all developed aesthetic theories which stressed notions of the archaic, the sublime and of artistic maturation.[9] In religion and philosophy, Lessing, Herder and the German romantics introduced evolutionist and historicist ideas, though many of their assumptions were present in the work of philosophers like Leibniz and Condorcet, as well as Rousseau, and in the conjectural 'natural history' of the Enlightenment in France and Scotland.[10] The idea that God works in and through human history, and that successive ages manifest His providential design, as well as mankind's religious progress, became important elements in eighteenth-century Deism, as well as the religious idealism of the nineteenth century.

From its first flowering in eighteenth-century Western Europe, the new historical outlook soon came to be applied to the intellectual creations of every European, and, later, nonEuropean, ethnic com-

munity. Historicism fertilised their linguistic revivals, their litera-
tures, their art and music, their religious philosophies, as well as
research into their respective pasts. For the peoples of Asia, Africa
and America, history furnished the vital clue to their identities, and
historicism provided a framework of meaning to their distinctive
characteristics. The historical and evolutionary framework has
served the essential purpose of endowing with meaning and coher-
ence what might otherwise so easily be seen as unrelated pieces of
cultural information or 'markers'. These typical nationalist endeavours, the quest for a viable literary language and the manipulation
of myths and traditions of an ancient religion, are really vital props
in the historicist drama. Language and religion may serve other purposes – delimitation of territory, definition of the population unit,
unification of communal sentiment, and cementing the sense of belonging to distinctive social groupings. But all of these uses are subordinate to, and take their meaning from, the overriding historicist
vision of entities which unfold their identity and purpose in time, of
which language and religion are but two expressions.

THE EDUCATORS

Why has the rediscovery and repossession of one's communal history, the cultural springboard of ethnic nationalism to this day, become so widespread and necessary a feature of the modern political
landscape? The short answer is that historicism is a logical outgrowth
of the Enlightenment and of all subsequent enlightenments. The
longer answer is that such historical concerns spring from the characteristic divisions among secular intellectuals in search of a viable
faith.

Essential to the European Enlightenment, as to its nonEuropean
successors, are the twin cults of nature and reason. Within Western
and Central Europe, these cults stemmed from a revival of interest in
classical antiquity and its models of thought and society. Shaftesbury, Bolingbroke, Diderot, Voltaire, Montesquieu, Rousseau, Lessing and Herder, to name but a few, shared a common faith in humanity, in the power of rational thought to shape man's progress,
and in the regenerative qualities of Greco-Roman thought and life.[11]
Increasingly, too, they and other enlighteners were impressed by the
evidence of human diversity and perfectibility. If reason demonstrated the essential unity of humanity, of *homo sapiens*, nature
showed us the range of types and the ladder of progress, or chain of
being, which differentiated humanity. The attempt to strike a balance between these viewpoints became a key characteristic of en-

lighteners in other parts of Europe and later in other continents. Educators such as Korais in Greece, Obradovic in Serbia, Palacky in Bohemia and Alfieri and Mazzini in Italy, attempted to reconcile their sense of ethnic diversity with their ideals of a united, progressive humanity devoted to rational and beneficent ends.[12] In each case, the educator sought to lift his unregenerated and downtrodden ethnic community or category, his ignorant and unredeemed folk, into the mainstream of civilised humanity. That, too, was the aim of Kemal Ataturk, and before him of the pan-Turkists and Young Ottomans around Namik Kemal.[13] In Central Asia and among the Tatars of Russia, Ismail bey Gasprinki and his followers founded the modernist schools of the *jadid* movement at the turn of the nineteenth century, and imparted to the younger generation the fruits of European secular thought and science.[14] In Lebanon, slightly earlier, Christian Arabs like Butrus al-Bustani and al-Yaziji preached an increasingly secular patriotism based on western education and the use of a modernised Arabic language. Indeed, Bustani's dream was to 'witness the progress of his compatriots in learning and civilisation through the medium of our noble language', an ideal common to many educators in Africa and Asia.[15] We find the same sentiments and aims among the early Indian educators, Roy, Dayananda and Banerjea, all of whom saw it as their aim to rescue a fallen community by rejoining it to the one and only civilisation of humanity through the medium of a secular and rationalist education combined with a respect for traditional values.[16] And in West Africa, in the same period, the later nineteenth century, Edward Blyden tirelessly preached the need for a racial regeneration of the African Negro through a marriage between African values and western science and education, which would nevertheless preserve the distinctive character and 'race integrity' of the Negro.[17]

Even this brief recital reveals the ambivalence at the heart of the aims of the educators. On the one hand, they clung to the rationalist ideals of the original Enlightenment and to its belief in mankind's progress through science and education. On the other, they sensed the gap between this ideal and the reality of the situation confronting the area and community with which they were linked. On the one hand, they felt it necessary to raise the status and lot of their community through western education; and the other, they rebelled against any universal panacea or 'grid' which would anaesthetise the unique experiences and annul the distinctive nature of their communities. It was the attempt to resolve these contradictions which so divided the educator-intellectuals and prompted their increasing recourse to historicism.

To grasp these divisions and their resolution, we need to look more closely at the role of secular intellectuals in the modern era. Analysts, creators and elaborators of ideas and systems of ideas have existed in every literate civilisation.[18] Before the modern era, however, these intellectuals have usually operated in the context of religious systems of thought and an ecclesiastical hierarchy.[19] It was therefore necessary for the first modern secular intellectuals to ground their raison d'etre and the legitimacy of their endeavours in the sole known example of a prestigious civilisation with a secular orientation among many of its intellectuals, namely, the Greco-Roman world. The spectacular rise of the secular intellectual in the modern era was made largely possible by the immense prestige of classical thought, art and science, and the humanist rediscovery of much of the classical heritage during the Renaissance.[20] During the Italian Renaissance, it was still possible for humanist intellectuals to marry their classical ideals and learning to a framework of Christian faith; but the religious wars which followed the Reformation, the growth of religious pluralism and tolerance, and the growing interest in empirical research into the natural world, gradually brought the classically trained intellectuals into conflict with the Church and encouraged religious scepticism and a secular faith in progress and unaided human reason. As this conflict developed, the intellectuals generated alternative idea-systems such as Cartesian philosophy or Newtonian science, as well as the specific metaphysical systems of individual philosophers.

The ranks of the educators were also growing rapidly in the later seventeenth and early eighteenth centuries, aided by the rise of a regular press, the mass publication of printed books and the spread of literacy among the aristocrats and bourgeoisie. This allowed the formation of a well-informed and reasoning reading public; by the mid-eighteenth century, the intellectuals could not only exchange ideas in their coffee-houses and salons, but influence a much wider audience through the printed word.[21] They were united by a common background and by an increasing community of aims: their classical background of learning, the rise of universities, the growing prestige of scientific research, the conflict with ecclesiastical authority, all contributed to a sense of unity among the secular intellectuals. So did their almost universal exclusion from politics and administration. In addition, there were the new ideals, the commitment to human reason, the belief in Nature, the dream of humanity perfected in a civilisation that would outstrip that of classical antiquity. Such ideals and backgrounds helped to raise the status of the secular intellectual in eighteenth- and nineteenth-century Europe; and, while there were significant variations outside Europe, many of these factors operated in similar fashion to raise the status of Asian and African intellectuals in the late nineteenth and early twentieth centuries. And just as the programmes of the *philosophes* found an echo among some of the 'enlightened despots' of late-eighteenth-century Europe, so today the ideals of their philosopher-king successors outside Europe have won political acceptance in many of the new states. [22]

THE EROSION OF FAITH

Central to this transformed position of the secular intellectual was the impact of rationalism and science. The significance of science as an 'effective' mode of cognition lay as much in the social as the intellectual sphere. [23] It was not simply that science was a mode of cognition open to inspection and verification of results and capable of rational exposition and training; its wide range of practical applications in all kinds of circumstances, and the innovative spirit which its successes encouraged, nurtured a self-confidence in purely human faculties that most religious thought and traditional wisdom had denigrated. Faith in human powers of observation and reasoning demanded, moreover, complete freedom from any artificial constraints – social, religious or political – as well as from any intellectual dogma which might deflect or impede rational argument and rigorous experiment.

It was therefore of signal importance to the position of secular intellectuals, both in early modern Europe, and later on in Asia, Africa and the Americas, that rationalism and the scientific temper emerged within the matrix of societies still dominated by religious assumptions and traditions, and usually by ecclesiastical authority. This meant that the quest for scientific truths necessarily took on the nature of a crusade on behalf of freedom of enquiry and the superiority of human reason to divine revelation. It also meant that the educators had to count on opposition, and often repression, by traditional authorities who feared this challenge to their social and political position, as well as to their intellectual monopoly. Powerful, therefore, as the position of the secular intellectual might be, it was also precarious. Though rationalism and science had the potential to destroy the hold of faith on public life, and even disestablish the church, the danger which it constituted for the social fabric evoked immediate and deep antagonisms, which were to set their mark on the ethnic revival.

The very challenge which the educators posed also contributed to their political isolation. Kings, aristocrats and bureaucrats feared the attractions which their ideas might have for wider sections of the population, as much as the radical connotations of the ideas themselves. In some cases, 'enlightened' rulers might coopt a few of the intellectuals and implement aspects of their programmes of reform; but more shrank from such hazardous paths.[24] Nevertheless, even the most reactionary could not remain totally immune to the new ideas or the pervasive influence of the educators. For one thing, few societies enjoyed complete isolation from alien influences; and, in any case, none were free of those social discontents, or political divisions, which allow new ideas to gain access and take root. Nor could rationalism and science be easily divorced from the technological successes which were its fruits in spheres as diverse as armaments and communications or manufacturing industry. Rulers could not easily reject the opportunities for greater effectiveness of control and political action which these technical innovations offered; and, while it was clearly preferable to adopt the techniques without the underlying assumptions, rulers soon found it necessary to compromise with the expertise disseminated by the educators, with consequences which we shall explore in the next chapter.

Let us return for the moment to the collision between rationalism and religious authority. The social context of this conflict was dominated by the emergence of powerful centralised government in a few key political units, usually under absolute monarchs or colonial bureaucracies representing centralised metropolitan states. The fact that the most advanced of these states were historical neighbours and came to constitute a well-defined diplomatic nexus or system of states in the selfsame early modern period which saw the birth of science and rationalism, meant that the new ideas and techniques, and their propagators, had more chances of adoption and dissemination than under feudal or imperial conditions. By its nature, the absolutist territorial state was a competitive unit; the hold of the ruler over his subjects depended upon his ability to succeed in the contest for wealth and power and prestige played out in European and colonial theatres. The Baroque splendours in which the kings lived were designed to impress their counterparts abroad even more than their subjects; but their success in this interstate rivalry in Europe and the colonies depended increasingly upon their ability to incorporate techniques and norms of efficiency into their political apparatus and social fabric. Interstate competition bred, therefore, not only the new 'national' sentiment which we noted in the last chapter, but also those drives for scientific and technical modernisation which became so characteristic of western bureaucratic states.[25]

How did this interstate competition affect the position of science and the educators in their conflict with established religious authority? On balance, it helped their cause far more than it impeded it. True, most rulers shied away from coopting the educators into government, and their reform programmes were often timid. In a direct clash, rulers tended to favour the ecclesiastical authorities as part of the established order, which it was unwise to undermine. But, equally, the incorporation of scientific techniques and ideas into the ruler's bureaucratic apparatus – his army, administration and legal system – and the need to encourage secular education among wider circles, in order to produce enough qualified professionals to meet internal and external requirements, consolidated the position of the secular intellectuals and boosted their morale. The rapid growth in the number of such professionals, and the proliferation of educational institutions to train them, served further to entrench the role of the educators. Finally, the spectacular results achieved by the new kind of 'scientific state' with its streamlined and rationalised bureaucracy, confirmed the status of the intellectuals at the cost of religious authority.

At the spiritual level, too, there was a decisive swing towards rationalism and away from revealed authority. The very success of the rationalised bureaucratic state undermined both the negative evaluation of human capacities propounded by traditional religions, and, even more important, the efficacy and legitimacy of divine authority itself.[26] Impressed by the effectiveness of collective action centred on the bureaucratic state, educated men and women began increasingly to doubt the religious assumption of God's omnipotence and His ability or desire to intervene in man's daily life or even in collective crises. At this point, the age-old problem of meaning, the philosophical antinomy of worldly evil and divine omnipotence and perfection, took on a new social and practical relevance.[27] Doubting the efficacy of God's power to intervene in a mechanistic universe, the enlightened also began to question the justice of His dispensation and the legitimacy of His authority. Unable to accept traditional theodicies, and impressed by the evidence of human suffering and injustice, many secular intellectuals embraced radical ideologies which looked to man's collective efforts and political institutions to redress the world's wrongs.[28]

At the centre of this intellectual and emotional revolution lay a crisis of authority. The enlightened replaced the authority of religion and its cosmic dramas with that of the scientific state clothed in the garb of intramundane ideologies of progress. This new construct, the 'scientific state' and its centralised administration, was, after all, enormously impressive. It was also entirely man-made, a human and therefore flexible engine of social change. In the hands of a wise legislator, or well-attuned educators, this motor of modernisation, this solvent of backwardness and tradition-bound structures, could set mankind on the road to that rational harmony of his interests and fulfilment of his talents which had so long eluded him, denied as it was by his dependence upon the deities of conservative and pessimistic faiths. Hence, for many intellectuals, the state came to symbolise the opportunity for a breakthrough towards modernity, and out of the trough of dependence on outside forces beyond their control. And the more the absolutist state had become entrenched in an area or community, the greater the faith that secular intellectuals came to repose in its efficacy.[29]

What this revolution, therefore, entailed was a transposition of the ancient problem of meaning away from the spiritual sphere onto a material and social plane. Injustice and suffering were not divinely ordained instruments of man's spiritual betterment, or inevitable components of earthly imperfection; they were mainly man-made problems with human solutions which men of good faith and intelligence could arrive at and implement for their less fortunate fellowmen. Such a conclusion sapped the vigour of traditional faiths, as it undermined the intellectual edifice of revealed dogma. Above all, it eroded the social and political relevance of religion, and the basis of ecclesiastical authority. Religion became more and more the expression of private convictions, an inspiration or consolation for the inward crises and joys of an individual's life, rather than a matter of public concern or communal action.

THREE ROUTES TO ETHNIC HISTORICISM

Of course, the actual processes by which faith was sapped and religious authority displaced, in the areas where this occurred, varied greatly in different communities. There was nothing inevitable, either, about the process itself, or about its trajectory. A good many 'modernised' or 'developed' nation-states have powerful ecclesiastical hierarchies, even in communist countries, and a vigorous religious life, private and public.[30] Some intellectuals, and educator-statesmen, have found private ways of reconciling some of the premisses of religion with a commitment to social progress through science and rationalist education.[31] Nevertheless, the basic choice between a social structure dominated by religious authority or by 'rational-legal' authority of the scientific state has remained fundamental, at both the intellectual and the social levels. With the advance of secular education and science, more and more people have come to feel the need for some sort of choice or harmonisation between these two polar principles; and this perception of a fundamental choice has had vital social repercussions in the histories of a great number of communities.

Certainly, the discussions of so-called modernist intellectuals were dominated at the outset by such perceptions. Historically and logically, three main positions on the question emerged out of the welter of speculation; and intellectuals have tended to divide along their lines ever since, with a good deal of interchange and even blurring in individual cases between the three options.

I have described these three responses to the crisis of religious authority elsewhere; and will therefore confine my remarks to showing how each of them has tended to encourage the growth of an historicist outlook, and to discover in the resuscitation of the ethnic community as an historical subject some sort of resolution of their intellectual and emotional dilemmas.[32]

The first route, that of neo-traditionalism, tries to accept the technical achievements and some of the methods of western science and rationalism without any of its underlying assumptions. Socially and politically, it utilises modern methods of mobilising people but for traditionalist ends. A traditional*ist* is, of course, a self-conscious ideologue; he knows perfectly well that he is manipulating scientific techniques in order to defend traditional values and dogma. He also approaches tradition 'from the outside'; he has seen it through the eye of the unbeliever, if only to reject his error, and of the foreigner, if only to be confirmed the more securely in the sense of what is his own. The neo-traditionalist is, moreover, politically self-conscious: he deliberately chooses secular political means for achieving traditional, religious goals. Thus al-Afghani organised a pan-Islamic crusade, agitating through the press and politically, and mobilising thinking Muslims from Egypt to Pakistan to revive and purify Islam and the Islamic *umma* in the face of western materialism and imperialism.[33] And in India, slightly later, Tilak and Aurobindo were appealing to the masses in an attempt to revive the fortunes of Hinduism at a time when Christianity and westernisation appeared to be eroding traditional faith; and they did so by politicising the tradition and organising the faithful into a modern-style crusade against alien unbelievers.[34]

It is not difficult to see how this kind of modernised religion and politicised tradition lends itself to ethnic historicism and outright nationalism. To use political means to revive one's religious heritage and faith, and to organise the faithful into a political movement, demands a clear conception of the origins, laws of growth and identity of the unit whose solidarity is being sought, in this case, the community of the faithful. It requires, moreover, a sense of the passage of ethnic time and the vicissitudes of the faithful during the course of the centuries. The faithful must be given a history; they must be endowed with a foundation charter; their identity and destiny must be fixed; and their decline from past grandeur and present misfortunes must be explained. The religious congregation must increasingly be turned into an ethnic community, as has happened to the Jews and the Iranian Shi'ites.

There are, however, difficulties in this metamorphosis. The populations of the faithful may not easily fit into this kind of historicist scheme, being either too large or too small or too scattered and divided for ethnic convenience. That has been the trouble with many 'pan' nationalisms, but none more so than that of pan-Islamism, which has had to compete, not only with other linguistically based 'pan' movements like pan-Arabism or pan-Turkism, but also with the nationalisms of the several states into which Arabic- and Turkic-speaking peoples have been divided, many of whom possess their own specific histories apart from the general history of the Islamic *umma* or the 'Arab nation'.[35] These complications weaken the binding power, if not the fervour, of latterday pan-Islamic crusades, and make it well-nigh impossible to organise the Muslim faithful into a politically coherent movement. Similar, if lesser, problems affect Hinduism in India, since the latter must compete with both a secular conception of Indianness which would embrace the Muslim population, and also with the various linguistically defined ethnic units into which the subcontinent is divided.[36]

There are other problems for neo-traditionalist ethnic nationalisms. Nationalism itself is a secular ideology: its referent is the nation, the salvation it proposes is strictly of the here and now, its elect includes all who 'belong' historically and/or politically, and its programme is one of practical regeneration. By contrast, neo-traditionalism utilises the nation for religious and traditional ends. It may feed on xenophobia, but its referent is the deity, its salvation is not of this world, and its elect includes only those who are counted among the faithful. Though it employs the language and techniques of modern political movements, neo-traditionalism puts them to the service of theological dogmas and religious passions of an ultra-orthodox strictness and puritannical zeal, which rejects, on principle, everything modern and rationalistic. Hence the unease between nationalism and neo-traditionalism, which we find, in practice, stems from the vast disparity between their goals and ideals.

Small wonder, then, that the 'neo-traditionalist' solution to the crisis of religious authority, though it encourages ethnic historicism and nationalism, is also the most unstable and flawed. The extremes to which it runs testify to this deep rent in its fabric. The neo-traditionalist has tasted the fruits of modernism and feels their attraction enough to employ modern techniques and slogans; his rejection of the underlying assumptions is all the more frenetic and bellicose for the temptations he experienced. The intense theocratic regime he espouses is an embodiment of that rejection.

And yet neo-traditionalism still remains a popular resolution around the world. Under the guise of defying the West, its rejection of rationalism offers hope and comfort to those whom social changes are plunging into uncertainty and instability, especially in areas plagued by weak or corrupt government or held down by externally imposed regimes. Here the potent mixture of a revitalised and fervently held religion with a militant, even xenophobic nationalism has its greatest appeal; for at one stroke it identifies the enemy of the community with the alien and corrosive power of the enemy of its faith. Rationalism and alienity are completely fused – with revolutionary impact.[37]

Neo-traditionalist intellectuals reject, on principle, the rationalist assumptions and critical language which they simultaneously require, if they are to communicate that rejection to their fellow-intellectuals and others. The other two positions, those of the reformists and the assimilationists, accept science and rationalism together with their associated modes of critical reflection, systematic observation and open argument. But, while the assimilationist accepts such rationalism wholeheartedly, his reformist counterpart does so with many reservations. Assimilationists embrace with an almost messianic fervour the rationalist and scientific principles embodied in the modern state, principles in which they not only believe but which also validate their own aspirations for power and prestige. From their ranks have been drawn most of the 'educators', self-styled secular intellectuals bent on regenerating their communities through rationalist education. To these people there was really only one modern, worthwhile civilisation, that of the modern West with its rational discourse and scientific expertise; and they saw their task as that of assimilating themselves and their communities to the norms and lifestyles of that one global civilisation. Assimilationists are, therefore, essentially cosmopolitan in aspiration, even if, in practice, they must always assimilate to a particular cultural variant (English, French, German, American, Russian) of 'modern' scientific civilisation. The point is that, to the assimilationist would-be educator, the 'scientific state' is a universal construct whose effect is the potential solution of the problem of meaning on a global scale. By means of this engine of modernisation, all mankind can pool its resources for the common good, thus rendering the old transcendental and cosmic problems essentially social and practical. Through self-help and collective planning, men can hope to solve problems that are really terrestrial and practical, but which till now had been represented by the traditional theodicies as supramundane, divinely ordained elements of the cosmos. The first task of assimilationists was, therefore, critical and destructive: the breaking down of transcendental mysteries into earthly, practical problems, so that men might be taught the scientific temper and techniques required for self-help programmes of collective regeneration.

But, how then could an assimilationist stance contribute to the rise of ethnic historicism? Is not their critical cosmopolitanism, their future-oriented messianism, incompatible with the cultural foundations of the ethnic revival? It is indeed incompatible. And it required a major reorientation of assimilationist aspirations, before they could lend themselves to an historicist resolution.

That change came for many with the disillusion of their cosmopolitan dreams and messianic ideals. Of course, a few assimilationists managed to slip into the advanced western societies, which they felt embodied their aspirations to be world-citizens. But many more were refused entry. Curiously, the process of rejection began in the western heartlands – in that initial contest between the *philosophes* and the *ancien régime,* which was soon replicated in much of Central and Eastern Europe.[38] Exclusion was even more overt for the messianic intellectuals of the 'Third World'. If they did not come to sense their rejection in the metropolitan lands which they visited, they were left in no doubt of it on their return home. And yet it was not the insults of junior colonial officials that restored the assimilationist intellectual to his community and its history; it was far more the subtle but pervasive sense of distance which European exposure instilled in him, the gulf between his own traditions and the rational-critical discourse of the West.[39]

And so the assimilationist-in-retreat from the scientific state in the West poured all his messianic fervour and ardent hopes back onto the community which he had sought to abandon. Painful though this transformation might be, it was made easier by the fact that the ideology of rational progress, which the assimilationist intellectuals had embraced, furnished them with an evolutionary outlook, which in turn could be harmonised with the history of particular ethnic communities. An ideology of progress entails, after all, a commitment to a linear conception of social development, in which some societies, the 'advanced' ones, are blazing the one and only trail for their 'backward' brethren. A global pioneering ideology implies a theory of stages of advancement and rules of improvement. Given also their revolutionary impulses, assimilationists would be predisposed to an interventionist view of the historical process, one in which the educator could speed up the movement of history. It was therefore not so difficult for a disappointed assimilationist to transfer his progressive and revolutionary ideology from the stage of world history to that of his community within that larger framework. In that way, his disillusion and rejection could be rationalised, even justified, by arguing that progress is slower, more piecemeal and fragmented, and requires a more active intervention in each area; in a word, by being more 'realistic'. Besides, the revolution of reason had not really occurred in the advanced states, even if early enthusiasms had misled many into believing it had; might not their own communities succeed where the advanced western nations had failed? And might not the secular educators fashion a more rational, progressive and scientific state in their own backward areas, than any yet seen in the West?

Such reasonings, at any rate, helped to soften the disillusion of the assimilationists and turn them back to their ethnic homelands. A residual messianic cosmopolitanism still lingered in their hearts; but now it came to inspire their efforts to regenerate their respective ethnic communities and restore their past splendours. The arena of emancipation and revolution was no longer the world at large; it had narrowed itself down to the 'scientific state' of particular ethnic communities, and to the history and destiny of those communities.

But here, too, there were problems. The assimilationist route to ethnic historicism is split between cosmopolitan assumptions of its rationalist culture and attempts to immerse itself in the historical culture of a particular, time- and place-bound community.[40] There is always a residual yearning to break free from the constraints of the local community. Assimilationists are always trying to remould their communities in the ideal image of one or other 'advanced' nation. Moreover, they are ill at ease with the religious traditions which usually form so large a part of the ethnic heritage, underpinning its distinctive identity and character. They have, after all, decisively rejected all religious authority, all cosmic salvation-dramas and every transcendental theodicy; must they now make a tactical peace with all that they rejected for standing in the way of communal regeneration, just because they in their turn were excluded?

It is here that the third position, that of reformists, commends itself. For the reformist, despite his commitment to critical rationalism and science, does not completely reject all religious authority or cosmic theodicies. As I have argued elsewhere, the reformist acknowledges the situation of 'dual legitimation', the twin sources of authority in the modern world, that of the divine order and that of the scientific state.[41] To a reformist, God makes history; but so does the man-made 'scientific state'. Revelation and intuition show us the divine plan, even while reason and science allow man to become God's co-worker. Power and value are divided today; man, through the scientific state, commands much value and considerable power, but God, in nature and morality, is the repository of power and value beyond man and his comprehension. In his own terrestrial sphere, man can raise himself; he must not wait till death for emancipation. But, in the sphere beyond, on the cosmic plane, God still rules; and furthermore, He works in man's sphere through man's own efforts. Cautiously optimistic, the reformist believes that God works for man through the scientific state; and man must therefore embrace the collective good which the state furthers, so that he can work with God. And only within a reformed religion can man work with God.

The reformist attempt to reconcile opposites, to harmonise an ancient and profoundly ethical religious tradition with modern, secular rationalism, lies at the root of much liberal and even social-democratic thought. Yet it, too, lends itself to an ethnic historicism. But the process of transformation is more complex. Like the assimilationist, the reformist is asked to determine his own destiny, to raise the collectivity through his own efforts. Self-help, rational choice, collective planning, are therefore as much a part of the mental armoury of reformists as of others. But that is only a predisposing factor. It does not explain the turn into historicism or the return to ethnicity.

Once again, it is a failure that provides the impetus to historicism. Reformists, working to reform their religion so as to adapt it to modern rationalism, necessarily run foul of the ecclesiastical authorities and their neo-traditionalist champions. Only a truly reformed religion, which returns to its original inspiration and sweeps away all meaningless accretions and superstition, along with archaic priestly hierarchies, can reconcile the basic ethical revelation with the demands of reason; and this brings reformers into direct conflict with the ecclesiastical authorities.

In the ensuing conflict, which has often been prolonged and violent, reformists have had only limited success (and that often for quite extraneous political or economic reasons). The inherent difficulties in their position have also been mercilessly exposed. After all, if every feature of traditional religion which fails the 'test of reason', which cannot be reconciled with rationalism, is abolished, what is left of the religion? Why not cross over into an assimilationist secularism? Does not a religious community require continuity and stability in the face of the ever-changing 'spirit of the age' and fluctuating social needs?

One way out of these problems and conflicts is to look to the community itself, its history and culture, for the essential elements of the religion and the criterion of religious reform.[42] In the still-meaningful traditions and beliefs of the community, the reformist discerns the 'essence' of a modern faith. Dead and meaningless rituals and superstitions can now be swept away, on the ground that they no longer play a part in the life of the ethnic community. Furthermore, the reformist looks back to those ages and periods of the community in which religion was pure and the community itself was great. He searches in the past for communal dignity inspired by true faith; and seeks to recreate both through a modernised religious education. In this way, the reformist is led back towards a reconsideration of his ethnic past, in order to salvage the true, the underlying, the pure religion of his people. He becomes more conservative, more defensive, more concerned to preserve a sacred island of ethnic values in a profane world. He historicises the religious tradition, and in the end comes to see the religion as an outgrowth, a creation, of the genius of his community. To save the genuine religion, what is required is not merely a religious reformation, but a spiritual purification which will stem the community's present decline and restore it to its former grandeur. Through spiritual self-help, the dejected ethnic community can be raised up anew. Through a cultural ethnic nationalism, the situation of 'dual legitimation' can be overcome, and the ethnic community can regain its former faith and dignity in a rationalist world.[43]

Each of these three positions – neo-traditionalism, reformism and assimilation – continue to be espoused to this day by intellectuals in many lands; and each in its way continues to lead its devotees, under the pressure of external circumstances, towards an ethnic historicism. For they all concede the twin premises of such historicisms, that entities have origins and purposes in time, and possess identities and boundaries in space, in a world composed of analogous entities. The spiritual situation of intellectuals is, therefore, at once open and circumscribed; they operate within a set of assumptions, yet within that circle can choose between alternative interpretations.[44]

What, then, were the circumstances that precipitated adherents of all three positions toward an historicist resolution? In Europe, a sense of linear time and the quest for origins stemmed, first, from a comparison with the ancients and a growing belief in the possibility of social progress; whereas, outside Europe, this same quest originated from comparisons with former days of communal splendour, now brought low by European conquest and cultural influence. Second, within Europe, a new sense of diversity and cultural pluralism arose mainly from interstate rivalries and territorial warfare, followed closely by the discovery of other continents and civilisations and 'exotic' peoples, and the ensuing scramble for colonies; whereas, outside Europe, that selfsame sense of diversity emerged more directly from the 'parallel society' created by colonialism, and from the clash of western and indigenous cultures among exposed intellectuals.[45]

Perhaps even more fundamental for the rise of ethnic historicism across the globe has been the growing influence of the educators themselves. The secular intellectuals, as the vanguard of science and critical rationalism, have relentlessly challenged the claims of absolutism, semi-feudal ties and often ecclesiastical authority. Increasingly a transcultural, cosmopolitan community of humanists and scientists, united by books, travel and a common language of discourse, and freed from personal service to aristocratic and chiefly patrons, these secular educators have found a ready market for their ideas among a public hungry for knowledge and innovation. Even neo-traditionalists, who openly repudiate modernity, must operate within this language of critical discourse and address this new educated public.

But, along with these elements of unity, have gone deep internal divisions among the intellectuals. For the intellectuals are divided by religion, language and origins; by the varying degree of their community's backwardness; by the length of their exposure to rationalist, critical education and the level of skills attained; and by the positions which they adopt in relation to the crisis of religious authority, which I have outlined above. Their contact with other intellectuals induces invidious comparisons and makes them vividly aware of their internal differences. The very act of trying to improve their position relative to that of intellectuals in more advanced communities with higher standards of education, drives home the importance of communal differences and distinctive origins. Their consciousness of the gulf that separates the community they wish to educate and regenerate from other advanced lands, makes them all too aware of the separate histories of different communities, of the special needs of local areas, and of the importance of time in allowing the necessary growth and development they so ardently desire.[46]

Ethnic historicism, therefore, is a natural and probable outcome of the overall situation of secular intellectuals, of their rise to power and prestige, and of their internal differences. Unable to separate their own interests from those of the whole community, they tend to interpret these interests as those of the whole; and likewise, with their defects and special characters. The interests, defects and character of intellectuals *in* Germany or China are perceived as *German* and *Chinese* interests, defects and characters, through a process of global comparisons. The reference of the intellectuals is always outward, to other intellectuals of different communities; and always linear, to more 'advanced' intellectuals in more 'progressive' states. Hence, their rise to power and influence confronts the intellectuals with the fact of cultural and temporal diversity and induces an evolutionary outlook, in which they can plot their own progress on the cultural and political ladder, as well as that of their respective communities. In the last analysis, then, ethnic historicism is a function of the ascent of the secular intellectuals.[47]

COMMUNAL REGENERATION

But there is also an altruistic and collective aspect of the intellectuals' bid for status and power through ethnic historicism. The fundamental goal to which the three routes outlined above all tended was that of communal regeneration through self-discovery and self-realisation; and herein lies the core of ethnic nationalism. Without idealising their motives or minimising the partisan self-interest of intellectuals, we cannot ignore their multi-class appeal and their often genuine commitment to the whole community. If nothing else, such social concern is a logical outcome of the characteristic activity and cultural outlook of most secular intellectuals, namely, their educational activities and their ethnic historicism. Aspiring to the regeneration of the community, the educators aim to rediscover the self within a wider community and fulfil individual potentialities in the distinctive social whole. Only through the autonomy, the self-propulsion, of the individual, which the intellectual assumes in his own being and activity, can the community find itself, its identity, once again; and only through the rediscovery of that communal identity can the individual find his own particular fulfilment and inner rebirth.

Hence, the intellectual is the prototype of individuals in the modern world and of the whole community. For he is the first self-propelling, self-based and self-fulfilling man. His task is to mould others, and the whole community, in his own image. That is the meaning of modern, secular education: to create individual and communal identities through a rebirth of the self.

To this end, teachers, writers, poets, musicians, artists and other intellectuals bend their creative efforts. To regenerate the community, and endow it with an original personality, writers and artists institute periodic folk revivals; they go out among the peasants and farmers, commune with nature, record the rhythms of the country-side, and bring them back into the anonymous city, so that rising urban strata may be 'reborn' and possess a clear and unmistakable identity. To this end, the musician creates the dramatic spectacles of historical opera and oratorio; the poet narrates his historical epics; the artist pictures ethnic customs and native landscapes, along with national histories, always to teach and instil the regenerative impulses.[48] Through these channels, the historicist message of the intellectuals is diffused to wider strata, and stamps their outlook and character.

Central to the historicist conception is a contrast between urban corruption and decay, and the healing powers of nature. For, if the community, like every other entity in nature, is subject to the laws of growth and development, then its regeneration must be sought in the unfolding of its organic identity, its peculiar nature and character. That identity and character are in danger of being submerged and lost in anonymous cities and their mechanical, artificial cultures. That is why the road to communal regeneration must lead away from the city and, with Rousseau, back to the simplicities of agrarian life.[49] To save modern, urban civilisation, men must forsake urbanism and rejoin the culture of its rural hinterland; for only in the countryside and villages have the genuine ethnic traditions persisted, albeit in their religious chrysalis, waiting to be rediscovered and explored by the educators. Part of the intellectuals' programme is, undoubtedly, populist: to find a bridge to the peasant masses, and rejoin the alienated of the city to their agrarian 'roots', by interpreting the forgotten rhythms of the countryside to an urban public that has lost its ancient traditions without finding yet a surrogate historical vision. But, beneath this social programme, lies a cultural vision which seeks to endow the community with a deeper historical consciousness, so that modernism and all its works can serve the ideal of a regenerated and purified community, and thereby restore to its members the dignity and glory they have lost. In each community, 'going to the people' and the return to nature was allied to a vivid recreation of past epochs, such as we meet in the great musical dramas of a Verdi or Mussourgsky, in the national nature symphonies of a Sibelius or Vaughan-Williams, or the history painting of Delacroix or the Russian Vasnetsov.[50] Folk and agrarian elements have served writers as diverse as Dostoevsky, Ibsen and Adam Mickiewicz; while composers like Bartok and Holst collected ballads and folk dances, to bring the most modern, ascetic tendencies into a living relationship with ethnic traditions and rural rhythms.

Out of the logic of the intellectuals' situation, and their recourse to an ethnic historicism, the cultural basis of the ethnic revival is woven. The rise of early romanticism undoubtedly aided their endeavours, giving them a wider resonance and meaning. Later romantic movements and outbursts have similarly stimulated the historicist basis of the ethnic revival in the last two centuries, including the current resurgence of 'neo-nationalism'. But, in the last resort, it was the rise of the secular intellectuals, their crisis of dual legitimation, and their internal divisions, which drove them to fashion that historical vision which could assuage the crisis and furnish a new social and political ideal for the wider community.

6

Bureaucracy and the intelligentsia

If the intellectuals are the spearhead of the ethnic revival, the professional intelligentsia form its habitual infantry.

Everywhere, it is the rising professional intelligentsia who lend to the historicist vision of the educators a broad social significance and push it towards political fulfilment. Yet it is intellectuals who supply them with ideals and definitions most appropriate to a political resolution of their social situation. The social spring of ethnic nationalism lies in the translation of the intellectuals' message to fit the interests of the professionals, and in the redefinition and redirection of those interests by the vision of the historicist educators. In the tension of this complex interplay is located the dynamic of the ethnic revival until this day.

*

INTELLECTUALS AND PROFESSIONAL INTELLIGENTSIA

Who are the intelligentsia? Originally the term was used of Eastern European, mainly Polish and Russian, educated elites with a self-consciously critical stance towards the Tsarist regime and its official culture.[1] Since then, the term has acquired new meanings, both in the West and in the Third World; and so I propose to use it to refer to all who possess some form of further or higher education and use their educational diplomas to gain a livelihood through vocational activity, thereby disseminating and applying the ideas and paradigms created by intellectuals. In other words, professional intelligentsia live off (literally as well as figuratively) the cultural capital generated by intellectuals. They utilise, they apply and they disseminate the culture created by others. They are professionals; they link theory to practical needs and problems. They neither originate the basic paradigms of knowledge nor create the images and insights which reinterpret reality, as do the intellectuals; instead, they innovate by applying these paradigms and insights to the practical world, by codifying new techniques and applying with the care and thoroughness of professional 'experts.' Their province is a purely professional expertise.[2]

The distinction between intellectuals and professional intelligentsia is not one of respective occupations, nor should it be confused with the division between technical and humanistic professionals. The latter division is important, but it belongs to a later phase in the development of the professional stratum, to which I shall return. The distinction between intellectuals and professional intelligentsia, between creators and analysts of ideas and paradigms, and their disseminators and practical appliers, is more far-reaching. To be an intellectual is to engage in a type of mental activity, manifest a state of being and personality type, and have a special kind of outlook and mode of discourse, without thought for its practical consequences or for personal gain. To be a member of the professional intelligentsia is to have a vocation, but also to engage in a certain kind of occupation in order to gain a livelihood; it is to live off one's education and become a member of a particular 'guild' or profession, and accept its code of conduct.

There is, of course, a good deal of overlap between intellectuals and professional intelligentsia. A professional may also be an intellectual. But, again, he need not, and many indeed are not. A professional need not be interested in ideas and knowledge for their own sake, nor in their disinterested analysis, except insofar as it may bear on his specific professional expertise and narrow specialism. Conversely, an intellectual may become a professional; today, he often must be. Characteristically, he becomes a teacher or academic; and in that purely professional capacity, he is one of the intelligentsia, though by no means all teachers are intellectuals. Even in the academic world, we find that there are some who are more interested in the creation and critique of ideas *per se,* and others who are more concerned with the transmission and dissemination of those ideas, and hence with pedagogical rather than strictly intellectual values. In fact, not many manage to combine the two in equal measure.

Intellectuals as a type of personality and mental attitude can be found in every walk of life. Some creative intellectuals engaged in trade or were artisans and workers, like the goldsmith Benvenuto Cellini or the docker Eric Hoffer or the Talmudic sages of ancient Palestine. Some composers, especially in Russia, worked as technical or humanistic professionals. Intellectuals also vary in their source of income. Some, like Plato, have private means, others like Leonardo work free-lance, while still others like St Thomas Aquinas act as spokesmen for official organisations. It is neither their daily occupation nor their source of income that sets them off as 'intellectuals,' but rather their 'extra-mural' activity, their mental attitudes, their assumptions and their characteristic enthusiasms.[3]

Members of the professional intelligentsia may share something of these enthusiasms and attitudes, but many clearly do not. Their orientation is vocational and professional, an interest in a career structure based upon a special expertise and definite skills acquired through a rigorous discipline certified by recognised bodies; but, for this circumscribed purpose they have to turn periodically to those creations of intellectuals, the bodies of theory which have been imparted to them by mediating pedagogues.

These pedagogues form a vital link between intellectuals and professional intelligentsia, which their common etymological root suggests. For the pedagogues create the possibility of wider comprehension and serve the intellectuals somewhat in the manner of Aaron in Schonberg's opera, who served Moses, his brother; for Moses, unable to communicate in its purity and entirety the vision vouchsafed to him, had to rely on the partial and sometimes misleading translations of his brother, in order to reach his people.[4] Not that pedagogues necessarily mislead in paraphrasing the ideas of intellectuals; and, besides, there are intellectuals who need no translators. They are the true educators. Others are not born pedagogues; their novel and sometimes obscure thought requires some mediation to make it intelligible and acceptable to a wider public. Hence the growth in numbers of teachers and academics who try to purvey in suitable language the path-breaking ideas and paradigms of creative intellectuals, to a broader constituency.

In this chain which moves from abstract theory to daily practice, from 'what is?' to 'so what?', the intellectuals are bound to the professionals by their translators, the pedagogues. Often, if an intellectual wants to reach the 'people,' he must find pedagogues who will translate his message to the wider constituency of the professional intelligentsia, who will in turn disseminate and apply its ideas among the populace as a whole. In this process, intellectuals are helped not only by the pedagogues with their technology of literacy and communications but also by the need of professionals to draw on the cultural capital created by intellectuals. They are also aided by what Alvin Gouldner calls the 'culture of critical discourse,' with its fundamental assumption of justification by argument and experiment alone, rather than by appeal to authority or position.[5] As Gouldner points out, the more removed are professional intelligentsia from what he terms 'humanistic intellectuals,' as technical intelligentsia tend to be, the more latent becomes their culture of critical discourse. But they too partake of its assumptions, its rationalism and common critical discourse. They too must rely on their own judgment and critical faculties, especially when accepted paradigms fail to fit the facts within their specialism. They may refuse to create new paradigms, but they must sift and analyse ideas in their restricted field, and occasionally even step outside their narrow specialism and its guild-like organisation to refer to a wider rationalist culture which legitimates and sanctions their particular expertise. The rules of procedure, logic, observation and experiment, which they normally take for granted, rest on general assumptions which they share with all professionals, pedagogues and intellectuals.

The rapid expansion of technical professionals raises the question of their relationship to other, more 'humanistic' professionals. Gouldner has suggested that we distinguish 'technical intelligentsia' from 'humanistic intellectuals'; but this omits the special role of the so-called 'liberal professions,' which have played an important historical role in social movements. It seems better to employ two distinctions: the first, between small circles of intellectuals and the broad, expanding stratum of vocational intelligentsia, as outlined above; and the second, between two parts of that broad stratum of intelligentsia, a 'humanistic' and a 'technical' part. The humanistic intelligentsia would include the old 'liberal professions' – doctors, lawyers, architects, academics, teachers – as well as the more recent professions of social work, journalism and broadcasting. Technical intelligentsia include such newer professions as engineers, agronomists, printers, pharmacologists, quantity surveyors, laboratory technicians, communications and ballistic experts, logistical and intelligence experts, and many others, whose knowledge of and interest in the older humanistic culture may be rather superficial, and who look for guidance and inspiration to scientific intellectuals, the physicists, mathematicians and biologists, whose paradigms have transformed our thinking about the universe and man's place in it.

Can we, then, speak of the professional intelligentsia and intellectuals as a 'New Class?'[6] I think not. Intellectuals come from all social classes and occupy every rung in the economic hierarchy; and their links with each other and with the professionals are often tenuous. Rather we should think of small circles of intellectuals, humanistic and scientific, veering between neo-traditionalist, reformist and assimilationist positions; and a large stratum of technical and humanistic professional intelligentsia. I would prefer *stratum* to class since, even among professionals, there are large economic differences, as, for example, between corporation lawyers and laboratory technicians on fixed contracts and low salaries. It seems more appropriate to characterise the intelligentsia as a 'stratum', because they are socially similar in work situation, education and perhaps life-styles, rather than in property or relation to the means of production. As for intellectuals, they are best thought of as a set of elites, with their cultural, national and scholarly subgroupings; for today they increasingly form coteries and cliques which serve as cultural models for elements in the wider society.[7]

Clearly, there is not enough unity of background and interests among intellectuals and professionals to treat them as a single undifferentiated economic class. But there are important links and much overlapping between their memberships. They do have in common a single language and a shared set of assumptions of rational discourse. They are linked by a subgroup of pedagogues who play a vital role in the expanding network of public education, which continually multiplies the membership of both intellectual elites and the liberal and technical professions. They are, therefore, increasingly exposed to the disciplines of tertiary education in universities and polytechnics. Through these disciplines, the ideas and paradigms of intellectuals are disseminated widely among the intelligentsia; and, closely related to this, there develops among both a common antagonism to rival strata. In what follows, I shall concentrate on this last factor, and try to show how the ideals and paradigms of the intellectuals win many adherents among the broad catchment area of the intelligentsia, largely as a result of their growing rivalry and conflict with the bureaucrats.

PROFESSIONAL MOBILITY IN THE 'SCIENTIFIC STATE'

The main channel for the rise of the intelligentsia is the bureaucratic organisation; and the chief reason for their growing role within it is their professional skill and ethic. Within the private sphere, professional intelligentsia have been employed in growing numbers and positions of importance since the Industrial Revolution, and especially since the rise of the large-scale firm. This is true not only of 'professional' organisations like the law practice or newspaper organisations, but also of the large corporation, bank or insurance company, with its accountants, organisation and methods experts and actuaries, not to mention sales and advertising research experts. No private firm or organisation could hope to survive without a large army of such diploma-holding experts, as is attested by the phenomenal growth of business studies and the almost universal necessity for some professional qualification for advancement in the private sector. In the public, non-governmental sector, qualified professionals are even more entrenched. In private schools and hospitals, parties, voluntary organisations, trades union secretariats, mass-media organisations, many important posts are held by diploma-holders with some form of tertiary education; while in local and central governmental institutions – schools, hospitals, armies, the judiciary, the legislature and civil service – the proportion and role of technical experts and humanistic intelligentsia, already considerable, is constantly increasing. And this, despite an amateur, gentlemanly ethic cultivated in the civil service in some countries. The truth is that this only masks the great reliance of all public bureaucracies on the expertise of trained technical intelligentsia or highly educated humanistic professionals. Gradually but surely, the intelligentsia, under the cover of professionalism, have climbed the bureaucratic ladder and infiltrated its positions.

How has this been managed? After all, no body is more jealous of its privileges and duties than the old hierarchy of bureaucrats. For the latter, authority rested not so much on expertise (though this was a valuable aid) as on legal position, seniority and the command structure itself. Not professionalism, but obedience to orders, not expertise but discipline, is the core of all bureaucratic organisation; and nowhere more so than in the nerve-centre of the state – the civil service itself. Organised on military lines for the swift transmission of orders by heads of departments, and nurturing an ethic of deference to legally constituted superiors, the central administration aimed at the most effective dispatch of the sovereign's will, the swiftest execution of decisions without questions asked.[8] How, then, was expertise wedded to discipline in such a way that the old bureaucrats could be challenged in their own lair?

Largely because of the growing specialisation of governmental tasks and the need for greater cost-efficiency. Both factors were conditioned by the growth of practical knowledge in early modern Europe, and the interstate rivalry which, in war and peace, spurred rulers to exert greater control over more resources – with a specialised, efficient bureaucracy as the indispensable instrument of such control. Both factors meant that a greater measure of scientific expertise and techniques had to be incorporated into the bureaucracy. In order that bureaucratic effectiveness should not squander resources and fall into the law of diminishing administrative returns, the rulers and directors adopt such ideas and techniques as will minimise economic and organisational costs while coping with the enlarged range of problems presented to the bureaucracies – usually by their counterparts in other states. Interbureaucratic competition is the fuel which feeds the scientific and technical spiral within governmental organisations, as well as in private firms. At the public level, these competitive forces gradually transform absolutist or colonial bureaucratic states into the *'scientific state'*, that is, a state whose bureaucratic organisations are increasingly pervaded by scientific and technical expertise and whose personnel includes a large proportion of technical professional intelligentsia. And, while few states today could be described as pure 'scientific states', given the still considererable power of the old hierarchical bureaucrats, the secular trend towards such a transformation is unmistakable.

The origins of the 'scientific state' are difficult to pinpoint; but certainly by the late seventeenth and early eighteenth centuries, the process of incorporating scientific and technical expertise and personnel into both military and civilian administration was well under way. As Michael Howard points out, there was a close connection between the development of rational administration and professional warfare in early-eighteenth-century Europe:

The development of state power and organisation [he argues], made such professional forces possible; but the development of military technology made them, functionally, almost essential. In noting this interaction one cannot ignore another which developed simultaneously: the manner in which the development of professional armed forces, itself made possible by the increasing control acquired by the state over the resources of the community, enabled the state to acquire yet greater control over those resources by serving as an instrument, not only of external defence but of internal compulsion.[9]

By the end of the seventeenth century, the French were able to take up the Dutch and Swedish examples and turn their blueprints into administrative and military reality. Two bureaucrats, Michel le Tellier and his son the Marquis de Louvois, worked tirelessly to turn indisciplined, corrupt bands into an efficient, centralised army with a unified administrative machine able to field a large and well-trained fighting body. The military model, where the incorporation of the most advanced military technology and expertise was inevitably at a premium, was profoundly influential for the 'scientific' development of civilian administration. This was partly because of the peculiar nature of the European system of states, which, as Poggi notes, was made up of 'coordinate, juxtaposed, sovereign units,' which generated the system.[10] It was, of course, a highly competitive, precarious equilibrium, quite unlike the more usual pattern of semi-dependent entities bound together by an imperial network in a given culture-area. Here, probably for the first time, a culture-area was divided into warring, autonomous and roughly equivalent political units, none of which, over a longer period, could establish an over-arching domination. As a result, armies and military technology played a vital initiating role in the scientific and technological revolutions, setting the pace for other areas of social life. The growth of discipline in the army paralleled the rise of rigid hierarchies within bureaucracies; similarly, the need to modernise and streamline the military demanded simultaneous developments within the wider administration.

But there was another reason for the influence of the military model: the growing prestige of its expertise, as evidenced in military successes. Inputs of technical expertise could be *seen* to effect results in the field, even to guarantee success. It was therefore possible to plan ahead, to make more-or-less-confident predictions, on the basis of science and rational technology. It was also possible to calculate the costs of alternative military strategies and techniques. Effectiveness could be balanced by efficiency, so as to deploy the minimum of resources for maximum results. Such plans and procedures, and their accompanying calculations, could be transferred to the civilian field, so as to maximise the resources at the disposal of the ruler and the state. By incorporating the relevant expertise – in such fields as law, taxation, demographic statistics, education, economics, regional planning and transport – the administration was enabled to define and appropriate for public use the greatest wealth and cultural resources within its territorial jurisdiction. In that way, the state could be 'built up' and 'constructed,' like an artefact. The state itself could be planned and engineered – unlike any society.

But the incorporation of expertise means the training and employment of professional experts, i.e. the technical (and sometimes humanistic) intelligentsia. In its power struggles with other states, and ensuing need for maximum control over internal resources, the modern, rationalised state must call on the services of the intelligentsia and nurture them within its bosom. It must draw to itself the most talented among those with practical knowledge; and where there are insufficient for its needs, the state must train them in public institutions. The state, therefore, founds or extends an educational system, taking over from private or ecclesiastical authorities, as the French state took over from the Jesuits in 1762, amid projects for a national system of education by La Chalotais and others.[11]

To survive the competition with other states, the absolutist state (and its colonial extensions) was increasingly compelled to train a force of technical intelligentsia, and to ensure their loyal cooperation through adequate rewards, financial and political. One way of doing so was to coopt sufficient numbers into the lower echelons of the central administration itself, so holding out possibilities of upward mobility for newly educated strata, and legitimating their new knowledge by conferring on them a commensurate status. Another way was to create auxiliary organisations of technical intelligentsia, alongside the main administrative hierarchy – much like the artillery corps in an army. In this way, an 'amateur' mandarin superiority of the ruling administrative caste can be preserved, with its central chain of command, while benefiting from the organised expertise around and beneath it. In this way, too, the bureaucratic ethos of discipline and legal authority can be implanted into the technical intelligentsia itself, making their members more amenable to internal bureaucratisation and so spreading its norms beyond the confines of governmental or public organisations.[12]

To recapitulate: prolonged interstate competition compelled European rulers to expand and centralise their administrations, and to incorporate new ideas and techniques into their bureaucracies, both civilian and military. To maximise control over resources, the state bureaucracy had to call upon the services of experts from the ranks of the technical intelligentsia, which, with the rise of science and its technological applications, was emerging as a social force. By implanting bureaucratic norms among the professionals and coopting some of their members into the central administration, rulers and bureaucratic managers opened new channels of upward mobility for them, and began to attract to the centre talent and expertise from even peripheral areas of their territorial domain. By founding schools and colleges to train technical intelligentsia, and provide a ready supply of loyal, competent and amenable professional expertise, the scientific state laid the basis for the expansion and organisation of the technical intelligentsia into a socially significant stratum. Under the aegis of the scientific state, the technical professionals began their slow climb to power. By rewarding the expertise of the intelligentsia, the bureaucracies acknowledged the latent power of educational qualifications; by recognising, indeed instituting within their own ranks, the examination system, the bureaucracies hallowed intellectual merit, regardless of class, region, language, religion or colour, and became one of the most powerful agencies of horizontal and vertical mobility for educated professionals.

RADICALISING THE INTELLIGENTSIA

However, the route to power would not be so smooth for the professional intelligentsia. Indeed, it could not. And that for three main reasons.

The first, quite simply, was educational overproduction. There was to occur a periodic imbalance between the number of highly trained 'clerks' and the number of bureaucratic posts available to such recruits. The growth of public education systems tended to produce more technically qualified personnel than could be absorbed into status-conferring and responsible administrative outlets. Even if there were no overt discrimination by bureaucrats or rulers, 'overproduction' of the intelligentsia was likely to occur, especially in societies in which forward planning tends to be partial and haphazard. It may, perhaps, be possible to minimise this imbalance in a totally planned socialist society that is also ethnically homogeneous; but the vast majority of societies are neither, and crises of educational overproduction tend to be recurrent.

The result of such imbalance is the thwarting of the professional intelligentsia's upward mobility. Its route to power is blocked, in proportion as its members fail to gain admission to the higher echelons of the bureaucracy. Already in the France of Louis XVI, the university system was greatly expanded, but more restrictions were placed on the entry of its products into the administration of the *ancien régime*, or into the more lucrative posts in the professions. Witness the career of many of the Jacobin leaders, notably Robespierre.[13] In Russia, too, blocked upward mobility helped to radicalise the Russian *intelligenty*, especially after the expansion of university education under Tsar Alexander II.[14] In Third World countries, too, educational overproduction on the part of colonial regimes, which needed a supply of local trained personnel to help modernise society, frustrated the ascent of indigenous intelligentsia in Asia and Africa. The oversupply of English-trained humanistic and technical intelligentsia was particularly acute in India, where it undoubtedly contributed to the rise of Indian nationalism in the late nineteenth century, as well as to the local linguistic nationalisms.[15] In Africa, too, especially in the British territories, educational production generally outstripped bureaucratic demand, and generated frustrations and career blockages, helping to radicalise several African intelligentsias.[16]

But here we must bring in the second reason for the blockage of the intelligentsia's rise to power, namely, the opposition of the old hierarchical bureaucrats. The bureaucrats who initially recruited the technical professionals to help them modernise the bureaucratic machine so as to control more resources more effectively, now find that they have unleashed a sorcerer's apprentice. For the intelligentsia, despite their many divisions, are united in their common rationalist assumptions and tertiary education. Though locked within their own, often narrow, practical specialisms, they adhere to general paradigms and critical procedures imbibed in their institutions of tertiary education; they are committed to the solution of problems within the boundaries of their specialisms, according to the general rules and paradigms they have learnt.

But the old-line bureaucrats are not committed to such procedures and paradigms. They have not necessarily been educated in institutions of higher education; and, even where they have, they are inclined to set its critical assumptions aside in the interests of 'policy' and under the dictates of 'authority.' For they do not hold office in virtue of a specialism, nor of a commitment to critical culture. They may be selected on the basis of competence and general intelligence; but their rise in the ranks is essentially conditioned by their attitudes to authority and their acquisition of the ethos of discipline. As transmitters of orders, as executives of policy, they are not employed to examine the assumptions of policies or analyse its effects. They are not even concerned with the problem of modernising the machine they control, only seeing to it that it is modernised – by the professionals they employ. They are concerned not with rationality or problem-solving, but with order and practical effectiveness. Hence, their deep suspicion of the arts of the intelligentsia.

A conflict of cultures is clearly in the making; and since the bureaucrats, almost by definition, are in control, they are able to use their dominant position to exclude, or curtail, the intelligentsia; and to admit only those who have shown that they are ready to adopt bureaucratic discipline above commitment to their own expertise and vocation. Though there may be no overt cultural discrimination on linguistic, religious or ethnic grounds, the managers of the main institutional bureaucracies tend to reserve for themselves the higher offices, calling in experts for specific tasks, but keeping them at arm's length from the nerve centres of decision-making. The usual justifications for this policy are, first, a stated preference for the general over the specific, for a coordination of the whole over a commitment to specialised professional knowledge of any part, and second, a belief in the superior virtue of 'experience' over theoretical understanding and knowledge. According to this view, what makes a good bureaucrat is a general view of policy of the organisation as a whole, bred of discipline combined with practical, day-to-day experience. Only those members of the technical intelligentsia who can be successfully 'bureaucratised' in this sense, who come to identify with the aims and methods of the organisation itself and place it above their own intellectual training and professional discipline, only such experts can be absorbed into the institutional hierarchy and be allowed to advance to senior positions. Indeed, some countries have even shown a preference for recruiting bureaucrats from students of liberal studies, i.e. the humanistic intelligentsia, on the grounds that their specific training and vocation (but not their general intelligence and logical training) would be 'irrelevant' to modern bureaucratic tasks, and hence they could be more easily resocialised in the relevant ethos and outlook.

The third reason for the blocked mobility of the intelligentsia is rather different, and at first glance unrelated to the other two. There is a good deal of historical evidence to support the view that various kinds of more-or-less-overt discrimination have been practised by rulers and bureaucratic managers alike. Indeed, many imperial bureaucracies tended to reserve their most senior posts to members of the dominant religion or tribe. It took the Roman empire some years before Gauls, Spaniards and Greeks were admitted to the topmost ranks of the imperial Civil service – under Claudius – and to the senate itself. Empires in early modern Europe varied considerably in their recruitment policies, with the Ottoman being much less discriminatory than the Romanov, at least in its later years. This latter difference would suggest that religion is not sufficient of itself to explain bureaucratic discrimination; and perhaps differences in the political and military strength of the two empires account for the more rigid ethnic policy of the Tsarist regime.[17]

But we may also suggest a connection between overt bureaucratic discrimination and the other two factors above. While some states and empires have bureaucracies with built-in religious or other prejudices from an earlier period, they may nevertheless resort to overt cultural discrimination, including the use of ethnic quotas, only when the technical intelligentsia has reproduced itself sufficiently to constitute a threat to the bureaucratic order itself. At this point in time, when competition for a shrinking number of senior posts becomes fierce, new types of cleavage – linguistic, racial or ethnic – are seized upon and politicised by rulers and bureaucratic managers, as barriers to entry or promotion in governmental or other public organisations. Thus 'ethnic' classification becomes one of a number of cultural lines of cleavage erected by modernising rulers to control the supply of scientific and technical personnel into their bureaucratic apparatus; and 'ethnicity' itself becomes a new focal point of solidarity among sections of the intelligentsia. More generally, cultural discrimination (of which 'ethnicity' is but one mode of classification) becomes a lever of power and prestige, and for the aspirants, a handicap in their ascent to power.[18]

It might be objected that cultural discrimination is itself very likely to breed discontent and resentment among professionals; and hence educational overproduction and bureaucratic suspicion are merely additional irritants. But such simplification overlooks a number of factors. To begin with, some bureaucratic orders have tried to practise a neutral ethnic recruitment policy, with a minimum of cultural discrimination and a maximum of communal self-rule within an imperial structure, as with the Ottoman *millets*.[19] In other cases, for example the French territories of West Africa, far from practising cultural discrimination, the French colonial regimes aimed to assimilate African elites into French culture and institutions, albeit in limited numbers and after careful preparation.[20] Second, cultural discrimination as policy is, as we saw, a venerable practice, which long antedates the birth of a technical (or even humanistic) intelligentsia; and besides, it is not at all clear that rejected aspirants for entry into ancient or medieval imperial bureaucracies were habitually filled with resentment and discontent. But that is exactly what began to occur with increasing regularity in the modern period, with the rise of the 'scientific state': rejected aspirants became more and more resentful, less easy to satisfy and reconcile, more restive and demanding.

The reason for this changing reaction to rejection takes us back again to the fundamental cultural assumptions and discourse on which the many professional specialisms of the intelligentsia are grounded. Like the intellectuals, whose paradigms they have often absorbed, the professional intelligentsia have experienced a crisis of faith and religious authority. Unlike the intellectuals, they have perhaps been able to achieve a more compartmentalised response to that crisis. Some have indeed suffered an erosion of faith, similar to that experienced by many intellectuals; but others have managed to remain outwardly orthodox, and even inwardly half-believing, while in their public and professional lives they adhere closely to the postulates of science and rationalism. Since they are professional specialists, they are not so concerned with overall consistency; at the same time, they are even less disposed to quietism and passive acquiescence in fate, when the public side of their existence is threatened or curtailed. Within the fairly narrow confines of their specialisms, they are even more fanatically rationalist and innovatory than the less 'expert' intellectuals. It is their very expertise that makes the intelligentsia so sure of their professional worth, and so uncompromising about their work; and as a result so indignant about their rejection. Unable to accept the validity of tradition and religious authority in their professional lives, they can no longer acquiesce in the public rejection or confinement imposed by the bureaucrats.

Radicalising the intelligentsia

In the past, religious authority and a cosmic world-image muted the pain of public rejection. Convinced that this world was an illusion or a vestibule to another, eternal existence, men could cheerfully bear the insolence of office and the rejection of individual worth. This is no longer the case. With the decline of religious authority, all authority appears capricious, and every rejection seems an attack on the validity of a particular type of knowledge and cognition. It is not just the individual who is rejected, and not merely his material interests that are injured. Rejection becomes a collective experience, and the damage falls more heavily on his new-found self-image and vision of reality. In rejecting him, bureaucrats and rulers are trying to assert the irrelevance of his culture, and his inferior worth as a diploma-holder. In elevating 'experience' above education, the bureaucracy attempts to undermine not just his claim to a livelihood, but also his self-respect and sense of professional worth. Even when they gained admission to the bureaucracies, professionals were often accorded lowly posts near the base of the organisational ladder, and their expertise was consequently wasted or under-utilised, except in a crisis. Either way, more and more members of the intelligentsia came to feel that their hard-earned diplomas could not bring them the status and dignity to which they deemed themselves entitled, and they often had to be content with low-status and even unprofessional employment, unsuited to their talents and training.

Here, then, was a potent and growing source of radicalism among the intelligentsia. That radicalism cannot be reduced to a simple failure to achieve material interests or even unhampered social mobility. It is much more a function of the sense of wasted efforts and talents, and of thwarted professional aspirations. Even harder to bear was the domination of bureaucrats who could not comprehend the often intricate reasonings and detailed knowledge of experts and yet presumed to give them orders. Although the professionals started their climb to power within the haven of the bureaucracy, they were increasingly to encounter the hostility of its senior incumbents, the men of the apparatus, for whom administration itself was the end, rather than a means to the achievement of external goals. To the intelligentsia, for whom all authority had now become suspect, and who admitted no sanction within their own specialisms except that of reasoned argument and critical analysis, the bureaucrat, who also rejected traditional types of authority in favour of legal ones, was particularly suspect. For he had 'gone over' to the enemy of rationalism, i.e. the mental closure of hierarchical discipline – and without even the excuse of religious believers! He had exchanged free, rational discourse and analysis for a circumscribed authority based on an unswerving, even blind, commitment to the institution he served: was this not a great 'betrayal'?

Hence the growing radicalism of the intelligentsia found its sharpest focus in opposition to the power of bureaucrats, and to the restrictions and exclusion of the bureaucracy. And insofar as the intelligentsia achieved any sense of unity as a stratum, and began to listen to the cultural and political message of the intellectuals, it was as a result of their growing conflict with bureaucracies and bureaucrats.

IN SEARCH OF HISTORICAL LEGITIMATIONS

The question still remains: why did the radicalism of the professionals turn to ethnic historicism? Why did it not always remain liberal, or opt for a marxist socialism? Why was the ethnicity solution of so many intellectuals ultimately persuasive for the intelligentsia, as it was to become for other strata, too?

Certainly, their professional training and specialisms cannot be said to have attuned technical professionals towards an historical outlook. Even the humanistic intelligentsia – the lawyers, doctors, teachers, architects and journalists – are not 'naturally' disposed to historicism by their particular professions. Yet, an evolutionary outlook and assumptions have often been adopted by practitioners in these fields; and, more important, among members of these professions we often find a vivid adherence to the concepts of historical identity and growth as a general framework for human development and scientific explanation. Historical and evolutionary paradigms appear to have a particular attraction for members of 'liberal professions' in the modern era; perhaps this is why the latter have figured so prominently in ethnic nationalisms.

But, if the attraction of historicism for the intelligentsia should not be sought in the nature of their training and specialisms, can it be the consequence of a crisis in the bureaucratic state and its elites, to whose position the professional intelligentsia were beginning to aspire, a crisis that was concurrent with, and partly responsible for, the rejection and subordination of that intelligentsia?

Undoubtedly, the growing demand for scientific and technological expertise by state machines and public bureaucracies, and the ensuing rejection and subordination of the experts themselves, was greatly aggravated by the crisis of the old social order and the absolutist state. The paradox of demand for expertise and rejection of experts which was part and parcel of the rise of the 'scientific state', was largely a result of the disruption of the legitimacy of the old order. The *ancien régime*, part-monarchical, part-aristocratic, part-clerical, was increasingly challenged by a combination of commercial, urban interests, the rise of a powerful stratum of bureaucrats and lawyers wielding formidable administrative powers, and by the advance of secular thought and education. Although there were many variations between communities and areas, we can discern a triple erosion of the powers of aristocrats, monarchs and clerics at the hands of an uneasy coalition of entrepreneurs, bureaucrats and intelligentsia, the latter often under the tutelage of free-lance intellectuals. In this process, state centralisation under the monarch played a crucial role, helping to curtail the powers of the nobles, and then delivering many functions into the hands of a bureaucratic stratum. It is at this stage, when the nobility have been weakened and their public role curtailed, that the crisis of the old order and the absolute state becomes apparent.[21]

Historically, this crisis of incipient democratisation took a variety of forms. In the classic West European instances, revolution destroyed the absolutist state and ushered in a constitutional monarchy or republican state. In Central and Eastern Europe, the old regime staged a come-back after the 1848 revolutions, although the manorial basis of the landowning nobility's rule was undermined.[22] In the end, large-scale war completed the final decay and overthrow of the old social order in Central Europe and Russia. The European colonies, too, were profoundly affected by events in the metropolis, with the growth of demands for democratic participation coming fast on the heels of debilitating European, and world, wars. At the same time, colonialism implanted a variant of the bureaucratic state in the interests of more efficient territorial and economic control, with the result that, as in Europe, the colonial variant of the absolutist state was capable of conversion into the framework for the new republican 'state-nations' of Asia and Africa.[23]

Now it was exactly this prolonged, and often dramatic, crisis of the absolutist state, first in Europe and then outside, that turned the intelligentsia, caught up in its midst, towards historicism. And not only the intelligentsia. The trend was first found among the bastions of the old order, among monarchs, clergy and aristocrats anxious to preserve their position in a changing world, whose climate of thought devalued their sources of authority. Divine right, noble blood, revelation and tradition, were all suspect to a growing number of the very secular strata whom the ruler and his bureaucracy had trained to meet their political and economic goals. External, interstate competition required a trained corps of loyal experts, so that the ruler and his bureaucracy could marshal his territorial resources more effectively and at less cost; yet the very training that would help him achieve these goals, also tended to undermine the legitimacy of the monarch and his court. In these circumstances, kings and nobles began to justify their positions in terms of precedent and custom, of legitimate descent and historical justice. In France, for example, the king and his ministers encouraged a cult of their medieval royal ancestors, notably St Louis, commissioning artists to glorify the royal pedigree shortly before the Revolution.[24] Aristocrats like the Comte de Boullainvilliers looked back to the early medieval kingdom of the Franks to justify the noble code and privileges of the French nobility, whose powers had been so curtailed by successive centralising monarchs.[25] And the same French aristocracy, sitting in the *Parlements,* championed the ancient 'liberties of the nation' and the rights of regional assemblies, in the name of historic precedent and ethnic tradition.[26] Elsewhere, other threatened strata sought to shore up the old order against the inroads of western secularism and bureaucracy; in the Balkan countries, for example, it was the clergy who fostered a nostalgic, historicist outlook, which could simultaneously justify their cherished idea of a religio-ethnic restoration.[27]

But not only did historicism penetrate the ranks of the old order in its crisis of legitimacy; it began to affect the outlook of aspirant strata. The bureaucrats, now that the authority of their formerly absolute masters was shaken, required a new kind of legitimation for their vastly extended operations. They too found it in history – the history of the dominant ethnic community from which they were mostly drawn. That history sanctioned their new role, it endowed them with some sort of identity by furnishing them with a 'national tradition', whose interests and character it was the State's duty to preserve and promote. For example, in Tsarist Russia, the bureaucratic machine even tried to impose a Great Russian 'national' tradition on all the ethnic communities in that heterogeneous empire, in the name of administrative uniformity and of an historic Russian Orthodox legitimacy.[28] In other European empires or overseas colonies, such attempts usually provoked vigorous resistance, constituting a powerful incentive to rival strata to discover an alternative and more acceptable historical pedigree for themselves.

Among these rivals, the most important were the professional intelligentsia. Recently created by the growth of science and rationalism, and its educational institutions, they suffered from the stigma of brash novelty. Lacking roots in the old order, they now found themselves excluded or subordinated by the new bureaucratic order. Moreover, they could no longer accept traditional explanations of their lot, which might have resigned them to their rejection. They were, in fact, doubly excluded – by the tradition of their own communities and by the 'western' bureaucratic states. In these adverse circumstances, many members of the intelligentsia began to refashion their commitment to rational progress of humanity at large into a more specific and circumscribed historicism. The old order had no place for their rationalism; the new only partly accepted their expertise and kept them at arm's length, because it rightly suspected the anti-authoritarian elements in the intelligentsia's outlook. So it became imperative to formulate a new identity for themselves and thereby legitimate their aspirations and activities. For the intelligentsia, the past was to be so constructed as to vindicate their role in the future; and this meant finding a version of evolutionism which would deliver the future into their hands.

Historicism became, therefore, an attractive and necessary framework for the professional intelligentsia, because the crisis of legitimacy under which the old order was sinking demanded that they too find a viable identity and role in the emergent new order. Their secular rationalism meant that they could not simply return to the religious traditions of their respective communities; many of them had been too deeply touched by the vision of global, human progress to revert to a simple traditionalism. They had to turn elsewhere for their new identity and historical legitimation – to the 'ethnicity solution' of the intellectuals.

THE ETHNIC SOLUTION

In fact, most of the professionals followed the path marked out by 'assimilationist' intellectuals before them. They turned back to a modernised version of communal identity, which the reformists had constructed to mediate between religious authority and the scientific state. The history of the community from which they hailed would now provide a rising intelligentsia with an 'ethnic' identity sufficient to legitimate their claims to high status and power.

There were a number of reasons for the appeal of this 'ethnic solution' of the intellectuals. By identifying their private concerns with those of the wider community, and sinking them in its sad history of neglect and oppression, the professionals could overcome their lack of a worthy pedigree and claim to speak for the whole collectivity, rather than some particular section. They could thereby overcome the stigma of novelty which attached to every new stratum – and the charge of selfish sectionalism.

Besides, an ethnic historicism, albeit born of disappointment, was not so far removed from the messianic belief in human progress, which had underpinned the rationalism of the intelligentsia. True, rejection had forced them back onto their own communities; nevertheless, they could endow their ethnic community with those qualities of growth and progress which they had formerly attributed to humanity as a whole. In their messianic enthusiasm, too, they could transform their ethnic communities from despised, passive objects of history into dynamic and active subjects shaping their own destinies in harmony with inward rhythms and characteristics. Something, then, could be saved from the wreck of the assimilationist utopia of world-citizenship, something definite and practical.[29]

But an *ethnic* historicism served the needs of professionals even more closely. An ethnic community, occupying normally its historic territory and possessing a unique culture, could furnish the intelligentsia with a rationale for their 'own' bureaucratic machines and a ready-made, enclosed arena in which their professionalism might have its due. An ethnic community provided a definite social space in which to construct a separate stratification system, complete with barriers against the unworthy and rewards for merit. It could also justify the setting up of separate and sovereign states, whose professional and bureaucratic apparatus would naturally satisfy the career aspirations of a multitude of hitherto excluded diploma-holders. By replicating the 'scientific state' across every continent and turning large religious communities – Hindu, Buddhist, Muslim and Christian – into several smaller sovereign bureaucratic states, the intelligentsia hoped to surmount the crisis of its own over-production and exclusion.

Yet career aspirations tell us only part of the story. Equally important are the 'ideal interests' of the intelligentsia, their vision of the world as it should be and their ideal of their own situation in it.[30] The ethnic community provides not only the basis of an alternative status system and power centre for an excluded stratum, but a resolution of their identity crisis through a revaluation of their function and purpose. For the professionals require a milieu which will place the highest premium on their education and skills, and the ethnic community, viewed as a 'subject of history' and a unique historical culture, provides that milieu. This is where the message of historicist intellectuals is so pertinent. They proclaim the need for education through self-discovery, and the need for self-discovery, individual and communal, through secular education. For the intellectuals, education is the sole and indispensable route to a true understanding of self and hence to self-fulfilment. But there is no 'self' outside the context of historic community. For we are the products of our histo-

126

ries, and these are pre-eminently communal or ethnic histories. Everything real and true in the individual self derives from the distinctive ethos and character of the history of the community to which the individual belongs and of which he forms an integral part. Education, therefore, derives its true meaning and purpose from the unique character of the community; while, conversely, the community can only 'realise itself', 'discover its identity' and understand its true worth through a secular education which will unfold to its members cultural self-understanding.[31]

Education, for the intellectual, is something more than the acquisition of skills and knowledge; for historicist intellectuals, it represents something even more than a scientific temper and rationalist outlook. True education is a process of self-fulfilment through self-understanding; and such a process is inevitably a collective or rather communal and historical project. It is a process by which the individual comes to realise his role in the particular historic culture in which he has been brought up, and simultaneously to understand the history and destiny of the community to which his fate is linked, by birth or residence or choice. There is no 'education' outside the community; and no 'community', properly understood, without the self-consciousness that education instils.

Seen in this context, the specialist skills and training of the intelligentsia, if put to 'proper use', assume a new and vital importance. They are the tools and instruments of a fuller communal, and hence individual, self-understanding. The theoretical principles of science and engineering, for example, may be universal; but their technological applications must be shaped by the exigencies and goals of each and every community, and that in turn requires a wider vision and self-understanding. With other specialisms, like the law or architecture, universal principles of reasoning and design are inextricably bound up with particular elements, peculiar to the traditions and character of each community; their study, therefore, demands an understanding of communal history and an even greater self-knowledge. But such self-knowledge is always an understanding of the culturally unique and the historically particular; and so specialist professionals are drawn by the new valuation placed on their skills into the ethnic vortex.

In the ethnic community, then, the specialist skills and education of the intelligentsia take on a new meaning and thereby acquire a higher valuation than in the 'alien' bureaucratic state. For the bureaucrats saw those skills and expertise in purely instrumental terms, and regarded their practitioners with suspicion, if not hostility. In the ethnic community, on the other hand, the intelligentsia are welcomed because only by means of their skills and specialist knowledge can a 'true' education arise, which will bring self-understanding and self-fulfilment for the whole community. Secular education is, therefore, more than a dispensable set of instruments; it represents the one and only route to self-discovery.

For the professionals, the new meaning accorded to their specialisms confers a genuine identity and a special role. By its urgent practical and spiritual need for the education and skills which the intelligentsia alone can offer, the 'ethnic solution' propounded by historicist intellectuals appears to transcend their divisions and resolve their identity crisis. The ethnic solution issues a summons to collective activity, an affirmation of purpose and function, for the intelligentsia. In the ethnic community, the historic culture-group, they are the men of the future, the key to collective progress and the means to self-knowledge. A 'subject of history' requires a modern institutional framework and outlook; the ethnic community, its roots deep in the past, must therefore place at its head the stratum of the future, the true representatives of modernism, who alone can restore it to its ancient dignity in the contemporary world – the intelligentsia. In restoring to the community its past dignity, the professional intelligentsia now find their true identity and function, and the only reward worthy of their educational attainments.

REJOINING THE COMMUNITY

The intellectuals' ethnicity solution may have resolved the material and spiritual crisis of the intelligentsia, but they also find themselves in a social crisis. They are virtually isolated. Their members represent a new stratum with suspect skills and knowledge, and they are usually greeted with hostility by the *ancien régime* and many bureaucrats. Here and there, circumstances may compel a bureaucratic state to take in more experts and professionals, and with time they may sometimes become less suspect to an increasingly professionalised bureaucracy. But, on the whole, their position is precarious and unenviable. Can they break out of this isolation, and find allies elsewhere?

In fact, the crisis of the old order presented an opportunity for other strata, too: above all, for the entrepreneurs, some of the lower clergy, and on occasion for some of the workers and peasantry. It is with one or more of these strata, or sections of them, that the intelligentsia habitually seeks to ally itself, and thereby to 'rejoin the community'.

Perhaps the most successful, and best-known, of these alliances has been between the professionals and the bourgeois entrepreneurs, although lately its popularity has declined in favour of an alliance with sections of the peasantry. By comparison, other types of alliance have had only limited appeal and temporary success. In some countries of Eastern Europe – Poland and Hungary, for example – the intelligentsia received considerable support from dispossessed minor aristocrats, although their understanding of the meaning and goals of an ethnic revival was rather different.[32] Similarly, a wide gulf separated the intelligentsia from the lower clergy, who were attracted to an ethnic solution by their sympathy for and proximity to the plight of the peasantry and by their dissatisfaction with the acquiescent attitudes of the higher priesthood. The Hellenic ideals which animated Greek intellectuals and professionals, for example, were far removed from the dreams of a restored Byzantine glory which inspired many a parish priest in the Morea.[33] In Burma, too, attempts to form an alliance between rationalist intelligentsia and the political monks (*ponggyis*) in the early twentieth century met with little success, and soon the intelligentsia looked elsewhere for support.[34] Yet, because the lower clergy have understood the western, rationalist challenge and fear a further decline in their status, they too are available for radicalisation along ethnic lines – though usually along the 'neo-traditionalist' route, rather than the assimilationist and reformist paths chosen by secular professionals. Their ethnic historicism is consequently a very different outlook and vision from that entertained by most of the intelligentsia.

More lasting and successful has been the alliance between the professionals and the entrepreneurial class. The latter, of course, have a purely practical interest in secular education – as a necessary grounding in basic skills required for business and industry. Their view of tertiary education, too, tends to be strictly instrumental: its products, the intelligentsia, provide high-level technologists for industry and teachers for the sons of the business class. The intelligentsia become an auxiliary stratum, a service class for business interests; they provide a general training in numeracy and literacy, and specialist skills for an industrial society. They are invaluable, indispensable instruments, but also useful allies in the struggle of the bourgeoisie against the aristocratic representatives of the old order. For traders and entrepreneurs suffer from all kinds of restrictions in the semi-feudal, absolutist states and empires from which they gradually emerged – ranging from ancient feudal and customs dues to the antichrematism of most aristocratic societies. They too have no pedigree and little culture; hence the trend among wealthy merchants and industrialists to support the scions of a new culture which is at the same time an ethnic one, and patronise artists and writers whose innovations will enhance the community's dignity and sense of individuality. Among the Tatars, for example, it was the great merchants who supported the modernist schools of the *jadidist* secular experiments of Ismail bey Gasprinski, because, through the skills and outlook of the professionals which those experiments would create, the merchants could shape the destiny of the new communal order which was emerging.[35] On their side, the intelligentsia welcomed the backing of such powerful figures, not merely because of their much-needed material resources, but also because entrepreneurs appreciated, after their fashion, the skills and secular knowledge and professional dedication of the intelligentsia. Both parties shared a commitment to 'western' ideas and 'modern' techniques, as well as a common faith in merit-based social mobility and the 'career open to talent'. That is what united the tiny Greek intelligentsia to the westernised entrepreneurs of the Philike Hetairia, the society formed in Odessa in 1814 to promote the interests of Greek Orthodox and Greek-speaking communities within the declining Ottoman empire, which proved to be the springboard for the subsequent Greek revolt and war of independence.[36] Among the Armenians, too, diaspora communities in India and Constantinople were led by an alliance of great merchants and intelligentsia, inspired by the historicist message of the intellectuals who had fashioned the Armenian renaissance of the nineteenth century.[37] And, in India, the native business class contributed funds and connections to the intelligentsia-led Congress Party, the spearhead of early Hindu Indian nationalism in the late nineteenth century.[38]

The essential link between professionals and bourgeoisie is their attempt to balance individual merit with community service. Both sides appreciated the limitations of an unbridled individualism and unregulated competition within the framework of an inimical *ancien régime*. Until the old order had been defeated and superseded, the collective interest must also be served and competition turned outwards. Without such competitive restraint and a measure of social solidarity, there was little hope of replacing the old order with its modern successor. Hence the need for a pooling of resources and personnel in the common struggle for an ethnic revival, which would give birth to a new merit-based order.

Yet, once the struggle had assumed open political shape, the strains in this uneasy alliance showed through. For one thing, many native bourgeoisies were too small and insignificant to provide much support for an isolated intelligentsia. For another, the intelligentsia developed a far stronger commitment to collective interests and communal solidarity than did the bourgeoisie. Though both sides were animated by a spirit of individualism and an ethic of competition, the professionals were more interested in maximising prestige and influence rather than incomes, and found solidaristic ways of doing so in the framework of leadership of an ethnic community. They were much more able and willing to convert their individualistic aspirations into collectivistic political ends, whose attainment would simultaneously satisfy their status needs. In those countries, too, where capitalists and the lesser bourgeoisie have triumphed and wield indirect powers in the political arena, they have done so mostly as a result of compromises with the old order; and this very fact increases the tensions already felt between business leaders and the intelligentsia. In pioneering societies which had little or no 'old order' to speak of, there has nevertheless also developed a contest between business owners and professional managers, as well as a wider struggle between business interests as a whole and intellectuals and intelligentsia outside the commercial and industrial sectors. By cultivating professionalism and 'welfare', ecology and planning, the intelligentsia offers a critique of 'amateur' entrepreneurs and their competitive waste, particularly in the United States.[39] In other words, new ruling classes such as industrial capitalists are as little immune from the radical critique of a rationalist and technical intelligentsia, as their counterparts in the old order.

Although collectivism and a communal ethic are not something native to an intelligentsia, they are kindled in the incipient political struggle, not only by their own rationalism and sense of rejected worth, but also by their social isolation and cultural shallowness. And as a result of this sense of being 'cut off' both in space and in time, both from other social groups and from previous generations and symbolic memories, sections of the intelligentsia, under the tutelage of radical intellectuals, attempt to break out and rejoin wider strata of the total community – usually, urban workers, the peasantry or the artisans and shopkeepers. All these alliances have proved unstable and temporary. In many countries, the urban wage-earning class is small and ill-organised, with considerable under- or unemployment and often seasonal or migrant labour, especially in Africa and Asia. Only where the working-class is large and concentrated enough to form stable trade unions, have the intelligentsia thought it worthwhile or necessary to join forces with them in an attack upon native aristocracies or alien colonialists. This occurred in some African countries like Tunisia and the Sudan, as well as in Israel and, more fleetingly, in India.[40] More often, the intelligentsia have steered clear of involvement with working-class demands, despite the novelty and rationalism of outlook of both strata. The professionals feel uneasy about a genuine working-class theory and movement – though it should be added that a number of socialist parties have, after some debate, opted for a strongly nationalist line, the most blatant example being the French and German parties on the eve of the First World War.

Of greater interest and moment has been the recent tendency to seek an active link with the peasantry. Actually, the phenomenon can be traced to the Romantic obsession with rural primitivism and folk customs; but it is really only since the end of the Second World War, that the intelligentsia has spawned radical populist groups who see in the organisation and mobilisation of the peasantry, not merely the surest route to power, but the sole means of resolving their identity crisis. Only the peasantry, the oldest oppressed class and often the vast majority of the population, can confer on a 'rootless' stratum like the professionals a genuine ethnic pedigree, and at the same time free them from their social isolation and political exclusion. This the working-class cannot do, since they too lack any historic validation. That is surely one source of that otherwise curious symbiosis of marxist communism and nationalism, which has taken hold in some of the most dependent and least advanced areas of the world. In Angola, Mozambique, South Yemen, Ethiopia and Vietnam, radicalised sections of the intelligentsia were able to forge guerilla organisations or political cadres which, with varying degrees of success, broke the barrier between themselves and the peasants or tribesmen, and place themselves at the head of a movement to regenerate the ethnic community by turning it into a territorial 'nation' through control of the bureaucratic State.[41]

RESHAPING THE COMMUNITY

I have argued that alliances between the intelligentsia and other strata, notably the bourgeoisie and peasantry, stem from the social isolation and lack of legitimacy of the professionals, whose novelty and rationalism make it suspect. There is, however, another side to this attempt to rejoin the community: the revolutionary impulse inherent in the intelligentsia's critical rationalism. Its very mode of discourse and conceptual apparatus are not merely qualitatively different from those of other strata, but inherently dynamic and active. They resemble engineering projects in their concern for the practical realisation of social blueprints; and undoubtedly one of the most appealing of these projects has been the ideal of 'nation-building'. This conceptual tool of the sociology of political development reveals itself as an ideological project of the practical intelligentsia, a blueprint of would-be consultants of the 'development process' (itself another of the intelligentsia's practical constructs).[42] The central idea here is that the nation must be 'built' in order to secure a balanced development of communal resources which will ensure self-sustaining economic growth, and a gradual but definite improvement in the material standards of living of its members. 'Nation-building' is therefore an indispensable framework and condition of social and economic development; without this national infrastructure there can be no social progress.

This intimate connection between 'nation-building' and social development provides the essential rationale for the real concern of the intelligentsia: to make its revolutionary mode of cognition and status acceptable to the community at large. Hence its frequent espousal of the sociology of underdevelopment and dependency. The picture of a world composed of a few large and highly developed nation-states 'underdeveloping' and inflicting a dependent mode of development upon a host of smaller semi- or pre-capitalist societies but lately come to statehood, undoubtedly legitimates the revolutionary strategies for autarchy and self-development propounded by radical cadres of the professionals, whose own position is apt to be doubly marginal – within their own communities and on a world stage dominated by the large, industrialised western or eastern states.[43]

Hence a social urge to rejoin their communities is allied to the intelligentsia's revolutionary cultural position and marginality; and this in turn propels them into forging blueprints for reshaping the structures and goals of the communities they seek to rejoin. That is the central meaning of 'nationhood' for the intelligentsia: a project which must be realised by transforming the components of the ethnic community they have rediscovered and seek to regenerate. It is not the community as such which draws the zeal and activity of the intelligentsia, but the community transformed according to a political blueprint, in short, the 'nation'. Hence, at the same time as the intelligentsia seek to rejoin the ethnic community, they do so only to the extent that they can hope to transform it into a 'nation'; and their alliances with other strata must be understood not merely in terms of tactical political needs, but also of the blueprints of 'nationhood' and 'nation-building' that they entertain at successive moments in their rise to power.

It is these visions and strategies that have shaped the movements for ethnic revival which we are witnessing today, both in the West and in the 'Third World' of Africa, Asia and Latin America, and to which I now wish to turn.

133

vwvwvwvwvwvwvwvwvwvwvwvwvwvwvwvwvwvwvwvwvwvwvwvwvwvwvwvwvwvwvwvwvwvwv

State integration and ethnic schism

In the preceding three chapters I have sketched a general interpretation of the social and cultural conditions of the ethnic revival. The
argument so far can be summarised as follows:

1. Throughout recorded history, ethnic ties and sentiments have
helped to shape men's loyalties and group affiliations, ever since the
initial transition from a nomadic to a sedentary agrarian existence.
Although such ties have always existed, being especially tenacious
in the countryside, their social influence and political relevance have
varied from period to period in different culture-areas of the globe.

2. Among the factors that have tended to crystallise ethnic communities and sharpen their political self-consciousness, interstate
wars and militarisation have played a particularly important role,
both in mobilising the population and in strengthening the centralised state apparatus in agrarian societies. Historically, we can discern a general correlation between intense interstate warfare and
contacts, on the one hand, and a growth in ethnic consciousness and
ethnic political salience, on the other; and both appear to fluctuate in
broad historical cycles prior to the rise of absolutist states in the West
at the close of the medieval era.

3. A new historical cycle of growing ethnic consciousness, in conjunction with the rise of rival bureaucratic states in Western Europe,
was given a fresh impetus and direction by several developments in
the field of culture, notably secularisation of thought and the rise of
science among humanist circles. Of particular importance in this
connection is the eighteenth-century flowering of secular intellectuals who pioneered the 'historicist' revolution. It was the educators
who supplied the ideals which not only revived, but also transformed ethnic ties and sentiments throughout Europe into a movement for national unity and statehood.

4. In response to the crisis of religious authority posed by the challenge of the 'scientific state', the educators have tended to adopt one
of three positions, each of which has contributed to the growth of an

historical vision of society: a neo-traditionalist, a reformist and an assimilationist response. Out of these differences as well as the new position of secular intellectuals, has come the impetus to an ethnically based communal regeneration.

5. The main constituency of the educators are the intelligentsia, or professionals with tertiary education, whose skills are needed by the expanding 'scientific state'. The latter's bureaucratic organisation provides their main channel of upward mobility, insofar as it incorporates scientific and technical expertise and methods, and creates an educational system to train experts in sufficient numbers.

6. But the rise of the intelligentsia has encountered several obstacles: a tendency towards overproduction of highly qualified personnel in relation to high-status, responsible administrative, business or professional posts; opposition on the part of entrenched hierarchical bureaucrats to the critical rationalism of the intelligentsia; and the use of ethnic or other cultural grounds for discrimination in admitting sections of the intelligentsia to public high-status positions. Coupled with their secular activism and sense of their own professional worth, these obstacles have radicalised large sections of the intelligentsia.

7. This radicalism has been channelled towards the ethnic historicism of the educators by a crisis of legitimacy experienced by the old order and the absolutist state; for the professionals, too, required a viable social identity supported by an historical legitimation, and they found it in the 'ethnic solution' proposed by their intellectuals. Besides providing a new bureaucratic arena for their career and status aspirations, the historic or ethnic community, suitably transformed into the active 'nation', resolves the cultural crisis of identity of the intelligentsia, places them at the head of an alliance with other aspirant strata, and breaks down their social isolation from the 'people', with potentially revolutionary results.

This interpretation of a general pattern underlying the modern ethnic revival and transformation covers mainly the social and cultural forces at work in each case. It stops short of more specific political factors and outcomes of the ethnic revival. Clearly, any ethnic revival carries with it the potential for political action, but of itself it does not determine the nature, extent or intensity of such action. As we saw, even nationalism, though it advances certain ideals of autonomy, unity and identity, does not indicate any particular strategy for attaining these goals. These may be communalist, autonomist, separatist or irredentist; and the adoption of any one (or more) of such strategies will depend on:

1. the relative strength and radicalism of the intelligentsia, and its ability to form alliances and break out of its isolation,
2. the extent of 'congruence' between the ethnic community and the state formation to which it is most closely related,
3. the general international context, both in its military and geopolitical, and its socioeconomic, aspects.

Considerable variations in all three respects exist between the ethnic communities and movements in the West (Europe and North America, excluding the Blacks and Puerto Ricans) and those of the 'Third World' (Africa, Asia and Latin America); and I shall therefore treat their patterns separately, before comparing them directly.

A 'GRID' OF 'STATE-NATIONS'

Perhaps the most important political attribute of many 'Third World' countries is the relative novelty and fragility of their present boundaries and state institutions, both of which in turn spring from their imposition by external forces.

In Africa, Asia and, to a lesser extent, Latin America, many of the new states received their territorial definition and administrative apparatus within the last hundred years, or even less. In Africa, especially, the colonial powers established after 1885 a 'grid' of artificially demarcated territories, each with its own administrative institutions.[1] The colonial powers of the time took little cognisance of the boundaries of the various ethnic groups and categories; and in several cases, such as the Ewe and BaKongo, they drew their new territorial boundaries across ethnic groupings so that the latter straddled two or more colonial units. Nevertheless, both the colonial administrators and their protégés, the African professional elites, regarded the redrawn territorial boundaries as the only legitimate ones, and defined the political community solely by reference to these administrative units.[2] African elites inherited both the boundaries and the state institutions at independence and have struggled to keep them intact in the face of various demands and pressures, usually those of dissatisfied ethnic communities incorporated within or straddling across the frontiers of the new states. Fearing a repetition of the fragmentation characteristic of the pre-War Balkans, African politicians have used every tactic to avert the break-up of their often fragile and precarious political units, in the hope that, given sufficient time, their present crop of 'state-nations' can be transformed into genuine 'nation-states' on the presumed European model.[3]

In Asia, the position is somewhat different and more varied. One pattern is the division of a large culture-area into several sovereign states: thus the Arab world in the Maghrib and Middle East is split into well-defined states, most of which owe their inception to the power politics of French and British colonialism, both before and after the Great War.[4] There is also a similarity with the African experience, in that many of these states were carved out without any regard to ethnic or historic boundaries and communities, and so incorporate two or more ethnic groups – Berbers, Copts, Druse, Alawites, Assyrians and Kurds. As in Africa, the creation of this colonial state-grid cuts across wider cultural–historical memories and sympathies, furnishing a rationale for pan-Arabism as a 'third level' of nationalist aspiration – much as pan-Africanism serves the same purposes in continental Africa.[5]

In southern Asia, the efforts of colonial administrators and indigenous elites to preserve state boundaries have been less successful. While Burma, Indonesia and the Philippines have so far held together, despite much ethnic and religious cleavage, India did not, and two new Muslim states – Pakistan and Bangladesh – cut themselves loose from the British colonial territory. So far, Pakistan and Hindu India have prevented further ethnic-linguistic fragmentation; but, as in Iran, the danger of ethnic secession remains real.[6] In all these cases, as well as in southeast Asia, the state boundaries and institutions, imposed by former colonial powers during the nineteenth century, have provided a continuing framework for the growth of a political community, but they remain relatively fragile and mutable by comparison with their European models.

Perhaps only Latin America has escaped some of the besetting problems of the 'grid' state system; and largely because the ethnic composition of the continent's population is not as heterogeneous as those of most African and Asian states, and because present state boundaries have tended to follow those of the provinces of the Spanish and Portuguese empires, which themselves were entrenched over a far longer period of time than were the later French, British, Dutch and Belgian empires.[7] Add to this the immense problems of communications and distances faced by the early Iberian settlers and their conquered populations, and the reduction of, or intermarriage with, the native Indian population; and the ethnic and religious challenges to the boundaries and institutions of the post-colonial states are reduced, despite several remaining ethnic problems.[8]

There is, of course, much variety in both ethnic composition and the relative strength of state institutions in Latin America. Before the Conquest, there was considerable ethnic diversity; and it is only recently that Latin American state structures have succeeded in moulding their different ethnic communities and 'racial' populations into distinctive national units; even here, the unity is sometimes precarious and the state structures fairly fragile, particularly in some central American states. On the other hand, a common Catholic religion together with processes of Hispanisation and mestizoisation have blunted differences that, in Europe, would today become cultural bases for autonomist or separatist movements. On the whole, ethnic revolts based on a rural hinterland have been rare in Latin America in this century, despite some populist movements led by urban intelligentsia. Instead, the leading Latin American states have managed to a considerable extent to weld their varied populations into a political community with a national 'political culture', and to accent cultural and economic rivalries with their neighbours or against the hegemony of external powers. As a result, the modern 'scientific' state has become less alien and remote, at any rate from the urban strata, than in Asia or Africa.[9]

In the latter continents, indeed, we find a high incidence of ethnic-political 'incongruence', and a fairly low level of legitimacy accorded to the 'post-colonial' state. There is here some resemblance to the situation in Eastern Europe during the last century, except, of course, that ethnic protest in Africa and Asia today is directed at the newly independent 'state-nations' rather than against old-established, if modernising, empires. The important point is that the ethnic incongruence of so many African and Asian states provides fertile ground for ethnic separatisms, even if it does not of itself generate ethnic movements. Moreover, the novelty, centrality and alien origin of many such states decreases their value for opponents and makes them ready targets for subversion and fragmentation.

INTEGRATION AND DEPENDENCY

Given the chance, most ethnic movements in Africa and Asia would opt for outright separatism. A number of factors combine to produce this outcome. The original nationalists who fought against colonial dependence selected from the European nationalist corpus those themes that emphasised self-government, autonomy and independent statehood.[10] Their successors have inherited such concerns along with the political apparatus of the colonies; but they have done so in a world whose balance of power was even more heavily tilted against the new states than for their East European predecessors after Versailles. For the European 'successor states' had, at least, a relatively higher level of both economic and cultural development – except perhaps in parts of the Balkans – and a more favourably balanced geopolitical environment, until the rise of Nazism. Many post-colonial states are desperately poor, and the economic and military gulf between them and the leading industrial nations is growing annually. Even those that possess large populations, strategic resources and perhaps a more educated citizenry, find themselves extremely vulnerable to either economic or military pressures, or both. China excepted, the political advancement, even survival, of 'Third World' countries is tied to their position in a complex system of political and economic patronage.

Paradoxically, independence itself, in a world of client-states, encourages ethnonational disruption in the Third World. The quest for independence, enshrined in the concept of 'inter-nationalism', sharpens interstate rivalries and comparisons; growing interdependence, albeit unequal, increases the struggle for position in one or more of the competing international power systems. In order to face external pressures and achieve a higher status within a client system, national elites feel compelled to mobilise their populations for the tasks of 'development' and 'nation-building'. Similarly, theories of economic dependency and structural underdevelopment can serve as rationalisations for political and economic failures and chronic problems, and incite the citizenry to greater efforts to achieve autarchy; moreover, by transferring the grounds for dependence from political and military to economic levels, national dignity is less compromised, and the state's powers can be increased.[11]

Once again, interstate pressures play a primary role in the genesis and maintenance of 'integration' nationalisms. Anxious to maximise their internal resources and present a unified front in the competition for markets and status, leaders of new states aim to weld their often diverse populations into a unified citizenry, whose loyalty to the post-colonial state and commitment to an overriding 'political culture' will, hopefully, supersede more localised allegiances and affiliations. Such political integration, however, need not preclude a considerable degree of cultural federalism; and several states, such as India, Mexico and Yugoslavia, have enacted provisions for safeguarding cultural and regional rights of ethnic minorities, on the 'Swiss model', while trying to create a single 'political culture' at the state level and in public sectors.[12]

And yet, because they hope to achieve that shift in identification to the state level in a few decades which it took the Swiss several centuries to attain, the ruling elites of the post-colonial states must rely far more heavily on the institutions and technology of the scientific state itself. It is the state that, as in Western Europe, will form the crucible of the nation – but with a quite novel speed and deliberation. Hence the ruling sectors of the intelligentsia and the bureaucrats will utilise the centrality and relative 'over-development' of the post-colonial state to compensate for its alien origin and fragile boundaries and weld, by force if necessary, and in league with the military, a heterogeneous population into a unified body politic.[13] The intelligentsia will make use of its advanced social position and try to overcome its isolation by channelling economic allocation and development through the state organs and institutions which it controls. Given the relative weakness of other classes and strata, and the legitimation accorded to their territorial state by outside powers, post-colonial bureaucracies and professionals can afford to adopt an authoritarian style in order to convince outsiders that they can turn their artificial top-heavy states into genuine societies or 'nations' with a grass-roots allegiance to the new political community.

An 'integration nationalism' is, therefore, a necessary concomitant of the central role and the paradoxical nature of the post-colonial state, at once precarious and over-elaborated in relation to its 'society'. Given the relative lack of consciousness of strata, the post-colonial state and its controllers, the bureaucrats and intelligentsia, are dominant; yet in relation to pre-colonial ethnic communities and categories, this same state appears fragile and divided. In relation to both strata and ethnic groups, however, the post-colonial state occupies a central and pivotal role in both economic allocation and political authority or mediation. It therefore attracts an even greater degree of aspirations and dissent than its well-established European counterparts; and its failure to satisfy these demands and centripetal pressures evokes an immediate crisis of legitimacy which turns quickly into fissiparous channels. To counter such tendencies, the intelligentsia must resort to authoritarian single-party or military regimes in order to create a unitary society with a single political allegiance to the state.[14]

Unfortunately for elites in the new states, their very commitment to political integration in a plural setting and fragile framework, fosters ethnic protest and revolt. Usually a single strategic ethnic community wields political powers and allocates resources, often on an ethnic basis, and with the best intentions. But, typically, the resources of new states are meagre, they are subject to large-scale external trade fluctuations, and elites cannot therefore attend to the special needs of peripheral or neglected ethnic groups. Worse, the novelty, arbitrary power and alien origin of the state casts doubt on its legitimacy in the eyes of groups who feel they cannot reap sufficient rewards from the post-independence regimes. There are, moreover, few well-established procedures for voicing and dealing with sectional or ethnic grievances; the power, yet fragility, of the state allows little in the way of constitutional outlets for securing ethnic redress, even where there is a commitment to 'ethnic arithmetic' policies. And where there are such outlets, as in Malaysia, the political dominance of one ethnic community and its commitment to the pursuit of a 'national' political integration is easily perceived as an attempt to subvert the position or even cultures of the other communities. In such inauspicious political and economic circumstances, coercive attempts to create a single 'political culture' overriding ethnic cultures, yet drawing many of its symbols from the heritage of the dominant ethnic community, appear simply to reinforce the sense of grievance and exploitation felt by the non-dominant communities. And if this is true of multiparty regimes with some constitutional safeguards, how much more likely is this sense of ethnic discrimination in states like Iraq and Burma and Ethiopia, where military regimes have adopted a 'hard line' towards the aspirations for greater autonomy shown by Kurds, Shan and Eritreans.[15]

ETHNIC POPULISM

One potent source of ethnic separatism lies, then, in the very nature and origins of the 'new state' in Africa and Asia, and in the crisis of legitimacy that inevitably sets in once the euphoria of the immediate post-independence years has evaporated.

But there are other factors, internal and external, which tend to push the ethnic revival towards the goal of political separatism in Africa and Asia. For the internal sources we need to return to the general model which posited a growth of the intelligentsia in line with state needs, until a point of educational overproduction was reached which laid the basis for the turn towards the ethnic historicism propounded by the educators. This general trend applies within most African and Asian states; but the intelligentsia here are far more isolated, and operate in a greater social vacuum, than their European counterparts. As a result, their ethnic revival has a much more populist flavour, and even tries to combine elements of an adapted marxism with their ethnic historicism. In both cases, there is a more marked tendency to push forward to political separation.

Most African and Asian societies on the eve of independence exhibited a tripartite social structure: first, a pre-colonial – semi-feudal, tribal, caste or *millet* – order, with a pre-capitalist, agrarian mode of production and with a landowning class, chiefs, monarchs and clergy ruling over the peasant masses; second, a departing colonial order of administrators, missionaries, entrepreneurs and technicians, some of whom stay on after independence; and finally, the rising urban strata, usually a small native bourgeoisie, an incipient wage-earning class, the military and the professional elites or intelligentsia, many of whom have been admitted to the lower rungs of the colonial bureaucracy and who are destined to provide the ruling cadres after independence.[16]

Now, whereas in Western and Central Europe the intelligentsia operated within a dense network of urban interests among whom they could find ready allies, in many African and Asian states they find themselves bereft of such support because of the 'underdeveloped' state of the urban capitalist strata and of the urban economic and political institutions and networks. In Africa, especially, professional elites had to create their own support networks, in the form of urban and 'tribal' or ethnic associations, which often became the basis for ethnic movements.[17] Of course, there have been exceptions to this pattern. In India, for example, the bourgeoisie was numerous and well-developed, and, perhaps because of its economic subordination to the British bourgeoisie, developed a strong political consciousness.[18] To a lesser extent, cash-crop farmers played a significant role in the Ivory Coast struggle for independence; while in other African countries like Tunisia and Guinea, the intelligentsia could turn for support to a powerful wage-earning class, organised in ably led trades unions.[19]

But, in many more cases, colonialism had not encouraged a native capitalist class; and the intelligentsia, products of elite schools and universities, or educated abroad, found themselves not only culturally marginal in their pre-colonial society, but without a modern infrastructure of institutions and strata which could support their critical rationalism and messianic historicism.

In these circumstances, they sought to break out of their social isolation through alliances with elements in the pre-colonial order. In some cases, there was an uneasy alliance with the clergy. In Burma, for example, the first wave of the independence struggle was led by the Buddhist monks or *ponggyis* under U Ottama; only later did the intelligentsia break away to form the Thakin society of the 1930s, after the messianic peasant revolt of Saya San had been suppressed.[20] In Iran, too, the *ulema* played a vital role in the struggle against foreign intervention, although, to this day, strong tensions exist between them and the rationalist intelligentsia.[21] More important has been the alliance with the peasant masses, or, at any rate, the peasantry of a particular region. Here the intelligentsia were attempting to put into practice the populist idea of serving the 'people', identified now with the rural masses, rather than the urban 'small man'.[22] This sort of rural populism fits perfectly with the educators' glorification of the countryside and rural virtues; and it also reinforces the ethnic and historicist elements of the ethnic revival, because, as we saw, it was in the countryside that cultural elements and historic traditions and sentiments were most persistent. This is why marxisant populists have recently returned to reconsider the question of ethnic 'mass sentiments'; and why communist strategy in the Third World has had to take increasing account of the ethnic profile and content of the peasantry from whom they seek support.[23]

It is also another reason why the ethnic revival in the Third World becomes politically separatist. For the crusade of the ethnic intelligentsia is also a social one, directed at the ruling regimes. Given the fragmentation of the peasantry along local and ethnic lines, and the need for their support in the absence of an urban base, there is a strong likelihood of similar ethnic divisions in the revolutionary intelligentsia. The new post-colonial state, like its colonial predecessor, cannot meet the occupational and status aspirations of the rising intelligentsia of the various ethnic communities which it incorporates; as a novel and fragile framework, its legitimacy is open to serious doubt; and, in these circumstances, the ruling bureaucracy tends to rely more heavily on force and repression than its well-established European counterparts. When, therefore, the disaffected intelligentsia turn to a rebellious peasantry, with which they share elements of a common history and culture, however dimly remembered, their opposition to the regime soon develops towards an open separatism; for the peasantry afford them both the social and the regional base they need, to carve out from the old plural state a new bureaucratic unit which can accommodate their career and status aspirations. Besides, the peasantry with their 'primordial' cultural ties and memories, their seasonal feasts and rituals, their celebration of the lifecycle, their myths and superstitions, their cults of ancient heroes and ancestors, lend to a rationalist, urban, parvenu intelligentsia a cultural aura and a depth of sentiment and solidarity, which gives force to their claim to a separate political identity. Is not their true 'nation' here, in the long-forgotten countryside?

By accepting an alliance, even forging one, with their ethnic peasantry, the intelligentsia also take over its traditions of truculence and revolt. There is much continuity, indeed, between peasant banditry and jacqueries, and the guerilla movements led by an ex-urban intelligentsia. Already, this link was found in the Zapatista movement in Mexico in 1910; Zapata was befriended by intellectuals in the capital, like Diaz Soto y Gama and the Magana brothers, but they supported his policy of relying on the Nahuatl-speaking Indian peasant community in the south, and like him looked back to Morelos' campaign in the same region against Spain in 1810–15, taking also as their symbol the dark-faced Virgin of Guadalupe.[24] Later in the century, the urban Chinese Communists took advantage of the radical, rebellious traditions of the regional peasantry in their gentry-led clans, and of their links with heterodox secret societies. They too looked back to earlier peasant rebellions like the Taiping near Canton, or the Nien in the north, both of which broke out in the 1850s.[25] And in Africa, too, an assimilationist intelligentsia in the Algerian cities forged an alliance with Berber-speaking peasants from the Kabyle mountains, who had been uprooted from their homes by the decay of sharecropping and the need to supplement their livelihood from a declining agriculture. When the nationalist revolt broke out in 1954, it was based first on the Berber region of the Aures mountains, the seat of ancient tribal feuds and dissidence.[26]

It was not long before this explosive mixture of nationalism and peasant regionalism, also found in the Balkans in the early nineteenth and the mid-twentieth centuries, was taken up by a more ethnically conscious intelligentsia. Among the Karen of Burma, as early as the end of the nineteenth century, there developed a Christian missionary-trained intelligentsia, who carried their Baptism to Judson College at Rangoon University in 1920.[27] During the Second World War the Karen resisted the Japanese invasion fiercely, unlike the Burmese; despite the promise of an autonomous state for the Karen in Aung San's new Burma, the Karen – Burmese relationship deteriorated and the Karen formed a Karen National Defence Organisation based on their villages, in a period of guerilla warfare.[28] During U Nu's period of office, all the main minorities in Burma – the Shan, Karen, Kachin and Chins – formed their own guerilla movements, but the succeeding military government of Ne Win suppressed these together with the autonomous states guaranteed in the 1947 Constitution. The new political departure of 1973 gave fresh impetus to separatist insurgency, with guerilla movements in the countryside and strikes in Rangoon; ideological and political centralisation merely fanned separatism in a repressive, precarious state which lacks legitimacy in the eyes of the incorporated ethnic nations (the Karen and Shan number over two millions each). Burma, indeed, is a good example of the way modern forces of westernisation, an intelligentsia and the new bureaucratic state have revived ancient ethnic sentiments and, by promoting an alliance with a mobilised peasantry or tribes, have encouraged separatist nationalisms among the ethnic communities.[29]

Pakistan has also been plagued by insistent ethnic problems since its founding in 1947. In the province of West Pakistan, formed in

1955, there emerged a party campaigning for greater autonomy, the National Awami Party, which in 1972 formed a coalition government in Baluchistan. But, as opponents of the central government in Islamabad, this provincial government was disbanded, causing much discontent among the 1,300,000 Baluchi. Typically, many Baluchi students left the university in Quetta, the provincial capital, and joined the militant mountain tribes in a guerilla war against the central government. Although the Baluchis are a predominantly pastoral and semi-nomadic people with only a tiny stratum of professionals or petty bourgeoisie, the pattern of resistance by an alliance of intelligentsia based on the university and the Baluchi Academy, with tribal pastoralists against the 'artificial' and 'illegitimate' state, is gradually emerging even in this remote hinterland – as it has among the neighbouring Pathans.[30]

A classic instance of this syndrome is furnished by the Kurds who straddle the frontiers of Iraq, Iran, Turkey, Syria and the Soviet Union, though they constitute only tiny minorities in the last two states.[31] The most persistent Kurdish ethnic nationalism is to be found, as one might expect, in Iraq, the state which owes most to western imposition and definition. There have also been Kurdish uprisings in Iran and Turkey, going back to 1880, and particularly after 1918; but most of these were 'feudal' and 'tribal' in character, rather than pan-Kurdish. Even the later and better-documented war between the Kurds under Mulla Mustafa Barzani and the Iraqi governments after 1961 mixes pre-modern 'tribal' factionalism with an ethnic movement for home rule in Kurdistan; Mustafa himself was a tribesman from the remote north of Iraq, but he managed to form an alliance with the left-wing intellectuals of the Democratic Party of Kurdistan, and led a coalition of mountain tribesmen and ex-students in his long guerilla campaign. Over the years, the older-style 'tribal' resistance of Kurdish sheikhs in their mountain fastnesses to any kind of alien interference has given way to a more general ethnic nationalism, based, in the first place, on the late nineteenth-century cultural nationalism formulated by Haji Qadir, the poet, and the Badr-Khan family, and later on the adherence of an intelligentsia increasingly trained in Baghdad and other, including western, cities. It is this intelligentsia that has formulated the ideals and guided the programme of the rural guerilla movement in the field.[32]

In subSaharan Africa, the same pattern has developed since independence, finding a fertile field for reinforcing latent ethnic rivalries. As political forms, African states are generally recent and of alien origin, and their legitimacy was almost immediately called in question, when post-independence hopes failed to materialise. In Nigeria, the older Yoruba–Ibo rivalry was to some extent overshadowed by competition between Ibo and Hausa-Fulani for professional and bureaucratic posts in the state and regional administrations. When, after Ironsi's coup in early 1966, the regions were abolished in favour of a single unified federal public service, the Northerners felt at a disadvantage, particularly in respect of the Ibo intelligentsia, and engineered a series of pogroms of Ibo traders, civil servants and technicians living in the North.[33] They then replaced Ironsi with a Northerner, albeit a Christian, General Gowon. There followed a second, and bloodier, pogrom of Ibo living in the North; and with the flight of hundreds of thousands more Ibo back to their 'homeland', the Eastern region, and the refusal of the military governor, General Ojukwu, to accept Gowon's accession and new administrative plan, the Ibo felt compelled to secede and set up the independent state of Biafra. Insofar as the Ibo themselves were among the most committed to the concept of a united Nigeria, the act of secession was felt to be a last resort. But, in fact, it was a foreseeable consequence of the failure of the Ibo intelligentsia to gain the positions and rewards it expected as the result of its intensive drive to westernisation; with the breakdown of integration within the army itself, and the consequent massacres, it became clear that the superior weight of the Hausa-Fulani peoples of the North would always frustrate this expectation. In this case, there was little need for the Ibo intelligentsia to formulate a new populist strategy, since the massacres had united behind it most strata of the Ibo community.[34]

If the Ibo intelligentsia enjoyed the immediate backing of other new strata, the same cannot be said in the Congolese civil war. It is true that by the late 1950s, rapid urbanisation had helped to foster a large wage-earning class; but the Congolese elite on the eve of the Belgian departure in 1960 was tiny, and consisted mainly of clerks and students, or sergeants in the Belgian *Force Publique*.[35] Missionary-educated and isolated from their own communities as well as the Belgian regime, this intelligentsia rapidly subdivided along ethnic lines, as independence drew near, starting with intense rivalry between the BaKongo and the somewhat artificial 'ethnic category' of the Bangala, or Lingala-speakers.[36] By 1955, their respective cultural organisations, the Association for the Maintenance, the Unity and the Expansion of the Kikongo Language (known as ABAKO), and the Liboka-ly-Bangala, began to compete for high municipal posts such as the Leopoldville *Chef de Cité*; the BaKongo, in particular, attempted to bolster their claims by referring to the illustrious history of their Kingdom of the Kongo (with its capital at San Salvador, in

Angola) which had included the city, and had been allegedly divided up by the colonial powers at the Congress of Berlin in 1885.[37] This myth was carried into the countryside, and the intelligentsia were soon able to fuse their cultural vision and political claims with rural grievances, notably against large concessions of land to European interests. In the eastern Congo, too, urban ethnic nationalisms were fused with rural grievances; and similarly with the Lulua in Central Kasai province, whose Association Lulua-Frères, founded in 1952, linked rural pressures on land with complaints about job discrimination right from the start.[38]

As in the Congo, so also in Angola. The main factions and parties, although they possessed a state-wide territorial aspiration, were based overwhelmingly upon ethnic communities or categories with (increasingly) ethno-national sentiments. The largest such category is the Ovimbundu (base of UNITA), comprising some 35% of the Angolan population; they include some 22 tribes, and speak the Umbundu language. Further north are the Akwambundu, who speak Kimbundu, and number about 25% of the population; they form the main constituency of the MPLA, and control Luanda. Finally, there are, once again, the BaKongo near the Zairian border; they number some 20%, with the rest being made up of smaller ethnic groups. In 1961, the BaKongo leaders, drawn largely from the *evolué* community of Leopoldville, formed a BaKongo party in 1954, which led a major revolt against the Portuguese in 1961; after their defeat, they turned to the countryside, and (as the FNLA) to small-scale guerilla warfare, based upon the large BaKongo refugee population in Zaire during Angola's long war of independence.[39]

The other two parties were also founded by urban intelligentsia: the Ovimbundu UNITA by Jonas Savimbi, who in 1965 split off from the BaKongo FNLA; and the Marxist MPLA by assimilated intellectuals in the Angolan cities, who in 1956 attracted the local Akwambundu population in Luanda. From 1963, the MPLA launched guerilla campaigns against the Portuguese, first in the enclave of Cabinda, and then in the remote east, from bases in Zambia.[40] The pattern by which a small urban intelligentsia seeks a rural base among its ethnic community in order to achieve state control, or to secede, has become the norm in recent states like Angola, where the three parties continue their guerilla warfare to this day. In underdeveloped countries, the 'rural option' has become almost a necessity for an aspirant intelligentsia. But how far such mobilisation of tribesmen and peasants goes, and whether it achieves political success, as it did in China and Vietnam, depends on wider geopolitical factors.

State integration and ethnic schism

The success of ethnic populism in mobilising the rural population and achieving either state control, or political secession, depends in large part on the geopolitical climate and constellation at the time of ethnic revolt. And the fact is that, given the number of candidates for such control or separation, very few have actually achieved their goals in the era following decolonisation.

We are often told that the nuclear balance between the superpowers renders them impotent to deal with local border or ethnic conflicts, and ensures the proliferation of 'bush wars'. Actually, the truth is that geopolitical competition on a global scale feeds on border and ethnic conflicts, so long as they do not overstep the limits of the client-state system.[41]

Since the Second World War, there has accrued to each of the superpowers a system of client-states, acquired or inherited. Some of these clients fall directly within their geopolitical orbit, others are associated with a superpower by virtue of location, historical connections or ideology; or because local hostilities have forced each party to seek such association in order to protect themselves and further their aims. As these 'spheres of influence' and association have crystallised, an intense competition for any remaining, outlying areas has developed, as in the Horn of Africa, Angola and Afghanistan. At the same time, it is noteworthy that the superpowers have rarely sought to redraw existing state boundaries; although they have sometimes, as with Bangladesh, been forced to accept such a redrawing *after the event*. Generally, however, they do not seek to encourage ethnic secession or incorporation *per se;* this could all too easily destabilise their own client-systems, benefiting the other superpower, or a third party.

On the other hand, they are not averse to fostering ethnic movements or 'national liberation struggles' to provide a check on governments too antipathetic to their own system, or too powerful in a sensitive strategic area. Ethnic conflicts resemble pawns in the grand global strategies of the superpowers, to be fostered or damped down according to a calculation of political and economic interests, but rarely to be given unconditional support. Like pawns, ethnic conflicts provide essential openings for superpower advantage in the different theatres of global rivalry; but they may also bring setbacks and humiliations, such as the Americans experienced in Vietnam and the Soviet Union in Egypt.[42]

Such controlled rivalry between client-systems feeding on ethnic conflict and instability has become an essential structural element

148

within the emergent international order. Insofar as it has been institutionalised, this order is based upon a recognition of the legitimacy
of certain historic states and their ex-colonies. It has little to do with
'nations', except where they chance to coincide demographically
with the boundaries of territorial states. It is the state, not the 'nation-state' of official terminology, which has become the 'module' of
the misnamed 'international' order. 'Internationalism' as an ideology
represents merely the desirability of cooperation between states
which claim to reflect the aspirations of 'peoples' or 'nations' within
their borders; in practice, this means that they represent the interests
of some, but not all, of these peoples, except in the rare case where
a state is composed of a homogeneous ethnic population with a clear
national consciousness.[43]

It is obvious that such an interstate system can only exacerbate
existing ethnic tensions within and across state borders. Where ethnic aspirations are unsatisfied, and the incorporating state nevertheless claims to represent those aspirations in all interstate networks
and fora, this can only sharpen latent ethnic antagonism and whet
the appetites of neglected or spurned ethnic intelligentsia, who in
any case form the most internationally aware section of their communities. In the same way, the client-systems which divide up the
global interstate order, and take in a majority of its member states,
can only raise the expectations of ambitious ethnic professionals
without, in most cases, being able to satisfy their demands. Most
states are, after all, members or associates of one or other of the
client-systems; discontented ethnic intelligentsia within a given
state will naturally tend to look for support for their cause to leading
members of the opposing client-system, once it becomes clear that
they cannot secure redress within their own bloc. The opposing superpower, or its close ally, may on occasion take up the ethnic cause;
but only insofar as, and to the extent that, its own interests can be
advanced by such a move. In many cases it will refuse the request,
so as not to offend the incorporating state which it hopes to attract
into its client-system, or even an interested local third party. It is rare
to find a superpower giving full support to an ethnic nationalism;
proliferation of mini-states in sensitive strategic areas could rebound
to the advantage of its global competitors.[44] There is also the risk of
undermining the interstate order itself, which tacitly legitimates the
client-systems and superpower hegemony within acknowledged
spheres of influence. An attack on the interstate order could have
serious repercussions for the position of the superpowers in the long
run. Besides, neither superpower is ethnically homogeneous; both
contain self-conscious ethnic communities, even nations, within

their borders, and they are therefore likely to sympathise with the ethnic predicament of similarly plural states.[45]

The chances of ethnic populisms attaining their separatist objectives are, therefore, fairly slender. Even their ability to mobilise their rural populations effectively, through importation of weapons and acquisition of funds and training, is severely curtailed by such an unfavourable international climate and constellation of global interests. Where a superpower did intervene locally, either directly or by proxy, it was usually to stabilise a government under attack, such as the South Vietnamese or Ethiopian, or to assist the movement, which was likely to win control over a state, and maintain itself in power, as in Angola. Ethnic movements like those of the Kurds or Ibo, Naga or Moro, who have never achieved sovereignty over a sizeable territory, or who seem unlikely to be able to do so by their own efforts, are generally denied the aid they seek, particularly when they encounter fierce state resistance. Only where the movement has been able to muster large-scale local support, as with the Palestinians, will a superpower interest itself to some extent in its cause; though, even here, it normally requires the tacit consent of the other superpower, if the claims of an ethnic movement can be met. Generally speaking, even where a superpower may support a 'national liberation struggle', it will calibrate such aid according to the degree of its control over the ethnic movement, and its calculation of the balance of advantage to itself. The dangers of involvement in open-ended conflict are becoming all too clear.[46]

And yet, there are factors in the geopolitical situation which give some comfort to potential ethnic separatisms. First, both superpowers and their allies are committed to 'democratic' and 'welfare' ideologies; they therefore tend to encourage ethnic populism if only as a means of ascertaining and demonstrating the extent of 'popular' support for the movement. But the majority of people in Third World states live and work in the countryside; urban elites, and especially an isolated intelligentsia, must mobilise the support of ethnic peasants and tribesmen through the establishment of rural branch parties and the formulation of agrarian programmes of reform, if they are to demonstrate their political credibility.[47] But agrarian reform is inevitably radical in the social and economic context of most Third World states; hence superpower rivalries and ideologies indirectly encourage the growth of marxist nationalisms. Second, there is the logic of global rivalry itself, which we have mentioned. This encourages both the superpowers, and the ethnic movement, to look for quick tactical advantages.[48] Even if this falls well short of satisfying separatist aspirations, because of the serious dangers to the overall system that

150

fragmentation carries with it, it nevertheless incites ethnic movements to more aggressive action, especially if they are favourably located in relation to the superpower spheres of influence.[49] And finally there is the 'demonstration effect' of other successful ethnic nationalisms elsewhere, and of the power of the ideology of self-determination, to which all, even the superpowers, pay at least lip-service.[50] Where the principle has been conceded, it becomes necessary only to establish the proper ethnic and national credentials to gain general acceptance and the support of the superpowers; or so it would seem. If it can be shown that the movement represents a fairly sizeable and well-delineated cultural and historic community with a strong regional base, and perhaps a tradition of former independence, then, surely, the principle of self-determination must be applied.[51]

And yet, in the vast majority of cases since the era of decolonisation, it has not found application. The aspirations of ethnic minorities to a separate sovereign existence have been neither stifled nor satisfied. Different aspects of the geopolitical field have both encouraged ethnic populism and socialistic nationalism, and contained their demands within a tight system of territorial statehood. At one and the same time, the international situation provokes ethnic and social discontent within subordinate states of the Third World, and fails to alleviate or remove it. Unquelled and unsatisfied, this endemic discontent breaks out in ever-renewed revolt and ethnic 'bush wars', which the superpowers try to turn to their advantage without too much risk to themselves. Like the interstate order itself, the superpowers must underwrite often-unviable state units whose central ethnic bureaucracies monopolise most of the state's resources and rewards and who therefore lose their last shred of legitimacy in the eyes of excluded or relegated ethnic minority communities, who together sometimes make up a majority of the total population. Small wonder, then, that the appeal of ethnic minorities to the great powers must continue, yet forever remain unquenched.

8

vwvwvwvwvwvwvwvwvwvwvwvwvwvwvwvwvwvwvwvwvwvwvwvwvwvwvwvwvwvwvwvwvwvwvwv

Accommodation and neo-ethnicity

In strong contrast to the trend towards political separatism characteristic of Africa and Asia, the experience of many ethnic communities
in the West, and notably North America, reveals a general tendency
towards accommodation within plural states. There are two major
exceptions to this generalisation: the case of Blacks, Indians and
Puerto Ricans in the United States, who have pursued various strategies in the past but seem now to be opting for a 'communalist' one,
and the regionally based ethnic communities of Canada and Western
Europe, which since the early 1960s have been pursuing a more aggressive autonomist line. Nor should we forget the coalescence of a
state 'bureaucratic nationalism' with an ethnic nationalism in those
European countries in which, to all intents, the state is ethnically
homogeneous, as in Poland, Portugal and Denmark.

In this chapter, accordingly, I shall focus on the accommodationist
trend in the United States, and also briefly consider Black communalism; and reserve for the next chapter an examination of the ethnic
revival in Canada and Western Europe.

ASSIMILATION AND PLURALISM

Early American sociological perspectives on ethnicity in the West
were predominantly 'assimilationist'. They assumed that over time,
usually a couple of generations, immigrant ethnic communities to
large plural societies such as America or Australia would first accul-
turate to the dominant secular culture, and finally, through intermarriage and socialisation, be absorbed into the larger society.[1] In turn,
this line of reasoning assumed that the several ethnic communities
and their traditions would gradually disappear into the melting-pot
of the overarching society; and that even those with sacred cultures
would shrink into fringe sects or retain only the most shadowy memories of their former religious traditions. Such arguments were, of
course, closely akin to the assumptions of 'modernisation' theory
with its unilinear scheme of development towards a fixed target of

the secular, industrial nation-state and the modern, participant society.[2] Both modernisation and assimilation theories recognised that successive waves of immigration, or the uneven diffusion of social development, would delay the final absorption of various ethnic communities, or societies, into a single dominant culture of modernity; yet they held that the process was inexorable and irreversible over the long run, and that mobilisation and incorporation would dissolve all primordial, communal bonds.

In recent years, a number of studies have revealed limitations in the assimilationist perspective. The much-vaunted return to ethnic 'roots' has demonstrated a depth of sentiment about ethnic identity and affiliation which surprised some and delighted others. More important, it soon became clear that 'Americanisation' described an extremely varied set of cultural patterns, and that the former cultural domination of white Anglo-Saxon protestant immigrants had given way to a much more heterogeneous continental culture. Indeed, America and other settler societies were today increasingly to be seen as cultural mosaics, in which ethnic pluralism was fast replacing the ideal (let alone the reality) of a single-state culture and society.[3] Besides, immigrant ethnic groups have varied greatly in the extent to which they have adapted to a presumed dominant culture, or, conversely, clung to their ancestral traditions and communal identities: those with a strong religious and national tradition, like Polish or Irish Catholics, or Jews, have tended to retain their identities, whether or not they adapted rapidly to new conditions in the host society. In these communities, especially, ethnic organisations and cultures remain flourishing, intermarriage is still a minority practice (albeit growing) and ethnic self-esteem is strong.[4] Moreover, ethnicity remains an important indicator of political and other attitudes: thus, Italian immigrants to the United States tend to be more 'fatalistic', less politically active and more conservative in family matters than Anglo-Saxons, while Irish immigrants were more 'trusting' (though also 'fatalistic') than Anglo-Saxons, more politically active and held more conservative views on the role of women.[5]

Two further points have reinforced the 'pluralist' view. The first is that ethnicity persists most strongly among lower classes, who are less exposed to acculturation and who make use of ethnic organisation and symbols to combat exploitation and inequality in American society. Here, ethnicity is instrumental rather than expressive: it serves new class functions in the prevalent socioeconomic order, functions which have given ethnic culture a new lease of life, retarding further any trend towards assimilation. Secondly, the new upward mobility of many ethnic members has brought their communities into the public eye. Catholic academics and Jewish writers and actors in show business have not only influenced the general patterns of 'American' culture in different cities and areas; they have highlighted the image of their ethnic community, and given it a new salience and visibility. Perhaps, too, there has been some return to ethnic affiliation and identity among such third-generation intelligentsia; they are at least curious and drawn towards the ethnic culture their parents had rejected in their rebellion against the first generation of immigrants.[6]

All this adds up to a different picture of colonisation societies than that presented by a simplified assimilation theory. It no longer assumes a goal of an undifferentiated American (Australian, Canadian) culture to which all subcultures will sooner or later conform. On the contrary, it sees the new American culture as essentially plural, a network of subgroups and subcultures, each with its own contribution and distinctive ethos, and thus quite unlike the more homogeneous cultures found in European states. Nevertheless, this sort of pluralism is not incompatible with assimilation theory, since it does not rule out a gradual process of at least partial fusion and intermingling, in which the 'sharp edges' of ethnic communities will be blunted and allegiances and identifications will gradually be transferred to the wider 'national' unit. Indeed, the very pluralism of such a 'nation' will facilitate this secular trend, making the choice less painful, the renunciation less salient.[7]

'NEO-ETHNICITY'

The question remains, however, whether such an 'accommodationist' picture as the theory of pluralism presents, can account for all the features of the present return to ethnicity in plural, colonisation societies; or whether we are not witnessing the first stage of a much more pronounced break with the hitherto prevailing trend towards acculturation and assimilation.

One argument in support of a revival of ethnicity in America centres on the idea that, with the present decline of class allegiances, ethnic communities have taken over their 'interest group' functions for those who feel disprivileged and relegated to a subordinate position in society. In other words, earlier class and religious conflicts have been displaced by vertical ethnic ones, at the very moment when uneven modernisation and more intensive communications make people more aware of ethnic inequalities.[8] To this analysis, Daniel Bell has added a larger dimension when he seeks to place the rise of ethnic identification in the world in the context of major macro-social trends, such as the growth of more inclusive identities, the shift from market to political decision-making, the decline of authority and redefinition of equality, and the rise of an external proletariat and anti-imperialism as an ideology. As a result, there has been a growth in competition between the main groups in 'plural societies'; for there the political arena has now become the salient one for working out rivalries between interest groups, particularly with the 'shrinkage' of the economic order, itself a consequence of the growth in State interference and of modernisation by elites 'from the top'.[9] With the subordination of the economic to the political order, class conflict has become institutionalised and 'class' no longer carries any affective tie; it has become merely a 'group interest', especially in America. This has allowed ethnicity to become more important:

> Ethnicity has become more salient because it can combine an interest with an affective tie. Ethnicity provides a tangible set of common identifications – in language, food, music, names – when other social roles become more abstract and impersonal. In the competition for the values of the society to be realised politically, ethnicity can become a means for claiming place or advantage.[10]

In America, especially, this new importance of the ethnic 'site' for the disadvantaged is a consequence of the decline of the white Anglo-Saxon supremacy and of white cultural imperialism. Add to this the desire for a primordial anchorage within a more bureaucratic social structure and more syncretistic culture, and the need for an effective communal organisation to defend rights or make demands; ethnicity provides both and has become a legitimate mode of self-expression and means of self-advancement. Ethnic groups have succeeded in wedding status issues to political demands, and their salience will last as long as prosperity allows status politics to predominate over class and economic issues.

By concentrating specifically on the *salience* of ethnicity, as opposed to its scope, intensity or social and political weight, Bell tends to view the ethnic revival as a more temporary and less far-reaching trend than the evidence would suggest outside white America. Where there are competing sets of ties and communal allegiances, the 'salience' of any one is likely to be subject to considerable local fluctuations; at the same time, salience tells us little about the penetration or depth of such ties and allegiances, nor about their extent, nor their intensity. And even information about the latter components omits the elements of persistence or durability over generations, that has characterised the recent cycle of the ethnic revival and transformation.

155

Among the white communities of the United States, however, the situation is quite different from that which has supported an ethnic revival elsewhere. In the United States, white 'neo-ethnicity' is partly a response to the Black Power movement of the mid-1960s, partly a retention of communal attachments by older, poorer sections who fear too-rapid change, and partly a return by younger, more educated strata to the symbols and traditions of their forbears. As such, white 'neo-ethnicity' is largely conservative and nostalgic, a desire to restore a dwindling ethnic cohesiveness in the face of assimilation and rapid change associated with upward mobility. [11] The social composition of such 'neo-ethnic' movements is varied; working-class, 'lower-middle-class' and marginal-income urban whites appear to be most prone to a traditionalistic neo-ethnicity with anti-Black overtones, yet the symbolism and nostalgia for a traditional identity also attract more educated, higher-income members of ethnic communities like the Jews of New York. [12]

This suggests that 'neo-ethnicity' in the United States, with the exception of Black, Indian and Puerto Rican movements, is essentially 'accommodative' to the system of the country as a whole, and is in particular a vehicle for group upward mobility or for the defence of rights for the disadvantaged, rights which seem particularly under threat in a period of rapid change. It is not, on the whole, a product of the thwarted aspirations of intelligentsia or other elites, although some intellectuals are involved in defining the content of 'neo-ethnicity' for particular communities. [13] Rather, it is a rearguard defence of attachments threatened by modernisation, led by traditionalistic intellectuals and appealing especially to the urban poor. The lack of an autonomist, let alone separatist, nationalistic component in the ideology of 'neo-ethnicity' underlines its difference from the norm of 'ethnic revival' and transformation, which we find elsewhere.

A 'SYMBOLIC ETHNICITY'?

It may well be that, for these reasons, 'neo-ethnicity' in the United States may be a more temporary, less deeply rooted phenomenon. With a decline in prosperity, or an increase in superpower conflict, the *salience* of ethnicity may wane, and with it ethnic communities and cultures, to the point of extreme attenuation. 'Neo-ethnicity', then, would have been merely a temporary wave, a last-ditch attempt to delay the secular trend of assimilation.

Other evidence, however, suggests that ethnicity as such will be a more durable factor in American society for some time to come. For one thing, educational overproduction is on the increase; the professions and academic community cannot absorb its graduates with their high qualifications, and neither can the bureaucracies.[14] We may yet witness the ethnic division of this new intelligentsia, and their return to their communities with demands for greater ethnic autonomy. We are already witnessing a sort of 'voluntary ethnicity' in which young educated third- and fourth-generation ethnics are inventing new modes of ethnic identification, despite the growth in intermarriage across ethnic lines and the loss of any remaining ethnic occupational ties.

For third- and fourth-generation ethnic members, the original ethnic cultures brought to America by their grandfathers and great-grandfathers are irrelevant to their everyday lives, but retain an emotive aura and provide materials out of which they can construct for themselves and their present needs a new ethnic identity. Ethnic roles have almost disappeared, though ethnic neighbourhoods still abound in large cities; yet third- and fourth-generation ethnics still *feel* Italian, Irish, Polish or Jewish, and they seek to express their ethnic sentiment in ways that suit their individual or small-group needs. Hence, they feel free to experiment with ethnic and traditional forms, and to choose from their ethnic heritage those aspects and traits that will most vividly express their own ethnic 'authenticity', without letting that heritage and those forms dictate their workaday lives.

This sort of attenuated ethnic sentiment and sense of identity, which Gans has dubbed 'symbolic ethnicity', is now on the increase, especially among younger generations, including the ethnic intelligentsia. It is to be found in such diverse phenomena as ethnic *rites de passage* and ceremonial, ethnic foods and consumer goods, ethnic characters on TV and films, and ethnic identifications with the 'old (or new) country', especially if distant from America; above all, an interest in ethnic histories, at a distance.[15] Even traumatic historical events like the Armenian massacres or the Holocaust may be serving the function of providing a symbolic identification for those Armenians and Jews of the current generations who are experiencing the threat of acculturation and assimilation, and who no longer possess a real group identity or practise a genuine ethnic culture.

Because those who adopt 'symbolic ethnicity' are also more upwardly mobile, and because the national media in America highlight ethnic symbols and convey them to a nation-wide audience, ethnicity as such has become much more visible and respectable, something that the wider society fosters and legitimates. That is why 'symbolic ethnicity' is likely to persist, even while ethnic cultures and organisations decline and disappear, over the long term.

On the other hand, can 'symbolic ethnicity' be treated as a local variant of the ethnic revival? Can a 'neo-traditionalism' of the salient few, or the revivalism of a minority, however visible or educated, be taken as evidence of a broader 'ethnic revival', even if it helps to keep ethnic identities alive into the fifth and sixth generations? Have not the oldest immigrants to America lost all trace of their original ethnic cultures, even where they retain something of their ancestral religion?

Gans himself is mindful of the possibility of such a revival, though he considers the evidence so far makes it unlikely. Yet, as he says, 'the history of religion and nationalism, as well as events of recent years, should remind us that the social process sometimes moves in dialectical ways, and that acculturative and assimilative actions by a majority occasionally generate revivalistic reactions by a minority'.[16]

When we couple his own analysis of a return by more educated strata to a 'symbolic ethnicity' in the much more open and innovative American environment, with the growth of an inflated intelligentsia and the new interest in ethnic histories which it is beginning to display, we may ask ourselves whether, even in the very different situation of America, we are not witnessing something analogous to the ethnic revival in other continents. How far this new interest will go, and to what extent it is likely to politicise attenuated ethnic identities, are debatable issues. Clearly, there are important differences from European or Third World experiences. America itself is not as long-established a state as its European counterparts, but its political community is much less fragile and much more legitimate in the eyes of most of the population than its African or Asian counterparts. Its social structure is also much more developed and balanced than those of most Third World countries, despite the persistence of major inequalities. Besides, centralising pressures by the federal bureaucracies are still, to some extent, held in check by the powers of the local states and the provisions of the Constitution; the targets for criticism and attack are therefore more diffused than in most other countries. Moreover, as one of the superpowers heading a client-system, and a plural state itself, America's situation encourages a high degree of internal tolerance for ethnic diversity, especially at the political level.[17] Although there is still some social discrimination against some white ethnic communities, at the political level there is considerable latitude for ethnic interests and communal action in furtherance of those interests. Ethnicity has, therefore, been woven into the fabric of American society to a far greater extent than in most other states, and this is perhaps a natural effect of the geographical dispersion and 'scrambling' of ethnic communities in a larger society. Had these communities settled in a more concentrated fashion over extensive areas, we might be witnessing some demands for a measure of ethnic autonomy, such as is found in Europe today.

All these reasons tend to support the idea that 'symbolic ethnicity' among white ethnics in America is quite different from the ethnic revival elsewhere. Yet, even after we have accepted these differences, the notion of 'symbolic ethnicity' does not quite cover the American experience of ethnicity. I do not mean simply that, among poorer whites, ethnic cultures and organisations persist into the present generation. Rather, it is a question of an important shift from 'accommodation' strategies to more 'communalist' ones. In Chapter 1 I cited the American example where ethnic communities seek both to attain group progress through educational mobility, and to control those urban areas where they form a majority and influence the destiny of the state in which they are incorporated through communal action. The quest for communal progress by climbing the educational and social ladder has been the typical 'accommodationist' strategy of many white ethnic communities; it is dynamic but essentially adaptive. The other strategy of political control at the urban and national levels, which I call 'communalism', is more recent; it owes much of its inspiration to the Black revolt of the early 1960s. In practice, the two strategies coexist. Yet there has been a more regenerative impulse at work of late, which finds expression in this shift towards a more communalist strategy. There are clearly nationalist undertones in such a strategy, as I noted earlier; for ethnic communities whose memberships are so scattered, except in certain urban zones, communalism may be the most appropriate way to express a sense of revitalised and renewed ethnic identity, which uses elements from the past, yet forges a quite different culture from that heritage; as which nationalism has not?[18]

While, therefore, the 'ethnic revival' in America has taken entirely different forms, and has a different genesis, from those of other states, it has some affinities with those other revivals, once we recognise the very different environment in which white ethnics must operate in the United States. Such a revival may not be so strong and lasting as elsewhere, but it is clearly of wider scope and greater depth than the term 'symbolic ethnicity' conveys. It remains to be seen whether the growth and plight of the intelligentsia in the United States will have the sort of ethnic repercussions which they have had in other countries.

Accommodation and neo-ethnicity

BLACK NATIONALISM

How far do the Black (and Indian and Puerto Rican) ethnic movements fit into the various schemes proposed for the fate of the white ethnics? Certainly we can find elements of acculturation, if not assimilation, of accommodative pluralism, of 'neo-ethnicity', albeit radicalised, even of 'symbolic ethnicity' among sections of the Black and Indian communities at different times in their long histories of conflict with the white majority in the United States.[19] But we can also find much more nationalistic responses – in Delaney and the 'Back-to-Africa' movements, in Garveyism, among the Black Muslims and Malcolm X's organisation, in the long struggle of Martin Luther King and his followers, in the Black Power movement and the Black Panthers, in the return to African roots both in Harlem in the 1920s and in many cities today. The Black experience in the United States is so varied, and has witnessed such a succession of movements, that it is difficult to find a single all-encompassing characterisation of its ethnic revival.[20]

For an 'ethnic revival' is clearly what has been taking place among the uprooted Blacks throughout the last century and more. The first cultural wave of such a revival was already to be found, after Delaney, in the work of du Bois before the First World War, and again in the 1920s in the Harlem New Negro movement.[21] In the interWar period, Black intellectuals laid the foundation for the vision of a regenerated community and sought to rediscover its ethnic roots.[22] It was not, however, until after the Second World War that their vision was accepted by a new Black intelligentsia, and spread, partly through the Black Muslims, to other urbanised Blacks in the ghettoes.[23] A new wave of Black ethnic nationalism surfaced in the late 1950s and early 1960s, and it soon led to overt demands, mainly by Black Power and Black Panther leaders, for ethnic autonomy and even separation in one of the territorial states of the continent.[24] Though an extreme demand by only a tiny, shrill minority, the desire to evacuate white America and its racist oppression has a long and troubled history.[25] In recent years, central government has succeeded in heading off such demands by coopting Black intelligentsia and businessmen, and by giving opportunities for advancement to a 'talented tenth', so that today it would be more accurate to speak of Black 'communalism' rather than autonomism. Black leaders today seek control over their urban areas in order to decide their own priorities and communal self-development plans, and at the same time they insist on having a voice in shaping the destiny of the United States as a whole, even to its foreign policy.[26] Their nationalism resembles, in some respects, the middle-class Jewish Diaspora nationalism propounded by Simon Dubnow after the Great War; for the Jewish communities scattered in Europe, yet partly concentrated in certain areas of the Pale of Settlement, it was feasible to advance a concept of cultural and social nationalism for such despised enclave communities.[27] Similarly, for the scattered yet partly concentrated urban Black communities, the diaspora 'communalist' nationalism of the new intelligentsia and elites appears to be the most appropriate way of both solving the African–American cultural dilemma, and countering white hostility in what had become their own country.

The history and rise of Black ethnic nationalism embodies, to a considerable extent, the conditions and mechanisms of the ethnic revival, as I have outlined them. Ethnic communities in West Africa were uprooted, and their members herded together to form an agglomerated 'ethnic category', whose transformation into an ethnic community was largely effected by that equivalent of war, slavery and its racist institutions. In fact, of course, the Blacks were treated as a 'racial category' rather than an ethnic one; and it has taken much painful self-discovery and inner striving to find some, at least, of their long-lost cultural and historical heritage, intertwined as it inevitably is with the American experience into which it was set and partly dissolved.[28] To this day, there is much doubt and soul-searching about the extent to which this Afro-American heritage can be salvaged (let alone the original African heritages).[29] Yet the attempt is clearly being made, and not just at the level of 'symbolic ethnicity', despite the fashionable 'Afro' cults. Nor is it simply a question of poorer Blacks retaining their sense of ethnicity through Christian Baptist organisations, though again these remain influential.

What is crucial for an understanding of the Black nationalist revolution is the growth of new strata, essentially rationalist and secular in outlook, above all an intelligentsia aspiring to break through the wall of prejudice and discrimination through education, but also by political means, if necessary. Since the Second World War, after the great migrations of Blacks to northern cities, the growing impact of federal agencies, starting with the army, have produced pressures for rapid integration in several fields, and have, as part of this demand, sought to create a new Black intelligentsia, impatient with the failure of public practice to accord with official pronouncements. A similar sense of frustration had already overtaken the Black intellectuals even before the War, so that would-be assimilationists among them were now turning their backs on the belated integration policies of the federal government and their liberal white civil-rights supporters. By the time the celebrated meeting between President

Kennedy and the Black intellectuals took place in 1963, they had already gone over to a fiercely autonomist, even separatist, frame of mind, which was soon to be translated into political action by their disciples among the Black professionals and students.[30] Hence the contradictions in federal policy, committed to integration yet practising or condoning discrimination, provided a perfect recipe for the radicalisation of the rising Black strata, which the scientific state was itself doing so much to foster and create, largely through its educational system. No wonder that, in comparison with white ethnics, Black intelligentsia felt themselves uniquely 'victimised', and saw in their own situation but a reflection of the exploited condition of the whole Black community.[31]

In some ways, the ethnic revival among American Blacks is analogous both to the classic instances of East European nationalism, and to the ethnic separatisms of Africa and Asia. It shares with the former the quest for cultural roots and historical self-discovery, as well as a desire to secede from what is seen as a necessarily oppressive and 'inauthentic' situation. With the Afro-Asian separatisms, it shares the intelligentsia's sense of isolation, and its feeling of helplessness, as a pawn in a great power conflict, although physically its community is located within the borders of one of the superpowers. On the other hand, the federal state to which it is opposed is quite unlike either the old European empires of the nineteenth century, or the fragile, if overdeveloped, states of Africa and Asia with their policies of cultural homogenisation or 'integration nationalisms'. Nor, as we shall see, is the Black revival to be compared with the experience of recent autonomist movements within other western states, though it too operates within a general context of high levels of mass education, industrialism and communications, within fairly well-established democratic states.

In short, the Black nationalism of North America partakes of elements from experiences elsewhere, but systematic comparison breaks down in the face of the unique historical context of slavery, segregation and overt racism, which have shaped the course and nature of the Black ethnic revival, and for which even the Jewish case provides only a very partial parallel.[32]

vwv

'Neo-nationalism'

Nowhere has the ethnic revival occasioned more surprise than in its European heartlands, and nowhere has there been such a proliferation of ethnic movements in the last two decades. This ethnic renaissance has taken two forms: a revitalised national sentiment on the part of dominant ethnic communities like the French under de Gaulle, the Norwegians, the Rumanians and the Poles, and, secondly, a surge of support for ethnic movements claiming autonomy on behalf of communities incorporated within existing state boundaries. The list of the latter is impressive: it includes such strong and well-developed movements as the Scottish, Welsh, Breton, Corsican, Basque, Catalan, Flemish, Ulster, Tyrolese, Croat, Slovak, Greek Cypriot, Maltese and, in Canada, the Quebecois, not to mention the special case of the Jurassiens in Switzerland. But there have also been autonomist stirrings among smaller, or less well-developed, groupings, some of them 'ethnic categories' rather than fully fledged communities. Examples of the latter include the Galicians, Andalusians, Cornish, Manx, Faroese, Shetlanders, Channel Islanders, Frisians, Gelderlanders, Walloons, Sardinians, Sicilians, Slovenes, Alsatians, Occitanians, French Basques, Bavarians and Lithuanians. And this is probably a conservative estimate.[1]

The questions that naturally arise are, firstly, what, if anything, do these movements have in common, and, secondly, why have they succeeded in attracting far greater support in the last two decades, especially in those states where it was thought that ethnic nationalism was a thing of the past?

AUTONOMY AND 'NEO-NATIONALISM'

The first point to notice is that the vast majority of these movements, whether they arise under democracy or dictatorships, in industrial or largely agrarian states, in the East or the West, are basically 'autonomist' in character and aims. That is to say, most of them want 'home rule', not outright separation. Their aim is coexistence within a federal state, but with complete control over every aspect of their communal affairs, both cultural and socio-economic. There are some significant exceptions: the Scottish National Party, the ETA wing of the Basque movement, and the Parti Quebecois have opted for complete separation. Yet, though they are, in their very different ways, important elements within their respective ethnic revivals, it would appear that, on this point, they do not represent the wishes of the mainstream of even their supporters, let alone the majority of their communities.[2] The remarkable fact about the present ethnic revival within Europe and Canada is that its adherents possess concentric loyalties – to their own ethnic communities, and to the states in which they have been incorporated for so long a period. The Flemish furnish an excellent example: although they have agitated for many years for linguistic autonomy within their region, and continue to press their claims within the contested area of Brussels, they, like their Walloon counterparts, remain committed to preserving the overall Belgian framework, and to the outside world present themselves under a double aspect, at once Flemish and Belgian.[3] And much the same is true for most Catalans, Scots and Welshmen, who see themselves as Spaniards and Britons, in however attenuated a sense, in addition to their ethnic-national identities.

Secondly, as I argued in Chapter 1, many of these ethnic movements had their origins in the period of the First World War or even earlier, while their cultural foundations go back to the early nineteenth century. In these cases, the present ethnic revival is a chronological continuation of an older nationalism, with some new emphases and ideological reorientations, to which I shall return. Basically, however, these movements are striving for the autonomy, unity and identity of their ethnic community, just as their early forbears; and in that sense deserve the label 'neo-nationalism'.[4] Even those ethnic movements which cannot point to a long nationalist pedigree, like the Occitanian, the Cornish or the Gelderlander, are set firmly within the framework of the classic ethnic nationalisms of the nineteenth century. There is, if not a chronological, at any rate a typological continuity, which also merits the label of 'neo-nationalism'. As Connor argues, the 'force field' of nationalism has now encompassed even these remote areas, stirring in its wake ethnic sentiments that everyone had presumed long forgotten and buried, and giving new life to what were deemed to be mere 'ethnographic monuments'.[5]

'Neo-nationalism', however, differs from its classic forbears in generally eschewing any desire to redraw the map of Europe. The classic nationalisms of Eastern Europe had generally aimed to secede from the large and oppressive empires in which their communities found themselves incorporated. Recent 'neo-nationalisms' prefer to retain the present state boundaries, with the exceptions noted above, and this may reflect the greater flexibility of modern political systems and perhaps the less well-developed sense of identity (and proportional numbers) of the ethnic communities concerned.

In preferring 'home rule' autonomy to outright separatism, western 'neo-nationalisms' stand mid-way between the communalism of the United States and the separatist movements characteristic of Africa and Asia. This is only to be expected. Being geographically concentrated or possessing a territorial base, European ethnic communities (and the Quebecois) resemble their African and Asian counterparts, and hence find a communalist strategy inappropriate; their aspiration for self-determination finds its natural expression in a territorial format. On the other hand, because they have emerged in more industrialised states with higher levels of education and communications and well-established boundaries and political systems, western ethnic movements do not feel impelled to demand outright separation; western political systems, moreover, tend to provide mechanisms for airing grievances without an immediate resort to violence being necessary. And yet, it is just in these democratic and constitutional western states that ethnic nationalisms have erupted once again, and this time with considerable force and far wider support for the ethnic communities concerned.

How has this state of affairs, so puzzling and paradoxical, come about? And why just now?

THE LOSS OF EMPIRE

While our basic model of the rise and overproduction of the intelligentsia within bureaucratic states undergoing a crisis of legitimacy throws light on the general conditions of ethnic nationalism in Europe during the last two centuries, we require an additional explanation for the timing and location of the current ethnic resurgence. Here again, we need to look at the three elements which we found to be relevant in the case of African and Asian separatisms: the degree of 'congruence' between ethnic communities and the boundaries of states, the degree of social isolation of the rising intelligentsia, and the overall geopolitical situation in which European ethnic movements must operate.

Let me start with the international context. Several observers have commented on the 'loss of empire' as a central feature of the post-War Western European experience. First Spain, then Holland, then

Britain, France and Belgium, and finally Portugal, have relinquished their overseas possessions within a remarkably short time-span, with a consequent loss of access to raw materials and, in some cases, markets, not to mention prestige.[6] The latter consideration is crucial. It is not so much the loss of empire as such, but the shift in the dominant centres of wealth and power, and hence of prestige, which accompanied the demise of empire, that has created the political conditions and climate in which ethnic movements can attract support and flourish. The formation of the two great client-systems has simply underlined this massive geopolitical shift away from the old European centres to the United States and Russia; even Canada has been overshadowed, economically and militarily, by its giant neighbour and the multinational companies based on its territory. And this at a time when systemic interdependence of the states within each client-system is rapidly growing, making it almost impossible for medium-sized states to pursue an independent economic or foreign policy.[7]

There are several relevant aspects of this recent massive geopolitical shift. The first is psychological: for the old medium-sized ex-imperial states it has produced a loss of self-confidence, a turning inwards, and an increase in self-criticism and self-doubt. There is also a widespread feeling of irreversible decline, expressed by the frequently stated opinion that the 'nation-state' is a modern irrelevance and obsolete in a world of regional superpowers and blocs. A second aspect is economic: loss of external markets has meant that it became necessary to create an internal European one, protected by tariff barriers, and this new interdependence has intensified economic rivalries between the constituent states. Such 'internal' rivalry both strengthens the state in its dealings with component groups within its borders, and weakens its ability to compete successfully on the external front. Thirdly, the medium-sized state experiences a political contraction, partly because of its linkage with the two superpowers and their client-systems, partly because its military capacity has shrunk to that of a largely dependent force. And all this with an unparalleled suddenness and rapidity which was so striking that it could hardly fail to evoke internal repercussions.

So dramatic a military shrinkage has perhaps given an exaggerated impression of the 'disarmed state'. Of course, nothing of the kind has happened; even medium-sized states are possessed of highly sophisticated weaponry and professional forces, which, as the French showed in Zaire, they are able to deploy quickly if need should arise. But this has not prevented the growth of a sentiment of military dependence and curtailment, as if the state were now 'muzzled' and shorn of one of its two essential functions, defence of the community and survival in a world of similar entities.[8] There is, after all, a good deal of evidence, of which the Suez adventure was only the most striking, that European states are really unable to carry through an independent military operation, without the tacit support of their superpower leaders. To disaffected minorities or classes, it has therefore seemed as if the incorporating state no longer commands the sanctions which can back its laws, and may be realistically challenged within its own domain.

This apparent crisis of coercive power has contributed greatly to the devaluation of the old order and its bastion, the state. It has been a major factor in the present crisis of legitimacy of the European state, though by no means the sole one. Moreover, it has occurred at a moment when an uneasy peace of heavily armed mutual deterrence links a divided world and its rival client-systems. Europe, above all, has experienced a stabilisation of state borders and conflicts relative to the pre-War period, as a result of this armed stalemate. Only in such geopolitical circumstances of coexisting and balanced zones of power, can minority groups with grievances against the constituent states within each bloc give vent to their discontent and advance their claims, especially where, for other reasons, overt state repression has been eschewed.

On the other hand, the stabilisation of relationships between states and their borders within Europe makes it difficult for ethnic minorities to effect any changes to the political *status quo*. Given the delicacy of the post-War settlement, and the need for European states to act in concert within their respective blocs, the chances of any ethnic movement with separatist aims achieving its goals are likely to be remote. Moreover, the fear of the military and political consequences of 'going it alone' must induce second thoughts for many a supporter of ethnic movements in Europe. But there need be no such fears where the demands are limited to autonomy within a federal state structure.

Hence the loss of empire, the geopolitical shift away from Europe, and the reduction in the economic and military capacity of the medium-sized European state, have created an overall context in which movements for ethnic autonomy could flourish, and the conditions in which they can press their demands.

PLANNING THE 'PLURAL STATE'

If we now turn to the second factor, the degree of 'incongruence' between state boundaries and ethnic composition, we find further specific grounds for the resurgence of ethnic movements in the West. For certain recent trends have brought this incongruence of the bureaucratic state to the fore, eliciting an ethnic response.

Paradoxically, political and military shrinkage of the European state has been offset by a vast increase in its powers of internal intervention. During the nineteenth century, western economic and political expansion, based largely on rapid industrialisation and the exploitation of overseas colonies, meant that the imperial state could afford to be liberal in its employment policies towards members of minority groups. The relatively small intelligentsias of 'peripheral' communities could be generally assimilated, without much regard to their origins or culture, though some restrictions on religion remained; Scots were frequently employed in the British imperial administration, and Corsicans policed French territory. Besides, the sheer volume of demand for admission to professional and bureaucratic posts was far less than in the twentieth century; indeed, the state had to set up institutions to train suitable personnel in the numbers needed for imperial tasks.

Western liberalism and expansion in this period went hand in hand with *laissez-faire* policies which, though not as unfettered as once thought, nevertheless tended to leave it to the laws of supply and demand to determine the numbers and skill-levels of experts employed in the bureaucracies and professions. But this period of expansion soon gave way to an era of state regulation and protectionism. The state increasingly intervened in the running of the economy, and a more powerful and centralised bureaucracy began to determine national needs for expertise and qualified staff. The pressures generated by the two World Wars greatly enhanced the role and powers of central bureaucracies, leaving a legacy of regulations and coordinating agencies of control, many of which were not dismantled in peacetime.[9] And all these developments occurred at a time when the military and political power of the major nation-states was waning, and when the state was turning out ever greater numbers of qualified experts to man its internal institutions of centralised control.

Inevitably, these contradictions began to generate a crisis, symbolised by the disillusion following the dramatic loss of empire. On the one hand, the European state was shorn of its external outlets for employing surplus expertise; on the other, it was strengthening its internal powers and proliferating agencies to keep pace with the expanding intelligentsia which its educational institutions were turning out. External contraction and internal centralisation inevitably

concentrated immense power in the hands of the old hierarchical bureaucrats, and increased tensions between them and the experts on
whose services they were compelled to call. The latter's critical rationalism increasingly conflicts with the hierarchical discipline of
bureaucracy at a moment of crisis, contraction and loss of external
prestige, when public confidence in government and the civil service
was ebbing and the performance of bureaucrats was coming under
growing public scrutiny. This crisis of confidence has contributed to
the enhanced need for the intelligentsia and professionalism; yet the
latter have not generally reaped the rewards and status commensurate with their vital function in modern society. Moreover, the loss of
external employment outlets following the demise of empire and the
geopolitical shift away from Europe, has undoubtedly increased
competition for professional and bureaucratic posts at home at a time
of severe economic contraction. Inevitably, the central region of each
European state has attracted qualified personnel from outlying areas;
and the inability to satisfy the aspirations of so many of the newly
educated has led to periodic emigrations by the highly qualified, especially to America, the so-called 'brain drain'.[10]

One other aspect of this growth in state power and intervention is
especially important for an understanding of the ethnic and regional
nature of autonomist movements. As state control has increased, and
communications have multiplied throughout its territorial domain,
even outlying and remote areas have been drawn into the bureaucratic networks. The process has, of course, been gradual and long
drawn-out; but, as Connor argues, it has been especially noticeable
within the post-War period.[11] Particularly important has been the
growth of educational systems in outlying areas, above all institutions of tertiary education. It is, after all, in the universities and
polytechnics that ethnic unrest is first likely to surface, where linguistic issues symbolise the deeper current of historicist sentiment
propounded by intellectuals and academics, as in the case of some
Welsh colleges and in the university of Louvain in Belgium. More
generally, the training of professional and academic personnel, who
are then compelled to emigrate to the capital in order to find suitable
employment, owing to the failure of the occupational system to keep
pace with educational production in the regions, has greatly expanded ethnic intelligentsias and rendered them susceptible to the
historicist message of their educators. It is, indeed, among emigré
intelligentsia who must be satisfied with posts on the lower rungs of
central bureaucracy or the professions that the cause of ethnic autonomy finds vocal support.[12]

The upshot of this immense growth in state powers and intervention within outlying regions has been to make the plural nature of the European state more salient and clearcut. While these states ruled multicultural empires, the ethnic pluralism of the state within its metropolitan borders was much less visible and important. With the liberation of the overseas territories, all attention becomes concentrated on the composition of the population within its own borders, just at the moment when central bureaucracy, after decades of neglect, obtains the power and shows the desire to intervene in areas and issues which it had until recently hardly bothered to treat. But this moment of state regulation of the economy is justified by the ideology of welfare and the trend towards collective planning from the centre outwards. And, as often happens, bureaucratic planners who look to the welfare and development of society and its economy as a whole, are impatient of local differences and historic peculiarities. In planning the plural state, they prefer not to have to take too much notice of cultural and historic diversity. Indeed, its very plurality is an obstruction to any rational plan of modernisation.

One might, of course, be justified in thinking that professionals and members of a rationalist intelligentsia would be sympathetic to such centralised bureaucratic development plans. Perhaps, indeed, they would be, if they could all be assimilated into the central professional and bureaucratic hierarchies, where, like Napoleon, they might exchange their local ethnic sentiment for a loyalty to the larger state. But, as we saw, many of them cannot be assimilated; and even when they are, they come into conflict with the reigning bureaucrats at the centre. Besides, such ethnic intelligentsia come to the capital with a sense of past discrimination; they know well that their culture is, if not despised, at any rate condescendingly belittled. Even where there is no overt discrimination by western states on ethnic grounds, negative stereotypes remain and may influence judgments. So that even those most committed to a universal discourse of rationalism retain an affection for their communities of origin and a slight sensitivity to such stereotypes.[13]

There may exist further grounds for the intelligentsia's opposition to central development plans. If the latter envisage the perpetuation of that neglect and secondary position to which their communities had been so long condemned, on the grounds that economic rationality demands rapid development of productive, industrial areas at the expense of relatively unproductive, decayed, non-industrial ones, then the reaction of ethnic intelligentsia is likely to be bitter and sharply critical. Thus, in 1962, Michel Debré's Group 1985 issued a report on regional development, which advocated the division of

France into industrial and expanding zones and poorer agricultural areas or 'deserts', including most of western and south-west France, with the recommendation that 'the conversion of these deserted regions into national parks should therefore be organised and accelerated'.[14] A similar, though rather more strategic use for Corsica, which showed as little sensitivity to local feeling, has produced a spate of violent opposition by some Corsican intelligentsia. In some other long-neglected areas like Brittany the intelligentsia have been joined by farmers and the fishing industry in well-supported parties bent on the economic reconstruction of their historic homeland.[15]

Not all modern European states seek to plan their plural societies with such mathematical rigour and centralised efficiency as the 'Jacobin' state in France.[16] But the long-term trend is undoubtedly towards such centralised planning, if only because of the need for advanced technology and investment in the new high-cost electronic and computer industries, in order to compete successfully in international markets. This will inevitably entail painful decisions about obsolete or declining industries, which, as with ship-building in Scotland, are often located in depopulated ethnic regions. More generally, collectivist planning carries with it a tendency to think in terms of the needs of the state as a whole rather than of its constituent parts, and hence overlooks special needs, particularly where these are as much cultural and psychological as economic.

The last point raises a particularly acute problem about the planning of a plural state. The tendency for economics and economic solutions to loom so large in modern social and political thought, carries with it a danger of insensitivity to less amenable and perhaps more subtle cultural needs.[17] Indeed, many ethnic intelligentsia tend to rationalise their cultural and political grievances in economic terms, if only to appear sensible, practical and 'realistic', lest they be castigated as 'wild' and merely 'literary' romantics. Not all do so, as we shall see; but their bureaucratic and political opponents consistently argue their case in economic terms, and it is economic rather than any other kind of 'planning' that exercises their minds. The assumption is that, given a favourable economic environment, social and cultural benefits will automatically follow. But, from an ethnic standpoint, this sort of planning necessarily fails to grasp, or even discover, the specific and unique nature of the social and cultural needs (and hence benefits) of each community, exactly because it only recognises the existence of regions and not of ethnic communities. To recognise the latter would require a very different kind of planning.

THE CRITIQUE OF CLASS DEMOCRACY

If the state's new interventionism and collectivist economic planning highlight the plural nature of the society it dominates, now that it is reduced to its heartland in Europe, the class nature of many western democracies exacerbates the ethnic problem and makes it that much more salient.

In most western states, democracy as we know it arose in the context of class struggles dating back to the political emergence of the bourgeoisie in the eighteenth century. The following two centuries have seen a gradual, if piecemeal, extension of civil and political rights to new strata lower down in the social scale.[18] The formation of parties in these parliamentary democracies was closely aligned with both religious and class cleavages, especially in the later nineteenth and early twentieth century. The disestablishment of the Church and the extension of the suffrage to the working-classes and women were issues that dominated the politics of many western democracies; but, once settled, these cleavages have tended to decline in importance. This is not to say that they have disappeared; religious divisions remain politically relevant, and class conflicts, in an era of recession and inflation, have retained something of their old vigour. And yet, if we compare their importance now to that of earlier periods, there has been a marked change in their salience and political relevance. Like ethnicity in previous eras, class cleavages remain deep-rooted but more controlled and latent than before. This is partly due to the institutionalisation of class conflict and the decline in the revolutionary potential of the European working-class; but it is also a function of the growth of a large service sector of white-collar workers, of which the most vigorous and politically relevant stratum is the intelligentsia. As a result, ethnic cleavages have come to the fore where religious and class conflicts have been, perhaps temporarily, displaced from the political arena.[19]

The decline of overt class conflict, despite much sectionalist industrial conflict, has tended to erode faith in the dominant class-based parties in western democracies. For ethnic minorities, in particular, the tendency of parties to act on behalf of state-wide classes at the expense of regions and ethnic communities, makes party platforms largely irrelevant and obsolete in their eyes. Such concerns are, moreover, divisive; they may, perhaps, benefit the problems of Welsh miners (in tandem with all other miners and workers), but at the cost of dividing off the latter from other inhabitants of Wales and from Welsh problems. Besides, once in power, class-based parties soon relegate their regional supporters' problems, since collectivist planning is necessarily general, and ethnic communities and regions must be subordinated to the overall needs of the whole territorial society. This is strikingly illustrated in the complaint of a Plaid Cymru manifesto that the Labour Party displayed a callous disregard of the coal and slate areas of Wales: 'It is on the backs of miners and quarrymen', runs one passage, 'that the Labour Party came to power. Once in power, the welfare of these areas had no place in its governing priorities.'[20]

Now, ethnic nationalists have always viewed the problems of class and class conflict with ambivalence. On the one hand, they have sometimes identified the nation with an oppressed class, and seen their struggle as one of liberating a proletarian nation; that was the case with Sultan Galiev's 'Asian socialism', and all who adopted a broadly Leninist interpretation of national liberation movements.[21] On the other hand, conservative or radical 'integral nationalists' sought to eradicate class conflicts and conceal class division, viewing them as detrimental to national unity in its struggles with other nations or with imperialism. We find this position, too, in some African state-nations today, as well as in the corporatist element of some 'integral nationalist' thought in pre-1914 Europe.[22]

In post-War Europe, however, the ethnic critique of class-based parties is part of a broader attack on the majoritarian nature of western democracy. For, in such a system, relatively small ethnic communities are unlikely to be able to affect governmental policy, unless larger class parties are evenly balanced in a 'hung' or coalition Parliament. Their sheer lack of numerical weight condemns them to a peripheral political position. Like other small but vocal interest groups – student movements, the ecology movement, even feminism – they can only bring their cause to public attention through extra-parliamentary methods bordering on civil disobedience and even isolated acts of violence. So, for example, the Welsh Language Society has found it necessary to engage in sporadic violence, in order to impress its protest against the relegation of the Welsh language onto the public consciousness; even within Wales, the speakers and defenders of the language as a symbol of Welsh historic culture are in a minority.[23] In other cases, such as the ETA wing of Basque ethnic nationalism, the majoritarian politics of parliamentary democracy is spurned on principle; head-counting in a 'bourgeois democracy' imposed by a socially and culturally alien authority is seen as a fraud, and popular participation in such an exercise is only one more example of false consciousness and distortion achieved by the agencies of foreign social control.[24]

This erosion of faith in class-based parties and parliamentary democracy as a whole is not, of course, confined to ethnic or other minorities. A degree of political apathy characterises the majorities in most western states, reflecting the failure of parties in government to fulfil their promises and deal with a deteriorating international economic situation. But political contraction and economic recession has fallen most heavily on those at the political periphery, who cannot invoke an electoral machine to deflect the effects, and are unable to muster countervailing pressure on central government, as can the major classes and status groups within the dominant majority. Moreover, the more stable and politically institutionalised class conflicts become, the more excluded and politically powerless do ethnic and other minorities feel; yet the very stalemate that such a situation produces, coupled with the armed interstate peace abroad, creates new temptations to pursue minority demands and aspirations, by legal or extra-legal means, but not through the class-based parties in the legislature. This explains why the rise of 'mass' support for ethnic autonomy movements in the 1960s occurred when it did; for, by that time, it had become plain that the rival class-based parties could not, or would not, cater to minority needs, which they regarded at best as of secondary concern, at worst as a distraction and nuisance. So the emergence of Scottish and Welsh ethnic nationalism as a political and electoral force in the later 1960s followed immediately in the wake of disillusion with the Labour Party's regional performance and its failure to live up to its promises for Wales and Scotland.[25] And, similarly, the rise of a more militant Breton nationalism in the 1960s followed the realisation by many Bretons that none of the parties in Paris had any intention of addressing themselves to the special needs of France's historic regions and communities.[26]

THE TECHNICAL INTELLIGENTSIA

This realisation, however, could not have found a political voice unless a new kind of leadership had begun to crystallise within western ethnic communities. Such a leadership was now drawn from the rising technical intelligentsia.

In an earlier chapter, a distinction was drawn between the humanistic and technical wings of the professional intelligentsia. There I divided that broad stratum into two main subgroups, those engaged in the 'liberal professions', who looked for their inspiration to the humanistic intellectuals, and the rather more recent technical professionals, who look for guidance and paradigms to the scientific intellectuals. Without doubt, the technical intelligentsia has of late expanded far more rapidly and grown much larger than its humanistic counterpart, especially with the recent proliferation of high-technology industries and the demand for technological expertise in every walk of life. The services of technically specialised professionals, ranging from engineers and economists to pharmacists and laboratory technicians, have become indispensable to the running of advanced industrial society.[27] To meet this ever-growing demand, the state has had to encourage, even create, a special type of educational system alongside the older humanistic one, centered on technical colleges and polytechnics. Although the technological innovations of the so-called 'second' industrial or chemical-electrical revolution which made such an expansion feasible, occurred in the late nineteenth century, it was not really till after the First World War, and more especially the Second, that a really large supply of trained technical professionals could be produced and used, especially during the post-1945 economic reconstruction of Europe.[28] Once again, the two World Wars played a vital role in accelerating both demand and supply, and post-1945 interstate rivalries have maintained the pressure to a certain extent.

Can we correlate this expansion of technical intelligentsia with the sudden upsurge of ethnic activism in the 1960s? Only to a rather limited extent. For one thing, there is no evidence that the new technical intelligentsia have entirely displaced the older humanistic leaderships. Teachers, for example, continue to play a pivotal role among ethnic activists; a recent study of the social class of French ethnic activists claimed that they constituted 37% of the sample, being especially highly represented in Brittany and Occitania.[29] As we saw, teachers provided an essential bridging function between intellectuals and professional intelligentsia as a whole; likewise, given the range of disciplines that they represent, they cannot be assigned exclusively to either the technical or the humanistic intelligentsia. Nor were the 40% of professionals among the ethnic activists in this sample broken down into the two constituent subgroups; the French census bureau's category of professionals (*professions libérales et cadres supérieurs*) includes professors and liberal professions, literary and scientific professions, engineers and executives; while the white-collar workers (31.8% of ethnic activists) includes teachers, technicians and administrators, medical and social specialists, and other intellectual professions.[30]

Nevertheless, the figures convey clearly the over-representation of the technical intelligentsia and teachers in French ethnic movements; and there is some confirmation of a more general trend in this direction from other western 'neo-nationalist' movements. In the province of Quebec, for example, support for Quebecois nationalism appears to have come mostly from the urban and professional classes, especially those who have experienced some blockage of occupational mobility.[31] Indeed, the hallmark of Quebec's 'quiet revolution' which began in 1960 with the coming to power of Jean Lesage's Liberal government was the transfer of control in the province from rural and ecclesiastical elites to a new stratum of professionals, technocrats and industrialists committed to secular, rationalist values within the framework of a French linguistic and historic self-expression. The very struggle to break the hold of dominant elites and institutions added a radical political dimension to this ethnic transformation.[32] In Scotland, too, the leadership of the SNP has been largely in the hands of professionals and small-businessmen tied to neither of the two major British parties; and it drew much support from technicians and skilled workers in the new towns, as well as some farmers and fishermen. Once again, the categories used in many polls do not allow us to determine the relative proportion of technical intelligentsia among SNP supporters, much less among the Party's activists; yet most commentators agree that the technical and professional element is vital and active in Scottish 'neo-nationalism'.[33]

None of this evidence, meagre as it is, can be considered conclusive. It only *suggests* a connection between the rapid expansion of technical intelligentsia and western 'neo-nationalism'. How close are the links, and the mechanisms by which they operate, can at present only be subjects for speculation. In particular, we need to know how far this expansion has been accompanied by a blockage of professional and bureaucratic mobility, and, if it has, how widely and keenly such blockage has been felt by those affected. If the links are close, then this would further confirm the 'neo-nationalism' thesis, namely, that we are confronted in the West by a renewal of nineteenth-century ethnic nationalisms, which were also largely led by those strata most heavily involved in the production and distribution of knowledge and information, albeit today of a more technical nature.[34] And, if the last point is upheld, it would also go some way towards explaining the peculiar ideological cast of today's neo-nationalisms, their pragmatic and economistic, yet paradoxically 'neo-romantic' communitarian approach.

SOCIAL ENGINEERING AND NEO-ROMANTICISM

Perhaps the most striking feature of western 'neo-nationalisms' is their curious blend of realistic and utopian ideologies. Compared to the pre-War period, ethnic movements in the West have undergone a radical ideological metamorphosis: there has been a strong shift to the left, and a novel interest in 'bread-and-butter' economic and social issues, which had previously been neglected. Demands for autonomy have made much play of economic grievances like regional unemployment, declining industries, regional underdevelopment, inequitable transfers of resources to the centre and the like. Social issues, too, have figured prominently in the literature of ethnic autonomists. They decry the emigration of skilled personnel from the community to the capital, bureaucratic neglect in providing services or bureaucratic insensitivity to local social needs. In these respects, ethnic 'neo-nationalisms' evince a far greater social and economic awareness that was ever the case before the Second World War.

Concomitant with this new social and economic awareness, there has been a decisive ideological shift to the left among many ethnic nationalists. Not only have western 'neo-nationalisms' given birth to extremist marxist or left-sectarian wings, sometimes espousing violent methods; the mainstream organisations have often adopted social-democratic or even socialist platforms with a strong commitment to social welfare policies, and a belief in the virtues and necessity of social engineering in order to reconstruct neglected or 'distorted' ethnic communities. Quebec, once again, affords a clear example of this dual transition – from cultural to socioeconomic concerns, and from conservative to radical or socially progressive ideologies. Before the Second World War, French ethnic nationalism in the province of Quebec was largely conservative and traditional, being heavily influenced by the interests of the clergy and landowners, which kept the mass of the province's population in the status of Roman Catholic, Francophone farmers. Even the pre-War Quebec movement for secession led by urban students and humanistic intelligentsia tended to be rightwing in its orientation. It was only after the Second World War, when intensive urbanisation and industrialisation, especially in manufacturing, had created new strata, especially a more technical professional intelligentsia, that the Liberals adopted a new social-democratic kind of Quebecois nationalism in their desire to be 'maitre chez-nous'.[35] The new technical strata were much more committed to the secular values of social-democracy; yet they grafted such rationalist and socially progressive ideals onto a revived sense of French linguistic and historic identity, adapting language as the vehicle of that identity to the needs of a much expanded public sector. The Parti Quebecois, too, has adopted left of centre policies; they carry still further the avowed aims of Quebecois nationalism to expand 'French power' in the professional and senior executive categories of provincial and federal public services, by creating new posts in the bureaucracies of a hoped-for independent Quebec.[36]

In Brittany, the shift towards the left and towards a concern with socioeconomic issues is equally discernible. The Breton Democratic Union (UDB) which drew largely from students and professionals of the non-Communist left, has since its founding in 1963 linked Brittany's economic and social problems with the 'underdevelopment' fostered by France's capitalist system, which has created 'internal colonies' within France's borders. Like the extremist Breton Liberation Front (FLB) and the Group for Breton and International Political Studies, the UDB espouses a socialist solution to Brittany's ills, but within the same federalist framework as the older, more centrist Movement for the Organisation of Brittany (MOB), founded in 1957.[37] Stable rightwing government in Paris, coupled with the student uprising of May–June 1968, has tended to bring the excluded left and the neglected regions in France together; and just as the non-Communist French left has been to some extent regionalised, so have ethnic autonomist movements become radicalised towards the left.

In other western countries, too, social-democratic and welfare versions of ethnic nationalism have gained ground since the Second World War. In Spain, this trend existed in the pre-War period, especially in Catalonia, much less in the Basque provinces.[38] During Franco's long rule, this tendency was enhanced, though again it has been much more marked among the Catalan parties. The dominant Basque party, the Partido Nacionalista Vasco (PNV), has always been much more conservative and Catholic in orientation than its Catalan counterparts, and this has been one factor in the growth of the ETA (Euzkadi ta Azkatasuna) minority wing, with its declared revolutionary Marxist ideology, which broke away from the PNV in 1959.[39] In Britain, too, radical autonomist movements have adopted a social-democratic or socialist ideology. In 1946 the Scottish Nationalist Party (SNP) published a manifesto, which lacked a section on Scottish culture, unlike previous Scottish statements, and instead laid emphasis upon the small man and small-town democracy, in the style of the Social Credit movement in Canada and New Zealand or populism in the United States.[40] In earlier days, Scottish ethnic movements, such as they were, tended to be the preserve of romantic intellectuals and humanistic intelligentsia, usually academics or teachers; and their interest was largely in the preservation of Scottish culture through maximum autonomy. From the early 1960s, however, the SNP's leaders, who come from the professional intelligentsia and small businessmen, have shifted their attention to social and economic issues

like nature-resource conservation, pension rights, coal-mine clo-
sures, teachers' salary claims and land-use planning, all of which,
they claim, can best be dealt with in the framework of an independent Scotland. Their platform today can be broadly described as social-democratic, although there are considerable differences of opinion within the party ranks; they believe in government intervention
in the economy and in economic planning, as well as the provision
of extensive welfare services, but not in revolutionary class struggle,
and they adhere to a firmly constitutionalist mode of politics. The
discovery of large amounts of oil in the continental shelf of Scotland's
North Sea coast, gave the SNP an opportunity to show how they
would reconstruct the declining industries of Scotland and modernise its infrastructure; their thinking demonstrated the new professional and technical orientations of the majority of its leadership and
supporters.[41] The corresponding attempts by Welsh autonomists to
shift the ground of their aspirations from cultural to social and economic issues have been much less successful. Plaid Cymru, despite
its success in attracting members of the humanistic and technical
professional intelligentsia and its growing interest in economic issues, has so far not managed to bridge the gap between an older
concern with language and identity preservation and the new technical interests of a partially industrialised society. In a sense, the
division of labour between the politically oriented Plaid Cymru and
the cultural Welsh Language Society, which has on occasion used
extra-parliamentary methods, symbolises a split, both in the ecological and historical experience of Wales as a whole, and in the ideological character of Welsh ethnic nationalism, a split that impedes
the emergence of a fully modernist and dynamic autonomist movement.[42]

And yet, the Welsh (or Flemish) example is not unique.[43] What
appears as an ideological and organisational split in Wales, reap-
pears as a blend of disparate elements in other movements. None of
them is as 'realistic' as I have suggested; nor is their commitment to
rationalism and social-democracy so thoroughgoing. Rather, it is
shot through with streaks of neo-romanticism, and placed within a
cultural framework which draws for its sustenance upon a longstand-
ing historic legacy and identity, which time and modernity may have
eroded but have not dissolved. To broaden their social constituency,
the ethnic autonomists must tap this legacy and identity; not so
much by a populist appeal to a fast-diminishing peasantry (though
pockets remain in Highland areas), but either by a small-town populism, as in Scotland, or by an ecological ideology of nature and
resource-preservation, which strikes the chord of urban nostalgia for

its historic rural hinterland. Thus, in Corsica, the nationalists have made their case in economic and ecological terms. They have protested not only against the influx of *colons* who operate the wine trade and have large landholdings, but also against the use of Corsica for military and strategic purposes, against sea pollution and against tourism, all of which, they feel, threaten Corsica's unique historic environment and heritage.[44] Similar neo-romantic elements exist side by side with rationalist, even marxist, programmes and ideas in the Jura; the Rassemblement Jurassien was happy to mix de Gaulle's slogans about a 'Rassemblement du Peuple Français' with progressive social policies, while more extremist groups espoused revolutionary action.[45] There has also been a cultural revival among Bretons, which overlaps with their political organisations; there has been an expansion of Breton in the baccalaureate at the Academy of Rennes, a Breton school organised in Brest enrolled two hundred students in 1975, and Breton folk singers like Servat, Glenmor and Stivell have reached a mass audience. Music, dance and craft groups flourish in the Breton cities as well as the countryside, so that the cultural revival is not confined to an elite.[46]

But, over and beyond such specific manifestations, there is a more profound conjunction of 'neo-romanticism' with social engineering. Its most obvious manifestations occur in the reaction against bureaucratic centralisation and the preference for smallness; its deeper roots lie in the fear of a loss of participation and community and the desire to revive an allegedly decentralised historic community.[47] And yet only through government, through the scientific state of the technical professionals, will the past be recovered, and the dream of de-alienation and participation in a worker-controlled democratic community be realised.

'LIBERATION STRUGGLES' OF INDUSTRIAL SOCIETIES

The malady which recent ethnic 'neo-nationalism' believes it has diagnosed, the malady of anomie, in the sense of both powerlessness and normlessness, is largely a condition to be found in western or, more generally, industrial societies. The peculiar facets of social structure and its effects on social relations which Marx analysed as 'alienation' and Durkheim as 'anomie', different though they are, pertain nevertheless to capitalist industrial societies. Insofar as they are relevant in the 'Third World', they appear only in attenuated and derivative form, depending on the degree of economic growth and social development of the state in question. So it would be quite in order to relate the 'neo-nationalist' solution to the peculiar conditions of industrial society as a whole, or of its capitalist variety. Yet this would omit an important cultural and ideological element of recent 'neo-nationalisms'; their liberal borrowing and cultural debt to 'Third World' nationalisms.

Perhaps the most important of these cultural transfers is the notion of a national 'liberation struggle'. This is not to be equated with nationalism as a whole. It is an ideological construct of a particular kind of situation in which nationalists may find themselves, an interpretation of an historically specific yet widespread phenomenon. A national liberation struggle is directed against a colonialism whose main properties are viewed as economic and political rather than cultural, and which may continue in less overt economic form, after the demise of political colonialism. However, a national liberation struggle, though it stems from economic and political conditions, is also a psychological process for generating self-awareness and wholeness through collective mobilisation and struggle. To end colonialism, in Fanon's sense, requires more than physically ejecting the foreigner from the territory; it requires the rebirth of self within a new type of community of the socially aware and participant, by men no longer disfigured by oppression and dependence.[48]

During the 1960s, the idea of a 'liberation struggle' began to be applied within industrial societies. On the one hand, since so many states were plural, and the largest and dominant ethnic community could be viewed as a ruling class (or, at any rate, the base for that class), peripheral and subordinate regions could be likened to 'internal' colonies, and their ethnic populations to oppressed classes and nations. Fanon's ideas of dependence and liberation could also be transferred to the members of ethnic minorities within old-established western states. They, too, could be regarded as exploited regions of an alien capitalism from which the minority must struggle to free itself, in the manner of Che Guevara, if the terrain allowed, or by urban insurrection, like the students in Paris in 1968. In fact, it was in the immediate aftermath of the events in Paris that many ethnic organisations emerged, preaching the new non-Communist radicalism of self-liberation through collective praxis. Distancing themselves from the Communist bloc, whom they accused of bureaucratic repression after the Prague Spring, the New Left radicals also imbued the rising tide of ethnic activism with their neo-Marxist and humanist philosophy of liberation from capitalist alienation, which itself owed a good deal to the Left's analysis of 'Third World' liberation struggles.[49]

A second, closely related notion that sprang from study of 'Third World' developments was that of 'dependency'. Here, two uses were brought into a close relationship: the psychological idea of dependence upon former masters, as propounded by Mannoni and later by Fanon,[50] and the economic model of dependent development, which owed much to sociological analysis of centre–periphery relations within a world capitalist mode of production; here the work of Andre Gunder Frank on Latin American dependency, and later of Wallerstein on the expansion of a world capitalist economy, proved influential.[51] These ideas were partially assimilated by radical elements within movements for ethnic autonomy, particularly in France and Spain; they testify to the close ideological links which now exist between former colonies and metropolitan states, except that this time Europe is reimporting an ideological model in order to explain and legitimate its own somewhat different ethnic autonomy movements. In particular, western 'neo-nationalisms' found the notion of an 'internal colony' developing in a dependent mode upon an international imperialist capitalism, centred upon a few dominant states (and hence ethnic communities) and their multi-nationals, especially attractive; for it appears to solve the nagging problem of their own 'lateness' and relative 'failure' in developing a strong ethnic nationalism before 1914.[52]

Another 'Third World' preoccupation, that of ethnic power, also struck a chord in the West. Associated particularly with the pan-African and Black Power movements in Africa, the Caribbean and the United States, the ideal of ethnic power involved a reversal of status through a transvaluation of values. Spurning western materialism and rationalism, the pan-Africanists elevated intuition, harmony with nature, the community and the immediacy of physical experience.[53] Black nationalism in America was particularly potent in generating a sense of redemption through ethnic power; occurring as it did in the most advanced capitalist state in the world, the Black Power movement radiated a powerful hope for all oppressed minorities, that through their own efforts they could find a new dignity and integrity and rediscover themselves by rejoining their community.

'Third World' ideas were not the only ideological influences on recent 'Neo-nationalisms'. There was the example of socialist polycentrism, notably in Yugoslavia and, to some extent, Rumania; there was the crusading fervour of the student movements in western universities; there was the related movement of feminism, with its parallel emphasis on dignity through self-discovery and self-liberation; above all, there was the growing disillusionment with the effects of unlimited economic growth, of which the ecological movements and anti-consumerism were the most overt expressions. And yet, it was to the experience of 'Third World' liberation movements that recent western 'neo-nationalisms' looked for much of their conceptual framework and emotional inspiration.

That such a linkage of ideas was possible within so short a time-span was largely due to the immense advances in communications since the Second World War; but also to the long post-War phase of liberalism which followed the defeat of Nazism and fascism, and which underwrote the legitimacy of ethnic and other minority movements. Only in such a permissive and liberal climate, especially after the relaxation of the Cold War, could such minority movements blossom, as had the earlier liberation movement during the decolonisation of Africa and Asia. If Versailles had placed the question of ethnic nationalism on the agenda of the world powers, Yalta had begun to treat ethnicity as the mould and measure of the liberated states. The founding of the United Nations Organisation and its Charter had legitimated the process; and the Bandoeng Conference had given non-aligned communities fresh hope. And yet, all these political developments had failed to resolve the ethnic question. The interests of the superpowers and their client-systems, the territorial status of many new states, the difficulties of disentangling the conflicting claims of often antagonistic ethnic communities, made it impossible to satisfy every aspiration. But the claim had been admitted; ethnicity was increasingly recognised as the basis of state boundaries and statehood itself, if for no other reason than that to deny it would amount to rejecting the basic notions of popular self-determination and popular sovereignty, which even superpowers had to acknowledge, theoretically at any rate. This contradiction between an acknowledged right to ethnic self-determination, and the practical failure to meet it, only heightened ethnic aspirations among the forgotten communities. In a declining Europe, the result could only be a resurgence of ethnic nationalism.

vwv

Towards the scientific state

Although it takes different forms in each culture area, the ethnic revival always involves a political transformation in the modern era. In America, ethnic communities increasingly act as the main economic and social interest groups, and compete for wider political influence. In Canada and Europe, autonomist movements seek to turn their ethnic communities and homelands into the basic political components of poly-ethnic states, and politicise the sense of social solidarity among their members. In many states of Africa and Asia, ethnic movements go even further, claiming the right and duty to form their own states in an act of secession or irredentism. In each of these cases, however, the central aim of the modern ethnic revival is to subordinate social and political action to cultural imperatives and turn the state into a vehicle of the historic community, in the name of ethnic nationalism and its unrelenting quest for autonomy, unity and identity. In effect, such a revival involves a self-transformation, which will realise a new congruence between state, territory and historic community, such as was rarely achieved in the past, and then only in isolated instances. For only in the congruence of a true 'nation-state', can historic cultures and unique solidarities hope to survive the temptations and dangers of a hostile environment.

What are the chances of success for this national transformation, and what are the distances between aspirations and realities? What are the contradictions, and long-term significance, of such a global transformation? In this final chapter I want to explore some of the paradoxes and meanings of the modern quest for national survival.

BUREAUCRATS AND SUPERPOWERS

Powerful and widespread though this quest has been, it has encountered strong opposition and involved deep-rooted dilemmas. The external constraints have come from three sources: the policies of the superpowers and their client-systems, the vested interests of governmental bureaucracies, and, more ambiguously, from class divisions which often crosscut ethnic allegiances. Though analytically separable, these three levels of opposition – international, state and stratum levels – are empirically interrelated; and these links must be borne in mind in analysing the constraints on any national transformation.

From the Napoleonic era until the Second World War, the great powers of Europe have increasingly identified their *raison d'état* with the assumed interests of their dominant ethnic community, and have utilised the aspirations of subordinate communities for their own, often changing, ends. Sometimes it suited the great powers to support independence movements by oppressed ethnic groups; this was the case with Greece and, later, Italy. In other cases, they ignored the claims of ethnic communities, like the Kurds and Armenians. Even when they accepted the principle of national self-determination, at least in theory, they were often unwilling to accept its practical implications and remained wedded to the preexisting and 'normal' poly-ethnic state framework; despite some acceptance of President Wilson's principles, the peacemakers at Versailles generally created poly-ethnic states on the ruins of the dissolved empires, states like Yugoslavia, Czechoslovakia and Poland, which contained sizeable ethnic minorities.[1]

The policies of the superpowers who succeeded to world leadership after 1945 have been similarly animated by a combination of theoretical acceptance of national self-determination and a thoroughly calculative application of self-interest in practice. As we saw in Chapter 7, such calculations have involved a typical ambiguity, amounting sometimes to self-contradiction and apparent duplicity: superpowers have often seemed, on the one hand to be encouraging ethnic aspirations and discontents, and on the other to be curbing any real movement towards outright secession or irredentism. But, in taking this stance, the superpowers are not simply acting with the cynical duplicity of the powerful. For their very competition allows their more powerful clients considerable freedom of action, which in turn reinforces the scope and powers of these states and their governmental bureaucracies. The existence of client-systems underwrites the latter's pivotal role in the flow of economic resources and military power, and enhances the control of centralised states like Pakistan, Vietnam, Egypt, Ethiopia, as well as Eastern and Western European states.

As a result, superpowers find their own freedom of action circumscribed not only by their mutual interests and rivalry, but by the strength of the state apparatus of their clients, which their alliances force them to enhance. Competition for political influence by the superpowers may also involve economic rivalry between multinational companies; the latter may well reduce, in the short run, the freedom of action of post-colonial states, but in the longer term they may contribute to the role and position of indigenous bureaucrats, by expanding some sectors of the home economy and by developing resources through high-level technology, whose assets are always subject to nationalisation and the threat of a transfer of political allegiance to the opposing client-system.[2]

The policies and interests of superpowers also tend to promote the interests of privileged elites or classes at the expense of poorer strata. Larger ethnic communities with well-developed classes and deep class conflicts may well find their solidarity further undermined by international reinforcement of the power of the state and its bureaucratic elites, who allocate and administer economic and social benefits between the competing classes. In the case of smaller and subordinate communities, the interstate order and its client-systems tend to unite their members in opposition to the bureaucratic state and its dominant ethnic community, whom the superpowers generally support. In these cases, class position tends to coincide with low ethnic status; at any rate, in the eyes of ethnic minorities, they become 'proletarian nations', united in their sense of alien exploitation.[3]

Now the inveterate opponents of ethnic nationalism and its chief representatives, the professional intelligentsia, are the governmental bureaucrats, who control much decision-making in the centralised poly-ethnic state. (Even in monoethnic states, bureaucrats may become remote and unresponsive to the needs of key strata in their desire to curb the influence of the intelligentsia, precipitating a movement of national renewal by the latter.)[4] Suspicious of the critical rationalism and expertise of the professionals, the bureaucrats seek the support of the superpowers and the whole interstate order, on the one hand, and such privileged classes or elites as they can attract, on the other. If successful, they manage to form a tripartite alliance between the superpower system, privileged elites or classes and the organs of state; and this powerful coalition has shown itself capable of checking the trend towards national transformation inherent in the ethnic revival, both in the older, well-established states and, so far, in the new states of Asia and Africa. Both global and internal factors, therefore, operate to curb and moderate the quest for national congruence and survival.

DIVERSITY AND CLOSURE

Internal dilemmas also beset the quest for national transformation. An important motive in this quest is the desire to preserve cultural diversity, and the high value placed on the uniqueness of distinct ways of life and their artefacts, irrespective of the morality or otherwise of the cultures involved. This involves an all-embracing cultural relativism, which would entail support for values and customs that may not only be morally indefensible from a universalist standpoint (e.g. the low value placed on women and female education in many cultures), but may even impinge on the freedom and security of neighbouring ethnic communities, if they happen to place martial virtues high on their scale of values. In such a case, cultural relativism actually threatens the principle of cultural diversity and autonomy.

The principle of cultural diversity poses further dilemmas in polyethnic societies, which, as we saw, constitute a large proportion of modern states. One of the ways of preserving such diversity as a living fact rather than an object of study or contemplation is through group endogamy. As John Porter has pointed out, the linking of 'culturism' to descent-group solidarity carries with it the danger of new forms of inequality and closure. It is all too easy to rank cultures in a hierarchy of superior and inferior worth, and then slide into the notion that 'qualitative cultural differences are inborn'.[5] Ethnicity soon loses its cultural and historical basis and acquires instead a believed-in biological underpinning. Such incipient racism also limits individual choice for ethnic members, and runs counter to the very notions of full citizenship, which figured so prominently in the claims of ethnic minorities for equal rights and fair treatment by a discriminatory bureaucracy. The claim to equality of citizenship on the basis of ethnic diversity ends in a form of closure which denies the full exercise of citizenship rights by ethnic members and gives rise to invidious comparisons between different ethnic communities in poly-ethnic states.

Not only may too great an emphasis upon cultural diversity produce new forms of ethnic closure; it may also foster a new ethnic stratification within poly-ethnic states, as well as between states. Most poly-ethnic states have been created by conquest or colonisation and migration, which generally forced the aboriginal inhabitants into various forms of servitude; and recently, the massive migration of labour to developed societies has created new kinds of ethnic stratification.[6] The ethnic revival, in laying such store by cultural diversity and ethnic dignity, can only intensify the competition of ethnic communities for society's resources and for higher social status. Those ethnic communities, whose values and organisation are more attuned to 'modernist' values and the needs of an increasingly scientific state, will tend to prosper in this race for status and social benefits at the cost of less organised and less 'modernist' ethnic groups; this is certainly true of economically advanced, democratic societies like the United States and Canada.[7] The retreat from universalistic values to more ascriptive ones, inherent in the ethnic revival, and the emphasis upon group mobility rather than individual advancement, inevitably accentuates inequalities between ethnic communities, even if it alters their placement in the overall hierarchy of poly-ethnic states.

At the interstate level, too, the quest for a cultural identity sharpens global rivalries and competition for political standing. Culture become a political resource; the possession of a unique historic solidarity, insofar as it produces a determined political will and a strong sense of cohesion, becomes an important factor in fixing the relative positions of ethnic states in the overall political hierarchy of client-systems. That is why the quest for homogeneity becomes such a priority in many new states, whose leaders are only too aware of their other handicaps and of the political relegation which cultural disunity and ethnic cleavages entail. Even in small monoethnic states, the role of cultural uniqueness in instilling a sense of national dedication in the 'people' is fully appreciated, in the hope that it may help to compensate for an otherwise lower political status. Hence the quest for cultural diversity and solidarity carries with it new possibilities of group closure and inequality.

PARTICIPATION AND TECHNOCRACY

A second dilemma bears more directly on the role of the professional intelligentsia. As we saw, ethnic nationalism has generally helped to extend the rights of citizenship to broader social strata, and, in line with its belief in popular sovereignty and fraternity, has legitimated extensive participation by the mass of the people. This was, of course, partly due to its original emergence in the wake of a wave of popular unrest and emancipation during and after the French Revolution; but it is also a function of its multi-class character, and of the fact, previously discussed, that it draws on persistent and widely diffused ethnic sentiments.[8] In recent years, aspirations for political enfranchisement have been extended into the social and economic spheres, and populist movements have drawn the peasantry, and the recent arrivals to the city, into this broad trend of democratic participation.

But, though popular agitation has played its part, the trend towards popular participation owes a great deal to the leadership of intellectuals and professional intelligentsia in socialist and nationalist movements. In the case of ethnic emancipation, the leadership of the educators and trained professionals has been indispensable. The drive for mass participation has been everywhere undertaken under the aegis of the intelligentsia, if not by them. This has placed them in a powerful, if often isolated, position; and has opened up the temptation to form an exclusive elite in virtue of their possession of certain cultural and political skills. Their training in special educational establishments, their intellectual and social links with the intelligentsia of other lands, their monopoly of the critical, rationalist culture, all separate them off from the mass of the population whom they aspire to lead. Paradoxically, then, the trend towards mass democratic participation legitimates and throws up a new type of leadership, and a new set of criteria for an alternative status system.

Those criteria emphasise educational and technical merit. Increasingly, admission to the higher echelons of ethnic and nationalist organisations is based upon academic and technical qualifications, coupled with political and ideological loyalty. These attributes are, in theory, universally accessible. They make it possible for the poorest and most disadvantaged in the community to rise into the ranks of ethnic and national leadership.[9] The fact that one can point to some cases of such elite mobility lends an air of verisimilitude to democratic claims, even if in practice certain classes and status groups remain in control of most leading positions. To some extent, the sense of solidarity which the ethnic revival instils, offsets and checks the growth and crystallisation of a new educational status system, as do the educational criteria themselves. Moreover, an elite which owes its position to education rather than birth or wealth, finds it ideologically harder to deny the democratic and egalitarian presuppositions of its own success. Politically, as we found with many populist nationalisms, the professional intelligentsia must have frequent recourse to other broader strata, notably the peasantry or newly urbanised proletariat. And divisions within the professional stratum frequently take the form of appeals to the professed interests of other strata, in the name of greater democracy and participation. For, once the right of every citizen to participate in the political arena has become the norm, then mass participation becomes in turn a weapon in the armoury of cultural populism and an index of genuine national transformation.[10]

If ethnic revivals encourage the movement for democratic participation, they also indirectly contribute to the domination of technocracy. We have seen that bureaucratic states were forced by their mutual rivalries to rely increasingly on scientific expertise, and hence felt compelled to train and incorporate a growing army of experts.

We have also seen how this professional intelligentsia has become increasingly technical in its outlook and skills; although the liberal professions still retain a high status in some countries, they are being outstripped in sheer numbers, in the satisfaction of social needs, and in terms of the whole future-oriented ethos of 'post-industrial' society. It seems as if the future of economically developed societies lies with technical experts of all kinds, and that the role of the historic cultures, which the educators and humanistic intelligentsia were so keen to revive and propagate, will become increasingly attenuated. The ethnic revival, by encouraging educational criteria which are today more and more technical in content and scientific in method, now appears to legitimate an ever-expanding stratum of experts and specialists for whom history is often no more than a museum exhibit, and culture but a set of artefacts for conservation and recreation. The very weapon which the educators had forged on behalf of their ethnic community and its regeneration, may now be turned in on itself, as an arid technocracy completes that 'disenchantment of the world' which the principle of cultural uniqueness was intended to roll back.[11] In other words, the changing nature of the professional intelligentsia (not to mention its interests) poses a serious dilemma for the principles of cultural diversity and historic community, which fostered and sanctioned mass participation, and threatens diversity and community in the name of a universal rational expertise.

REPLICATING SCIENTIFIC STATES

Nor do the dilemmas of the quest for national transformation end there. The impact of a growing army of experts on the powerful bureaucratic state, though it brings serious strains and conflicts between professionals and bureaucrats at the apex of state organs, also raises the possibility of resolutions which are, in the final analysis, corrosive of any national transformation.

There are two kinds of resolution. The first is through the cooptation of technical professionals, in sufficient numbers, by the ruling bureaucrats into the highest administrative echelons, and even into government itself. Of course, bureaucrats frequently espouse national sentiments; and in a monoethnic state they may be closely associated with movements of national renewal, as were the *officiers* during the French Revolution who were among the most patriotic of the revolutionaries.[12] At other times, especially in poly-ethnic states, the bureaucracy appears rather remote from ethnic sentiments, identifying their interests with those of the state apparatus itself and embracing an *étatisme*, which is anathema to ethnic minorities. Or they may identify with the interests and sentiments of the dominant ethnic community, again at the overt expense of other ethnic communities.[13]

From the standpoint of the ethnic minorities, the only counterweights to the power of an *étatiste* or ethnically partial bureaucracy are the often disorganised and fragmented masses with their host of specific grievances, and the much better educated, organised and articulate professional intelligentsia. But if key members of the latter become associates or even instruments of central government and administration, usually through cooptation, and if the latter is increasingly pervaded by technical expertise, then the best hope of ethnic redress is to that extent diminished. Something like this occurred in Brittany in the early 1960s, when members of the CELIB organisation in Brittany, which had been set up as a regional economic pressure group of technical experts, were coopted by the French government; it was one of the factors that led to the formation of the Breton Democratic Union.[14]

In fact, bureaucracies and even governments in advanced industrial societies have become increasingly technocratic in orientation and composition. Though the cult of the amateur still persists in a few advanced countries, and though party bureaucrats continue to occupy high positions in both communist and capitalist states, they have had to come to terms with the invading army of professionals-turned-technocrats and in some cases even allow them to form governments to handle increasingly complex and intractable economic situations by the application of their technical expertise. This has occurred in France and the European Economic Community in its most developed forms, but in other countries economic, social and political 'advisers' have been frequently appointed to high ministerial or administrative positions.[15] With economic and industrial advance, the state has been increasingly transformed from a legal–bureaucratic into a scientific–technical state.

Insofar as the increasingly scientific state is able to cream off representative experts from ethnic minorities into central or regional bureaucracies, it deprives those communities of their best leaders and blunts the edge of their resentment. Often, however, it fails to coopt ethnic experts in sufficient numbers, either because it feels it cannot, or through some lingering (or lively) prejudice. In that case, the ethnic movement gathers momentum, and seeks redress through the creation of an autonomous regional bureaucracy and government, or even a separate scientific state, which will be able to accommodate the growing numbers of ethnic technical professionals. In poly-ethnic states, the replication and strengthening of the scientific state, to be staffed by one's own experts, becomes a key demand behind movements for ethnic autonomy or separatism. In fact, replication of the scientific state in the mirror image of the ethnic community and *its* intelligentsia, becomes an essential aspect of the quest for national transformation. 'Liberation from' the old polyethnic bureaucratic state is matched by 'redemption of' the culture community in its own scientific state.

But herein too lies a dilemma for ethnic movements. To safeguard their unique cultures and pre-modern histories, they must create a protective shell, their own scientific state, modelled on those of the units they fear and detest. But, by creating just such another state, they lay the basis for the inner erosion of that very culture and history they so wanted to safeguard and cultivate. For, of its nature, a scientific–technical state run by an army of professionals and technocrats is oriented to specialist concerns and universalist rational procedures and concepts, for whom the historicist vision and romantic imagination for past cultures is at best an irrelevance and at worst an obstacle to a computerised, future-oriented, scientific society. The whole power of the scientific state is then poised to drain away the last vestiges of that cultural uniqueness which it was created to serve.

This is the tragedy of the search for 'normalisation'.[16] Ethnic nationalism aims to cure the community of its historical deformities and self-estrangement. It sets out to liberate the chosen group from its historic exile and oppression, while preserving its unique identity. The community will no longer be a 'stranger among nations', unlike all other communities; it will be restored to its former healthy and 'normal' condition. Thus the slogan of 'normalisation' appears to resolve a deep inner tension. By creating a 'normal' society in its own scientific state, as a replica of similar societies and states, one can preserve whatever is historically unique and valuable in one's cultural heritage, while purifying the community of obscurantist and 'unhealthy' elements and rectifying anomalies inconsistent with rationalist norms and practices. Unfortunately, the standardisation and replication of scientific 'nation'-states that normalisation entails, preserves the outward show of national differences while eroding the community's historic way of life and attenuating the intimacy of collective action and the glow of shared myths and symbols. Culture is sundered from everyday life, as more and more areas of life become impregnated with scientific assumptions and rationalist norms. The quest for geopolitical security in a world of scientific states puts a heavy premium on interstate recognition of normalcy and bureaucratic order. But the price of such recognition is the creation of a type of state order and citizenship which has been stripped of those very elements of uniqueness and diversity, which provide the new-born state with its *raison d'être*. The ultimate beneficiary of the ethnic revival would appear to be the antiseptic technocratic state.

THE QUEST FOR NATIONAL CONGRUENCE

We appear to have come full circle. The old liberal assumptions appear to have been justified, after all. Ethnic loyalty and nationalism must wither as science and modernisation bite deeper into every area of social life. Though it may have helped to spur economic and social development, the ethnic revival can only be a temporary phenomenon, and must ultimately be self-defeating. Even the nation-state will be transcended.

Or will it? If the scientific state is the heir of the ethnic revival, and if the technocrats take over from the bureaucrats, may we not be witnessing the rise of a new kind of state-manufactured 'political culture' based upon political myths that buttress, and legitimate, the rule of the technocrats? Something of this sort is going on in some of the new states of Africa and Asia, or in some older states like Mexico and Turkey, which have experienced a revolutionary upheaval in the early part of this century. The Mexican revolution and the Cardenas period, and the Young Turk revolution and the rule of Kemal Ataturk, function now as political symbols of a recent state-inspired nationalism, which is at the same time more than just a rationale for a particular political system.[17] In time, such a politically inspired nationalism becomes itself a design for living in a political community and a means of creating and symbolising a particular national solidarity. For each of these myths, events, heroes and symbols remain peculiar to a given political community and awaken quite specific sentiments which cannot be shared by persons who do not belong to that community. Of course, this kind of 'political culture' with its strictly modern, and modernist, myths and symbols, is a far cry from the primordial and medieval ethnic cultures espoused by ethnic nationalists. For a technocrat, the notion of preserving an ancient culture in the cause of national survival is pure obscurantism and irrational romanticism. It is not better to break the links of the chain, and start anew?

But breaking those links has proved to be an uphill struggle. It has proved virtually impossible for future-oriented intellectuals and technocrats to impose their revolutionary political vision of the new community upon the great majority of the population. In those cases where the attempt was made to start afresh, whether in France or China, the United States or the Soviet Union, Turkey or Japan, the new political and scientific vision of the future has had to come to terms with older ethnic cultures and national sentiments, or, as in the United States, to accept the coexistence of subordinate, even conflicting, ethnic cultures within an overarching political culture and community.[18] This may well be the pattern in several Asian and African states, if ethnic separatism is contained. And, if it is, the likelihood of the new state 'political culture' increasingly resembling an amalgam of its several ethnic cultures, and drawing much of its sustenance and meaning from them is very strong, irrespective of the scorn and impatience of the technocrats. The pressing need to integrate culturally diverse peoples into a politically unified citizenry requires constant use of the mass media and educational system on the part of bureaucrats and technocrats, in order to instil the appropriate civil sentiments of fraternity and solidarity. But solidarity must be based upon an historic culture, which cannot be created by revolutionary fiat. Hence the need to incorporate pre-existing cultural traditions into the new political culture, secularising and changing their meanings to accord with the new vision of the political community. The political myths of the post-revolutionary, modern period, have proved to be insufficient to the task of welding poly-ethnic states together; even in more monoethnic states, there have been periodic rediscoveries of an historic culture as an indispensable basis for communal regeneration.[19] The advance into the future has frequently taken the route of a return to an ethnic past.

But this is only part of the story. If the most dynamic and future-oriented sectors of society are bound by visible and hidden chains to their ethnic pasts, so that their new political culture must incorporate much of the old ethnic ones, they may equally provoke an ethnic reaction against the scientific state and its failure to recognise the historic constraints imposed by a unique community and its specific solidarity. As one wave of technical professionals is coopted into the scientific state, or sets up its own rationalised state, another wave emerges to represent those they abandon and to protest against their exclusion. That protest is generally couched in the language of ethnic historicism, especially in poly-ethnic states. The chief beneficiaries of the scientific state are the technical professionals; the educators themselves, as well as humanistic intelligentsia and teachers, and the rural population, must be satisfied with the lower rungs of state institutions, with some exceptions, or with relegation of their needs and interests by an urban, industrial and technological stratum. As the scientific state and its technocrats tighten their hold on the community or communities within their borders, and as they promote policies that benefit the technical professionals and their immediate allies, so they lay the foundations for a fresh revolt by disaffected ethnic intellectuals, under-rewarded humanistic intelligentsia and neglected peasantries or farmers. And if the scientific state fails to expand sufficiently to meet the mobility needs of even the technical strata, then large numbers of them will be tempted to join an ethnic revolt which they hope will unblock their chances of upward mobility and higher status.

It follows that ethnic nationalisms and the scientific state are locked into a recurrent spiral of conflict. Every ethnic revolt expands the role and powers of the scientific state and the technocrats. Every ethnic revolt tightens their hold. At the same time, every act of repression and intervention in the community is liable to provoke further ethnic revolt and rivalry and strengthen the sense of ethnic solidarity among those subjected to the controls of the scientific state and its technical elites. This dynamic spiral is plainly visible in poly-ethnic states with regionally based minorities or competing ethnic communities, notably in large cities.[20] But it is no less applicable, at least in principle, to the most ethnically homogeneous of states. For they, too, experience the general problems of remote bureaucracy and unresponsive technocracy, of a technological sector cut off from its historic roots and denying its cultural traditions, above all, of the opposition of a mechanical, impersonal 'culture' of the state to the personalised, intimate, historical culture of the community; and they respond also with an ethnic revival, which demands a more radical 'national congruence'.

Here lies the nub of the conflict: the opposition between state and community in the modern world. On the one hand, an increasingly rationalised, technical and efficient machine, the 'scientific state', run by an army of impersonal officials and specialist experts; on the other, a kaleidoscope of historic, competing culture communities, unique, incommensurable, symbolically personalised, which apparently refuse to be packaged and standardised within the neat boundaries of identical, hermetic scientific states in the serried ranks of international diplomacy.

Can such a deepseated conflict be transcended in anything more than name? Can the quest for a genuine congruence between ethnic community and scientific state ever really succeed? Or are we doomed to remain locked for the foreseeable future within the dynamic spiral of this conflict?

My own view is that a genuine resolution is unlikely, at least in the short run and for the majority of cases. All kinds of factors, structural and temporal, militate against an early resolution. There are simply too many unsatisfied demands and too few resources, material and spiritual, to satisfy them, even without vested interests, insensitivity and other human failings. The ethnic revival is now too deeply entrenched to be easily reversed or eroded, at any rate for many decades; but so is the scientific state. The hopes of achieving an early 'national congruence' and true 'nation-states' do not look bright. The whole interstate order is, as we saw, premissed on the primacy of state over nation or *ethnie*. The political imperatives of most new states are, similarly, heavily weighted against the demands of specific ethnic communities and their cultures, even if they have to incorporate elements from those cultures to create some sort of political cohesion among their citizens. Even in the industrial and western worlds, opposition to strong ethnic demands is powerful and persistent. If anything, the hold of the scientific state is growing, with the likelihood of provoking further ethnic unrest.

The difficulties of implementing the programme of ethnic nationalism within genuine nation-states are, therefore, formidable and unlikely to be easily achieved. Yet the quest for national congruence between an ethnic culture and a scientific state, and the creation of full nations which is the chief goal of the national transformation or ethnic revival, does not appear to be abating. Ethnic conflicts are undoubtedly the most intractable of all; and this is because they involve so much more than a mere redrawing of the political map. They involve the implementation of ethnic nationalism's basic programme of national transformation, which would leave no state untouched, and would drastically alter the composition and mode of governing of most states in the modern world. For this programme involves humanising the scientific state, not only by binding its technocratic elites to the mass of the population and making them responsive to local ethnic cultures, but also by turning the scientific state into an *instrument* of the national community rather than its directive force. It is this radical alteration of the balance of power between community and state that makes the achievement of nationalism's goals, and the creation of true 'nations', so unlikely. For, to a nationalist, the nation represents more of an abstract ideal than a living reality, whatever the rhetoric employed. As an ideal, it has been widely accepted; and many have died striving for its attainment. Its realisation, however, has been faltering and partial; for the 'nation' is not to be equated with simple independence or political statehood. On the contrary, it subordinates the state and uses independence for cultural ends which will ensure the survival of unique solidarities. But, perhaps, its very lack of achievement, the vast distance between the ideal and its practical realisation, provides the motor of this quest for national transformation, and will ensure the proliferation of ethnic revivals in a world of scientific states.

Notes

vwvwvwvwvwvwvwvwvwvwvwvwvwvwvwvwvwvwvwvwvwvwvwvwvwvwvwvwvwvwvwvwvwvwv

(Full details of the references will be found in the Bibliography)

Introduction

1 This was the classical marxist assumption; see Marx and Engels (1959), 19, 26; and Davis (1967), esp. 44–61.
2 This was the classical functionalist assumption; see Kerr *et al.* (1962); Smelser (1968).
3 Engels (1859). The passage reads:
   > All changes (in the map of Europe) if they are to last, must in general start from the effort to give to the large and viable European nations more and more their *true* national boundaries, which are determined by language and sympathies, while at the same time the ruins of peoples, which are still found here and there and which are no longer capable of a national existence, are absorbed by the larger nations and either become a part of them or maintain themselves as ethnographic monuments without political significance.   (italics in original)
4 Mill (1861), ch. 16. The main passage reads:
   > Where the sentiment of nationality exists in any force, there is a *prima facie* case for uniting all the members of the nationality under the same government, and a government to themselves apart. This is merely saying that the question of government ought to be decided by the governed. One hardly knows what any division of the human race should be free to do if not to determine with which of the various collective bodies of human beings they choose to associate themselves.
5 For a critique and analysis of the neglect of ethnic nationalism in the nineteenth and early twentieth centuries by so many Europocentric social thinkers, see Berlin (1979), 333–55.
6 On this trend, exemplified by Nairn, Hechter and the theorists of 'internal colonialism', see Chapter 2.

1 An 'ethnic revival'?

1 But already in 1948, perceptive observers were forecasting further ethnic conflict in southeast Asia, e.g. Furnivall (1948).
2 M. Stephens: 'The Friulans', in Ashworth (1978), 48–51.
3 R. Holland and G. Mondrova: 'Bulgaria', in Ashworth (1978), 26–31.

198

4 M. Stephens: 'The Sorbs', in Ashworth (1978) 120–24.

5 N. Tapp: 'The hill people of northern Thailand', in Ashworth (1977).

6 J. Mercer: 'The Saharauis of western Sahara', in Ashworth (1977).

7 P. J. Viggers: 'Amerindian minorities in El Salvador, Honduras, Nicaragua, Costa Rica and Belize', in Ashworth (1978).

8 Connor (1972), a seminal article in the study of nationalism.

9 Neuberger (1976a).

10 Geipel (1970) lists many of these minorities, which have lately sprouted ethnic movements; see also Connor (1976).

11 On the African movements, see Argyle (1969).

12 Masur (1966).

13 Kohn (1961b), ch. 1, emphasises the attempt to realise the English ideal of liberty on American soil, but underlines the cultural affinity between the colonies and England.

14 On these factors, see Humphreys and Lynch (1965), especially 138–47.

15 Seton-Watson (1977), 196.

16 Weber (1968).

17 This expression is that of Zartmann (1965), and refers to new states that aspire to become nations, although they lack even ethnic homogeneity.

18 Warburton (1976); and Thürer (1970).

19 Steinberg (1976), especially ch. 6.

20 On post-exilic Jewry, see Tcherikover (1970); for the Guti and Lullubi, see Roux (1964), 146–8, 235–6, as well as on other ancient near eastern peoples like the Elamites, Kassites, Amorites and Mannaeans.

21 Frye (1966).

22 For these, see the essays by Cohn and Wagatsuma in de Reuck and Knight (1967).

23 Glazer and Moynihan (1964), Introduction.

24 Horowitz, in Said (ed.) (1977), 175–80.

25 W. A. Lewis (1965).

26 See Heraud (1963) for this term, for which there is no exact English equivalent. Here, I generally use the term 'ethnic community'.

27 On the pan-Turkist movement, see Zenkovsky (1960) and Hostler (1953).

28 Seton-Watson (1977), ch. 2, although he excludes Spain (but not Castile) from this group. For definitions of nationalism, see A. D. Smith (1973).

29 On the development of this strategy among the Blacks in the late 1960s, see Draper (1970).

30 See Fondation Hardt (1962) for Greek ethnocentrism; and Maccoby (1974) for the Jewish resistance movement in ancient Judea.

31 W. Beer: 'The social class of ethnic activists in contemporary France', in Esman (1977), 147–8.

32 On trends in the East, see Goldhagen (1968); and Szporluk (1973).

33 On this, see Argyle (1976) for an analysis of nationalisms' strength in the early nineteenth-century Habsburg empire.

34 Mayo (1974), chs. 3, 5.

35 Webb (1977), 64.

36 *ibid.*, 58–9.

37 Payne (1971).
38 Thrasher (1972).
39 Bracey, Meier and Rudwick (1970), Introduction.
40 Edmonds (1971).
41 N. Kasfir: 'Cultural sub-nationalism in Uganda', in Olorunsola (1972), 89–90; Rosberg and Nottingham (1966).
42 Bennigsen and Lemercier-Quelquejay (1966).
43 Mayo (1974), ch. 5.
44 For this debate, see Tipton (1972).

2 Uneven development

1 On this whole question, see Rosdolsky (1964) who has analysed the foreign policy of the *Neue Rheinische Zeitung* during 1848, when Marx was its chief editor and Engels its foreign editor. Engels, in particular, opposed the proletarian brotherhood of nations in the social sense to the 'old, elemental national egoism' of free trade, and to the backward small nationalities, see Marx and Engels (1955–63), II, 611–14.
2 Davis (1967), chs. 2–3.
3 Davis (1965); and Shaheen (1956).
4 K. Kautsky, in *Neue Zeit* (1886), 522–5, cited in Davis (1967), 142.
5 'England, it is true, in causing a social revolution in Hindostan, was actuated only by the vilest interests, and was stupid in her manner of enforcing them. But that is not the question. The question is, can mankind fulfil its destiny without a fundamental revolution in the social state of Asia? If not, whatever may have been the crimes of England she was the unconscious tool of history in bringing about the revolution', in K. Marx: 'The British Rule in India', *New York Daily Tribune*, 25 June 1853, in Avineri (1969), 94.
6 Lenin (1916); see also Fieldhouse (1967), especially nos. 16, 18, 22.
7 This, of course, is the standpoint of the main British parties, Labour according more weight to the devolution advocated by the Kilbrandon report than the Conservatives.
8 On the concept of relative deprivation, see Thrupp (1962).
9 Webb (1977), 110–15.
10 Payne (1971), 24.
11 Heiberg (1975).
12 S. Bridge: 'Some causes of political change in modern Yugoslavia', in Esman (1977).
13 T. Turner: 'Congo-Kinshasa', in Olorunsola (1972).
14 Frank (1969); O'Brien (1975); for a critique, cf. Laclau (1971); see also Stone (1979).
15 Wallerstein (1974) analyses the growth of this modern world system.
16 Hechter (1975), 30.
17 G. Balandier: 'The colonial situation,' in Wallerstein (1966).
18 Hechter (1975), 33–4; Hechter describes internal colonialism as 'a malin-

tegration established on terms increasingly regarded as unjust and illegitimate', *ibid.*, 34.

19 Hechter (1975), 38–9.
20 *ibid.*, 39.
21 *ibid.*, 271. The split is also a cultural one.
22 *ibid.*, 265.
23 *ibid.*, 310. Universalist principles of bureaucracy tend to favour the more advantaged groups within a plural state.
24 *ibid.*, 33, note 1, for Hechter's discussion of this problem.
25 Hechter and Levi (1979), 263 *et sqq.;* see also Hechter (1978).
26 Hechter and Levi (1979), 265; Hobsbawm (1971). See also Webb (1977), 121–7 for a critique of its application to Scotland.
27 On the application to Quebec, see McRoberts (1979).
28 Hechter and Levi (1979), 270–2.
29 For southern Italy, see Palloni (1979). For the Hungarian ethnic reaction *preceding* extensive economic dependency, see Verdery (1979), 391, who also notes the complexity of having more than one colonial master and colonised subjects in Transylvania, *ibid.*, 390–1.
30 On Brittany, see Reece (1979); on Ireland, see Norman (1973) and Moody (1968), chs. 1–3.
31 W. Petersen: 'On the subnations of Western Europe', in Glazer and Moynihan (1975), 198–208; and cf. parallels in Malaysia.
32 Nairn (1976).
33 M. Rioux: 'Quebec: From a minority complex to majority behaviour', in Tobias and Woodhouse (1969); Spry (1971).
34 Hechter and Levi (1979), 267.
35 Nairn (1977), 96.
36 *ibid.*, 97.
37 *ibid.*, 98.
38 *ibid.*, 100.
39 *ibid.*, 340.
40 *ibid.*, ch. 2, esp. 117.
41 *ibid.*, 101.
42 *ibid.*, 71–82, 177–81.
43 *ibid.*, 128.
44 *ibid.*, 337–8.
45 *ibid.*, ch. 1.
46 *ibid.*, 337.
47 Kemilainen (1964).
48 Baron (1960); Kohn (1967).
49 Cobban (1965). But cf. Shafer (1938) for a contrary argument.
50 Stavrianos (1957).
51 Frazee (1969); Campbell and Sherrard (1968), chs. 1–2.
52 Nairn (1977), 335–6.
53 *ibid.*, 104.
54 A. D. Smith (1979), ch. 3.
55 Gellner (1964), ch. 7.

3 Language and community

1 Under Mazarin in France, and through the language revival of Gottsched in Germany, see Kohn (1944); and Barnard (1965), ch. 1.

2 On Herder, generally, see Barnard (1969); on the linguistic element in German political romanticism, see Kohn (1965).

3 For Herder's cultural populism, the most incisive account is Berlin (1976), from which this quotation is taken.

4 Znaniecki (1952); and Kedourie (1960).

5 Gellner (1973), 7.

6 *ibid.*, 11.

7 *ibid.*, 12.

8 *ibid.*, 13.

9 *ibid.*, 14. Actually Gellner also adds that 'resignation' plays a part in this equation. In stable societies, communities tend to accept their lot; presumably, in mobile societies, they no longer do so.

10 Binder (1964); Sharabi (1970); and A. D. Smith (1973a).

11 Van den Berghe (1967), ch. 3.

12 *ibid.*, ch 2; and Masur (1966), ch. 5.

13 This applies especially to Afrikaner nationalism, see de Klerk (1975); also Munger (1967).

14 I. J. Lederer: 'Nationalism and the Yugoslavs', in Sugar and Lederer (1969). Also P. Brock: 'Polish nationalism', in *ibid.*

15 G. Arnakis: 'The role of religion in the development of Balkan nationalism', in Jelavich (1963). For the Jews and Tatars, see Baron (1964) and Bennigsen and Lemercier-Quelquejay (1960).

16 G. Ashworth: 'The Philippine Moslems', in Ashworth (1977), 125–30; Beckett (1971), on northern Ireland.

17 See Kohn (1957); and Kohn (1965) and Holborn (1964).

18 Deutsch and Foltz (1963), Introduction; also Deutsch (1966).

19 Mayo (1974), 1.

20 *ibid.*, ch. 1, esp. 11.

21 *ibid.*, 150.

22 *ibid.*, 156.

23 *ibid.*, 157 and *passim.*

24 For this important distinction between 'operational' and 'analytic' theories, see M. Yapp: 'Language, religion and political identity: a general framework', in Taylor and Yapp (1979).

25 See Kohn (1957); on the question of size of *ethnie* and nations, see A. D. Smith (1971), ch. 7, note 93, 322–3.

26 Lartichaux (1977); also Kohn (1967), Part I.

27 Markham (1954).

28 Mayo (1974), ch. 1, 12 (note 6).

29 Montagne (1952); for the West African case, see Crowder (1968).

30 Mercier (1965); and for the variety of usage and definitions of the term 'tribe' in the work of Africanists, see King (1976).

31 Rotberg (1967); and the case-studies in Olorunsola (1972).

32 Neuberger (1976b).

33 Lijphart (1969); and J. Steiner and J. Obler: 'Does the Consociational theory really hold for Switzerland?', in Esman (1977).

34 For a detailed analysis, see Connor (1972).

35 Connor, in Esman (ed.) (1977), 25–6.

36 *ibid.*, 25; on the history of this infection, see Connor (1973).

37 *ibid.*, 43. See also Connor, in Said and Simmons (eds.) (1976).

38 Connor, in Esman (ed.) (1977), 25.

39 Connor (1972), 331.

40 As Karl Kautsky had predicted; see Davis (1967), 142.

41 Deutsch (1966), but cf. his amended position in Deutsch (1969).

42 On the uses of the term 'modernisation', see Nettl and Robertson (1968). A typical example of culture contact was the process by which the ancient Near East became 'hellenised'. But the latter did not involve those processes of industrialisation, immense technological progress, vast urbanisation (except for Alexandria), the diffusion of mass literacy and the mass media, democratic participation and the like, that various theorists designate 'processes of modernisation'. On this, see A. D. Smith (1973b), and on the processes of hellenisation, see Tcherikover (1970).

43 Connor (1972), 334; and Connor (1978), esp. 383–6.

44 Connor (1972), 341; see Connor (1978), 388, where Connor writes: 'a nation is a self-aware ethnic group . . . until the members are themselves aware of the group's uniqueness, it is merely an ethnic group and not a nation. While an ethnic group *may*, therefore, be other-defined, the nation *must* be self-defined' (italics in original).

45 Connor (1978), 389–91.

46 *ibid.*, 387, where Connor notes the ill effects of the prevalent separation of studies of 'ethnicity' (usually equated with cultural *minorities* in the United States) and of 'nationalism', whereas an earlier generation of scholars, including Max Weber and Ernest Barker, had appreciated their intimate relationships.

4 *Ethnic consciousness in pre-modern eras*

1 This confusion of regionalism with ethnic community and sentiment has been a feature of the British debate on 'devolution'. On this debate, see Birch (1977) and Nairn (1977).

2 In other words, an 'ethnic group' as a type of community requires both a common culture and a coextensive 'sense of community'. On the disjunctions between culture and sense of community, see Rosh White (1978), 144–5, and, more generally, Burgess (1978).

3 Akzin (1964), 55 *et sqq.*; on the use of 'colour' by American Blacks, to symbolise and dignify their lost history, see Legum (1962), 96–7, and Geiss (1974), 319.

4 Connor (1972), 334; but cf. Connor (1978) for an amended definition.

5 P. R. Brass: 'Elite groups, symbol manipulation and ethnic identity among the Muslims of South Asia', in Taylor and Yapp (1979), 35–41.

6 On 'primordial sentiments' see Shils (1957) and Geertz (1963).

7 Schermerhorn (1970), too, stresses the role of history in his definition of the ethnic group as 'a collectivity within a larger society having real or putative common ancestry, memories of a shared historical past, and a cultural focus on one or more symbolic elements defined as the epitome of their peoplehood . . . A necessary accompaniment is some consciousness of kind among members of the group', 12.

8 Brass, in Taylor and Yapp (1979), 35, and Francis (1976), 6–7; van den Berghe (1978).

9 Debray (1977), 29–41; see Burgess (1978) for definitions of ethnicity.

10 On the Greek case, see G. Arnakis: 'The role of religion in the development of Balkan nationalism', in Jelavich (1963). On the Jewish case, see Baron (1960), ch. 7. On Czechs, Poles, Germans and other East European 'linguistic' nationalisms, see Seton-Watson (1977), chs. 3–4.

11 Welch (1966), ch. 6.

12 Armstrong (1963), chs. 1–2; and J. F. Zacek: 'Nationalism in Czechoslovakia', in Sugar and Lederer (1969); also Brock (1976).

13 On the role of peasants in revolution, see Barrington Moore (1967), ch. 9; and for the Chinese case, Johnson (1963).

14 On religion in China and India, see Levenson (1958) and D. E. Smith (1974), especially the essays by D. E. Smith and by Sharma and Sharma. On the Arabs and Jews, see Carmichael (1967) and Katz (1958).

15 On the Greeks and Armenians in 'exile', see Campbell and Sherrard (1968) and Nalbandian (1963); and on Black 'Back-to-Africa' movements, Brotz (1966). On the Jews, see Dinur (1969) and Grayzel (1968).

16 Braidwood and Willey (1962).

17 Frankfort (1954); Kramer (1963).

18 Bermant and Weitzman (1979), 27–33, 102–12; Moscati (1962), ch. 6.

19 Coulborn (1959).

20 Noth (1960), Part I, and Part II, ch. 1.

21 Associated with the legends of the Heraclidae, recounted in Schwab (1947); see Andrewes (1956), ch. 5.

22 Weber (1968), Vol. I/2, ch. 5.

23 Guthrie (1968), esp. 106–8; see Nilsson (1940).

24 Frankfort (1948).

25 On populism and marxist nationalisms, see A. D. Smith (1979), ch. 5.

26 Debray (1977) and Nairn (1977); see also Worsley (1964).

27 C. Johnson: 'Building a communist nation in China', in Scalapino (1969). See also Huntington (1968), esp. 334 *et sqq.*

28 Leiden and Schmitt (1968), ch. 10. On peasant wars, generally, see Wolf (1973).

29 E. Weber (1979), a detailed study of rural change between 1870 and 1914.

30 Zernatto (1944); and see Argyle (1976).

31 For general accounts of the relationships between war and society, see Bramson and Goethals (1964). The themes adumbrated in this section are discussed at greater length in A. D. Smith (forthcoming).

32 Malinowski (1941).

33 Simmel (1964), 101.

34 Weber (1968), vol. I/2, ch. 5; yet the initial political unit tends to include more than one community of culture, or to cut across the boundaries of a culture community, see Aron (1966), 292–7.

35 Weber (1952), 268; Noth (1960), Part III. On the religious interpretations of Judea's political position, see Kauffmann (1961), Part III.

36 Thürer (1970), chs. 2–3; and Kohn (1957).

37 Poggi (1978).

38 Easton (1953); and C. Schmitt (1963), both cited in Poggi (1978), ch. 1.

39 Poggi (1978), 11.

40 *ibid.*, 12; yet self-identification is closely bound up with denial and exclusion of other units.

41 Enloe (1980); on warfare and the sense of community in the modern era, see M. Howard: 'Total War in the twentieth century: Participation and consensus in the Second World War', in Bond and Roy (1975).

42 On Greek hoplite formations, see Forrest (1966), 88–97, and McNeill (1963), 198–200; on the interrelations of military formats and state- and nation-building, see S. Finer: 'State- and nation-building in Europe: The role of the military', in Tilly (1975).

43 R. Schlaifer: 'Greek theories of slavery from Homer to Aristotle', in Finley (1960); also Bacon (1961).

44 Marwick (1974), 33, 123, 132, 142, 153 *et sqq.*; also Enloe (1980), ch. 2.

45 See Finer, in Tilly (1975); and Parsons (1966), Part I.

46 These are the terms used by Levenson (1959). On ancient ethnocentrism, see A. D. Smith (1972).

47 Roux (1964), ch. 10; Bermant and Weitzman (1979), 33–5.

48 Moscati (1962), chs. 5–6; Pritchard (1958), for the inscriptions.

49 Roux (1964), ch. 19; and Moscati (1962), ch. 3. The modern Christian Assyrians of Iraq and the diaspora claim descent from the ancient Assyrians, see Cahnmann (1944) and E. Naby: 'The Assyrians', in Ashworth (1978), 12–16.

50 Grimal (1968), 210–41.

51 Grant (1973), ch. 2, and Part IV.

52 Sherwin-White (1952).

53 Syme (1970); admission of non-Italians to the Senate was conceded under Claudius.

54 Koht (1947).

55 There is a vigorous debate among medieval historians about the degree of national sentiment within the several European states during the feudal era and later. On the whole, I follow Kohn (1944), esp. 78–85, 93–6, and Shafer (1955), 59–63; for the debate, see Tipton (1972).

56 These coincide with what Seton-Watson terms the 'old continuous nations', Seton-Watson (1977), ch. 2.

57 See Koht (1947); Seton-Watson (1977), chs. 3–4.

58 On this, see Tipton (1972), especially the extracts from Hertz and Kirkland; and Kohn (1944), 112–15, 155–6.

59 Poggi (1978), ch. 4.

60 Kohn (1940).

61 Strayer (1963); also Poggi (1978), ch. 4.

62 On this European 'state system', see Wallerstein (1974); on the uneven-ness of 'national development' in the early modern period, see Seton-Watson (1977), chs. 2–4.

63 For example, Kohn (1944), ch. 1; Kedourie (1960); Gellner (1964), ch. 7. See M. Yapp: 'Language, religion and political identity: A general frame-work', in Taylor and Yapp (1979), esp. 5–7.

5 Historicism

1 See Nisbet (1969), Part ii; for a rather different usage, cf. Popper (1957).

2 Antoni (1959).

3 Walch (1967); Rosenblum (1967), ch. 1.

4 On Ossian, see Okun (1967).

5 Rosenblum (1967), 34, 42–51; and A. D. Smith (1979a).

6 Irwin (1966) analyses the contribution of English neo-classicists and neo-Gothic motifs; on the French contribution, see Loquin (1912).

7 Rosenblum (1967), ch. 3; and Mordaunt Crook (1972).

8 See Honour (1968); and, on music, Jacobs (1972), ch. 12.

9 On Shaftesbury's *Charakteristicks of men, manners, opinions, times,* Lon-don 1711, and *The judgment of Hercules,* London 1712, and on Winckel-mann, see Irwin (1972), Introduction, Parts iii and iv; on Burke, see Wark (1954).

10 On the background of German romanticism, see Barnard (1965), ch. 1; for eighteenth-century 'natural history', see Nisbet (1969), ch. 4.

11 On the appeal to antiquity, see Gay (1970), Vol. i, chs. 1–2.

12 On Korais and Obradovic, see Stavrianos (1961), esp. chs. 9, 14 and 15. For Alfieri and Mazzini, see Beales (1971) and (with brief extracts) Woolf (1969). For Palacky, see Kohn (1960), 20–23, 75–83.

13 On the varieties of Ottoman and Turkish nationalism, see Lewis (1968) and Berkes (1964).

14 Zenkovsky (1953) and (1960).

15 Tibawi (1963) and Sharabi (1970). The quotation from al-Bustani comes from a work of 1869–70, and is cited by Tibawi.

16 Heimsath (1964) and Pocock (1958); and more generally, Kedourie (1971), Introduction and extract (4) by Banerjea.

17 Lynch (1967); and July (1967), ch. 11. See also the extracts from Blyden in Wilson (1969), Part iv.

18 For a classic collection of readings on the subject, see Huszar (1960). See also Mannheim (1936), esp. 155–62 and (1940), Part ii; Seton-Watson (1960), ch. 6; and Lipset (1960), ch. 10.

19 Shils (1972a); and Eisenstadt (1972) and (1973).

20 Bolgar (1971).

21 T. Huszar: 'Changes in the concept of intellectuals', in Gella (1976).

22 On enlightened absolutism, see Beloff (1954); for the ideologies of leaders of new states, see Sigmund (1967) and Matossian (1958).

23 Gellner (1964), ch. 8.

24 An example of such enlightened despotism was the reformist monarch, Joseph II. On the general characteristics of absolutist states, see Poggi (1978), chs. 4–5, and for Germany, Bruford (1965).

25 On Baroque kings, see Friedrich (1962); also Beloff (1954).

26 Lively (1966); and Anchor (1967).

27 Obeyesekere (1968); for the philosophical arguments, see Pike (1964).

28 For the traditional theodicies of Kharma, Zoroastrian dualism and the predestination decree of the *deus absconditus*, see Weber (1947), 275, and (1965), 138–50; for the refusal to accept human suffering, see the figure of Ivan Karamazov in Dostoevsky's *The Brothers Karamazov I*, 287 (Penguin edition).

29 This is more fully discussed in A. D. Smith (1970) and (1971), ch. 10.

30 Poland is the obvious example, in the communist world; in western societies, too, Ireland and the United States, and to some extent Holland and Greece, continue to manifest a vigorous public religious life and hierarchies. On these and other European cases, see D. Martin: 'The Religious Condition of Europe', in Giner and Archer (1978).

31 Examples were (and are) U Nu of Burma, Nyerere, Kaunda, Sukarno, Sadat, Muhammad Abduh, Iqbal, Roy, Blyden and Martin Buber, each of whom, in their very different ways, worked out a personal synthesis of religious, national and socially progressive motifs in varying proportions. On some of these syntheses in southeast Asia, see M. Sarkisyanz: 'On the place of U Nu's Buddhist Socialism in Burma's History of Ideas', in Sakai (1961), and, more generally, Wertheim (1958).

32 A. D. Smith (1971), ch. 10, and (1979), ch. 2.

33 Kedourie (1966) and Hourani (1970), ch. 5.

34 M. Adenwalla: 'Hindu concepts and the Gita in early Indian national thought', in Sakai (1961); and Singh (1963). See also Embree (1972), chs. 2–3.

35 von Grunebaum (1964), ch. 9; see also Zeine (1958).

36 Harrison (1960) analyses these linguistic nationalisms, while D. E. Smith (1963) discusses the problems of Indian secularism.

37 This is especially the case with the current Islamic revival, which owes a great debt to the activities of the Muslim Brotherhood, see Halpern (1963), ch. 8.

38 Anchor (1967); Barnard (1965), ch. 1; Gay (1973), Vol. II, ch. 9.

39 Kedourie (1971), Introduction; Hodgkin (1964).

40 For a fuller discussion, see A. D. Smith (1979), ch. 2.

41 A. D. Smith (1971), ch. 10. For reformists in the Muslim, Hindu and Jewish worlds, see Gibb (1947), Heimsath (1964), and Hertzberg (1960), Introduction.

42 J. L. Blau: 'Tradition and innovation', in Blau *et al.* (1959).

43 An excellent example of such a position occurs in Egypt at the turn of the century, especially in the writings of Rashid Rida and the *salafiyya* movement; see Dawn (1961), and Abun-Nasr (1966).

44 It is important to stress that these three positions remain relevant and persistent options in the latter half of the twentieth century, as the Is-

lamic revival today clearly illustrates. It is also relevant that, once ethnic nationalism has itself become a much-publicised and successful option, each of the three intellectual positions tends to reinforce the trend towards an ethnic historicism; so that, increasingly, for all their differences, the three positions operate within a definite and circumscribed political framework. This may also help to explain why individual thinkers and writers may cross over from one position to another, without too much difficulty, and why an ethnic nationalism of one sort may, under changing conditions, give way to that of another kind.

45 On the European case of perceiving diversity, see Nisbet (1969), Part II, and Kedourie (1960), ch. 4.

46 See the discussion of Korais (and the extract cited from him) by Kedourie (1971), Introduction, 37–48.

47 A good example of this external 'reference group' is afforded by Slavophiles as well as westernisers in nineteenth-century Russia, see Thaden (1964) and Shapiro (1967).

48 Opera, in particular, has lent itself to the purpose of communal regeneration: Glinka's *A Life for the Tsar* (1836), Mussorgsky's *Boris Godunov* (1869) and Borodin's *Prince Igor* (1890), are examples of the Russian nationalist school, but there are analogues in several European countries in the late nineteenth and early twentieth centuries, notably in the operas of Smetana and Janáček in Czechoslovakia, in Grieg's setting of Ibsen's *Peer Gynt,* and in Sibelius' evocations of the *Kalevala* (c. 1895), see Robertson and Stevens (1968), Part II, ch. 3.

49 See Kohler (1970) and Cobban (1964), ch. 4.

50 On Vasnetsov and the Russian nationalist school centred on Abramtsevo, see Gray (1971), chs. 1–2.

6 Bureaucracy and the intelligentsia

1 A. Gella: 'An introduction to the sociology of the intelligentsia', in Gella (1976) discusses the history of the term.

2 In what follows, the term 'intelligentsia' refers exclusively to these professional strata, and the latter are distinguished from the 'intellectuals', although in practice there is some overlap. In fact, some writers (e.g. Kautsky (1962), Introduction) are really referring to these professional 'intelligentsia' when they describe the attitudes and activities of 'intellectuals'.

3 For portraits of such 'intellectuals', see Huszar (1960), Part III. Speaking of the 'intellectuals', Feuer (1975) 202, writes: 'On the one hand, the word denotes anyone whose ideas range beyond his profession or vocation; endowed with an enduring concern with the questions of existence, he ventures on the basis of his own experience to have opinions on the unanswerable questions of ultimate reality. On the other hand, the word refers to those persons who have a compulsive commitment to the criticism of the social order; . . .' For Feuer, these 'ideologists' embrace the 'intellectuals in politics', those whose 'avenue to power is ideology'.

Here I tend to use the term 'intellectual' in the first sense only; not all 'intellectuals' in this sense are critical of the social order, nor necessarily ideologues or 'misfits'.

For an illuminating analysis of the rabbinic intellectuals (*Hakhamim*) of ancient Palestine, see E. E. Urbach: 'The Talmudic Sage: Character and Authority', in Ben-Sasson and Ettinger (1971).

4 Schonberg's opera, *Moses and Aaron,* was completed in the 1930s, and upholds the prophetic tradition of ideology analysed by Weber (1952) and castigated by Feuer (1975), 197–202.

5 Gouldner (1979), esp. 28–43.

6 *ibid.,* 8 and *passim*. For a critique of such views, see Ben-David (1963/4).

7 Nadel (1956), and Keller (1968) on functional elites in general.

8 See Weber (1964), 329–41; and Gouldner (1979), 51–2.

9 Howard (1976), 55.

10 Poggi (1978), 88 *et sqq*.

11 Archer and Vaughan (1971), 151–9, on La Chalotais' *Essai d'education nationale* (Paris, 1763); and Palmer (1940).

12 For an account of the rise of bureaucratic states, see Jacoby (1973), Part I.

13 See Lefebvre (1947), 39–42; and Brinton (1952).

14 Pipes (1961); Confino (1972).

15 McCulley (1966), chs. 4–5.

16 Wallerstein (1965); see also Lloyd (1966).

17 On the Roman case, see Syme (1970). On Ottoman Turkey, see Davison (1963) and Karal (1965). On Russia, see Seton-Watson (1967) and Greenberg (1976), Vol. I, esp. ch. 6.

18 On this use of 'ethnicity', see Enloe (1980), ch. 2.

19 See Stavrianos (1961) on the *millet* system. Similarly with ancient Rome.

20 W. H. Lewis (1965) and Crowder (1968).

21 On this crisis, see Barrington Moore (1967) and Skocpol (1979), Part I, ch. 2.

22 Hamerow (1958), Part III; Anderson (1972), ch. 2.

23 See Rotberg (1967).

24 Cummings (1975), 31–43.

25 On the theories of 'racial' cleavage between Franks and Gauls in this period, see Barzun (1932); also L. Poliakov: 'Racism in Europe', in de Reuck and Knight (1967).

26 Palmer (1959), 86–99.

27 Frazee (1969); Campbell and Sherrard (1968), chs. 1–2.

28 Thaden (1964); Alworth (1967).

29 Kedourie (1971) illustrates this disillusion and transformation in some of the cases cited in his Introduction; for further discussion of the assimilationist case, see A. D. Smith (1971), ch. 10.

30 For this concept, see Weber (1965), chs. 6–7; Weber (1947), ch. 11.

31 This is closely allied to the German romantic concept of *Bildung;* see Barnard (1969).

32 See P. Brock: 'Polish Nationalism', and G. Barany: 'Hungary: From aristocratic to proletarian nationalism', in Sugar and Lederer (1969).

33 Frazee (1969), and Stavrianos (1961); also C. Koumarianou: 'The contribution of the intelligentsia towards the Greek independence movement, 1798–1821', in Clogg (1973).
34 D. E. Smith (1965).
35 Bennigsen and Quelquejay (1960); and Zenkovsky (1953).
36 Mouzelis (1978), 12–14, 94–5, and G. D. Frangos: 'The *Philike Etairia:* A premature national coalition', in Clogg (1973).
37 On this renaissance, see Sarkiss (1937); and Nalbandian (1963).
38 Seal (1968).
39 Gouldner (1979), 17–18, 42–3.
40 Davies (1966) examines some African alliances.
41 See Huntington (1968), esp. 334 *et sqq.,* and Seton-Watson (1978), ch. 3.
42 As in the title of Deutsch and Foltz (1963); see Kautsky (1962), Introduction, on the connection between intelligentsia and modernism.
43 For this strategy, see Frank (1969). For a critique, cf. Roxborough (1976).

7 State integration and ethnic schism

1 For an early analysis of this 'grid', see Montagne (1952).
2 Rotberg (1967); Emerson (1960b).
3 Neuberger (1976b); Gray Cowan (1964), ch. 1.
4 See Sharabi (1966); and Halpern (1963).
5 See Binder (1964); and Haim (1962), Introduction. On Pan-Africanism, see Geiss (1974).
6 J. Das Gupta: 'Ethnicity, language demands and national development in India', in Glazer and Moynihan (1975).
7 See Masur (1966); and Whitaker (1962).
8 Griffin (1964); and van den Berghe (1967), chs. 2–3.
9 Whitaker and Jordan (1966); and Morner (1967).
10 On the affinity between European, especially Rousseauan, nationalist motifs and those of latterday African nationalists, see Hodgkin (1961); all speak the language of self-determination, as Ronen (1979) argues, ch. 1.
11 On this national *atimia,* see Nettl and Robertson (1968).
12 For the Yugoslav case, see S. Bridge: 'Some causes of political change in modern Yugoslavia', in Esman (1977). On the 'Swiss model', see Steinberg (1976).
13 On the 'post-colonial' state, see Alavi (1972).
14 For some of the recent debates about the role of the State in Africa, see Saul (1979), ch. 8; and for an extended discussion of the post-colonial African state and its 'organisational bourgeoisie', see Markovitz (1977), chs. 6, 10.
15 M. J. Esman: 'Communal conflict in Southeast Asia', in Glazer and Moynihan (1975) explores some of the resultant post-colonial patterns of communal relations in Southeast Asia.
16 See Kautsky (1962) Introduction, and Markovitz (1977).
17 Little (1965).
18 Misra (1961); and Desai (1954).

19 Zolberg (1964); and Davies (1966).

20 Sarkisyanz (1964).

21 Keddie (1966).

22 P. Worsley: 'The concept of Populism', in Gellner and Ionescu (1970).

23 Debray (1977); but, officially, marxist nationalism attempts to obviate and encompass interethnic divisions in liberation struggles, as in Guinea-Bissau under Cabral's leadership; see Lyon (1980).

24 Wolf (1973), ch. 1, 28–32.

25 *ibid.*, ch. 3, esp. 113–25; and C. Johnson: 'Building a communist nation in China', in Scalapino (1969).

26 Wolf (1973), ch. 5, esp. 232–8; and Tillion (1958).

27 H. Tinker: 'Burma: Separatism as a way of life', in Ashworth (1977); and Anderson, von der Mehden and Young (1967), ch. 6.

28 On the history of the War and post-War period, see Cady (1958).

29 Esman: 'Communal conflict in Southeast Asia', in Glazer and Moynihan (1975).

30 DKH: 'The Baluchis of Pakistan', and 'The Pashtoons (Pathan) of Pakistan', in Ashworth (1977).

31 Edmonds in 1967 estimated the Kurdish population as: 3,200,000 in Turkey, 1,800,000 in Persia, 1,550,000 in Iraq, 320,000 in Syria and 80,000 in Soviet Transcaucasia, making about 7 millions in all, Edmonds (1971), 92 (note 4). In Iraq, they form nearly a fifth of the total population.

32 Edmonds (1971), esp. 88–90, 94–6, 100–2; Cottam (1964), 65–74.

33 John Gaisford: 'Nigerian Pluralism', in Ashworth (1977); and V. Olorunsola: 'Nigeria', in Olorunsola (1972).

34 Markovitz (1977), 314–19; Anderson, von der Mehden and Young (1967), 34–7.

35 Young (1965), 441.

36 T. Turner: 'Congo-Kinshasa', in Olorunsola (1972), esp. 203–7; and Anderson, von der Mehden and Young (1967), 31–4.

37 *ibid.*, 208–12; Young (1965), p. 247.

38 T. Turner: 'Congo-Kinshasa,' in Olorunsola (1972), 221.

39 T. Hodges: 'The ethnic conflict in Angola', in Ashworth (1978); and Davidson, Slovo and Wilkinson (1976), Part I, ch. 6, 53–5.

40 Davidson, Slovo and Wilkinson (1976), chs. 7, 9; on 'ethnic diversity' in Africa, see Seton-Watson (1978), ch. 3, 62–7.

41 Bloomfield and Leiss (1969), 4–9.

42 On secession and the interstate system, see Anderson, von der Mehden and Young (1967), 67–74.

43 On the noncoincidence of states and culture communities or *ethnie*, see Aron (1966), 292–7; see also Enloe (1980), chs. 1–3.

44 As with Biafra, Eritrea, the BaKongo and Ewe in Africa; or the Kurds, Naga and Pathans in Asia; although, from time to time, some of these groups received aid (usually indirectly) from one or both of the client-systems, as have the Palestinians. More often, the superpower systems support officially recognised and legally constituted states such as Angola, Vietnam, Korea and Ethiopia, or state-wide 'national liberation

struggles', as in Angola, Mozambique and Guinea-Bissau, see Davidson, Slovo and Wilkinson (1976). The one major exception is Bangladesh.

45 On the United States' ethnic composition, see next chapter; on that of the Soviet Union, see R. Pipes: 'Reflections on the nationality problems of the Soviet Union', in Glazer and Moynihan (1975); and also Goldhagen (1968).

46 Especially after Vietnam and, more recently, Afghanistan. There is also the lesson of the Middle East conflict, where both superpowers and their client-systems are careful to calculate their degree of support, not merely in accordance with their own interests, but with those of the interstate system as a whole.

47 See the statement by Amilcar Cabral:
    'The leaders of the liberation movement, drawn generally from the petty-bourgeoisie (intellectuals, clerks) or urban working groups (workers, drivers, other wage-earners), have to live day by day with various peasant strata in the heart of the rural populations. They come to know the people better. They discover at the grass roots the richness of the people's cultural values (whether philosophical or political, artistic, social or moral). They acquire a clearer understanding of the economic realities of their country, and of the problems, sufferings and hopes of the masses of their people.'
    A. Cabral: *National Liberation and Culture*, Syracuse University, New York, 20 February 1970 (memorial lecture to Mondlane), cited in Davidson, Slovo and Wilkinson (1976), ch. 6, 51.
    On 'Third World' populisms, see Gellner and Ionescu (1970) and A. D. Smith (1979), ch. 5.

48 On the dynamics of the interstate system and 'balance of power' mechanisms, see Spanier (1972), Part I, and Part II, ch. 3.

49 For some of these international repercussions and dimensions of ethnic conflicts, see Said and Simmons (1976), notably the essay by Walker Connor: 'The political significance of ethnonationalism within western Europe'.

50 On this, see Ronen (1979).

51 See Connor (1973) and in Said and Simmons (1976).

8 Accommodation and neo-ethnicity

1 See Lloyd Warner and Srole (1945).

2 As in Deutsch (1966) and Lerner (1958).

3 A view presented in Greeley (1974), ch. 1; see also Herberg (1960).

4 Glazer and Moynihan (1964), Introduction, esp. 12–21; indeed, they contend that ethnic groups in New York constitute new social forms.

5 A. M. Greely and W. C. McCready: 'The transmission of cultural heritages: the case of the Irish and the Italians', in Glazer and Moynihan (1975).

6 See Kramer and Leventman (1961) for the 'third-generation' thesis.

7 On the Canadian case, see Porter (1965); on America, see Greeley (1974) and Blau (1976), chs. 1, 7.

8 A. Lijphart: 'Political theories and the explanation of ethnic conflict in the western world: Falsified predictions and plausible postdictions', in Esman (1977), esp. 59–61.

9 D. Bell: 'Ethnicity and social change', in Glazer and Moynihan (1975).

10 *ibid.*, 169. For some comments on Bell's analysis, see Halsey (1978).

11 M. Kilson: 'Blacks and neo-ethnicity in American political life', in Glazer and Moynihan (1975), esp. 260–1.

12 *ibid.*, 260–6; on the position of New York's Jews, see Glazer and Moynihan (1964), ch. 4; 'The Jews'.

13 Roman Catholic academics and Reform Jews, for example; see Gans (1979).

14 Gouldner (1979), 60–73.

15 Gans (1979), esp. 9–13, to which this section is mainly indebted.

16 *ibid.*, 17. But 'revivalism' need not always imply 'neo-traditionalism'.

17 I. L. Horowitz: 'Ethnic politics and US foreign policy,' in Said (1977), 175–80.

18 See Glazer and Moynihan (1964), Introduction.

19 Here I concentrate on Black nationalism; but there has been a recent shift in Indian strategies, symbolised of course by Wounded Knee, see Svensson (1978), 113–16.

20 For a documentary history of these movements, see Bracey, Meier and Rudwick (1970).

21 Geiss (1974), ch. 12.

22 Cruse (1967), esp. Part I.

23 On the Black Muslims, see Essien-Udom (1962); see also Brotz (1964).

24 See Carmichael and Hamilton (1967) on the application of the notion of an internal colony to 'institutional racism' in America.

25 See Draper (1970), esp. chs. 6–8, for a critical analysis.

26 Kilson, in Glazer and Moynihan (1975), esp. 243–9, 257–8.

27 Dubnow (1958), esp. Introduction by K. Pinson.

28 On the American experience, see Cruse (1967) and Frazier (1948).

29 And not only in America. For African rediscovery of their past, see Geiss (1974) and July (1967).

30 Captured in Baldwin's *The Fire Next Time;* see Kilson, in Glazer and Moynihan (1975).

31 St Clair Drake: 'The social and economic status of the Negro in the United States', in Beteille (1969).

32 See Mazrui (1978) on this comparison.

9 'Neo-nationalism'

1 For these and many others in Europe (69 in all), see J. Krejci: 'Ethnic problems in Europe', in Giner and Archer (1978).

2 As witness the decline in support for Scottish separatism as put forward

by the SNP, both in the referendum and in the national (1979) and local elections; and the rejection by 59.5% to 40.4% of Levesque's (1980) referendum on 'sovereignty-association' for Quebec. But note, also, that the percentage of supporters for Scottish and Quebecois autonomy remained fairly constant.

3 W. Petersen: 'On the subnations of Western Europe', in Glazer and Moynihan (1975), esp. 198–208.

4 This is the label given by Nairn (1977) and discussed, critically, by Hobsbawm (1977).

5 W. Connor: 'Ethnonationalism in the First World: The present in historical perspective', in Esman (1977), 43.

6 This loss has not been as complete as might be supposed, in some cases. Thus France and Britain have maintained both political and economic links, as 'senior partners', if not as outright 'neo-colonialist' powers, especially in Africa. They have been aided in this by the role of multinational companies operating from France or Britain, or from the United States. For the African case, see Markovitz (1977), 87–97; and Amin (1973).

7 On this geopolitical shift, see Barraclough (1967).

8 The other being, according to Poggi (1978), ch. 1, State regulation of rewards and values within the community and the maintenance of law and order (see above, Ch. 4, page 76).

9 On these, see Marwick (1974), 63–8, 161–3.

10 In England, the Robbins Report on Higher Education of 1964 was designed to meet the demand for professional and academic skills by vastly expanding the tertiary sector of education; but economic outlets and the occupational system failed to keep pace with educational production, especially after the energy crisis of 1974 and ensuing recessions. Much of the discontent generated by economic insecurity in the 1970s has fallen on immigrant groups in Britain, and on 'guest workers' on the Continent, as witnessed by the 1974 Schwarzenbach referendum in Switzerland. On labour migrations in Northern and Western Europe, see S. Giner and J. Salcedo: 'Migrant workers in European social structures', in Giner and Archer (1978).

11 Connor, in Esman (1977), 27–8.

12 See Reece (1979) on Breton emigration. On the question of universities as the seat of Welsh ethnic nationalism, see Morgan (1971), 161–2; and on the university of Louvain's difficulties in 1968, see Petersen, in Glazer and Moynihan (1975), 205–6. There have also been complaints about the lack of a university in Corsica; and, in another context, there was a revival of Croat nationalism in the mid-1960s centred on Zagreb university, which led to the 1971 crisis of Croatian Party leadership, see Snyder (1976), 157–60, and S. Bridges: 'Some causes of political change in modern Yugoslavia', in Esman (1977).

13 On Napoleon's exchange of Corsican for French loyalty, see Markham (1954), ch. 1; Bretons, Irish and Welsh suffered under these negative stereotypes, see S. Berger: 'Bretons and Jacobins: Reflections on French re-

gional ethnicity', in Esman (1977), 159–60, 166–7; and Hechter (1975), 74–7.

14 Cited in Mayo (1974), 45.

15 On Corsica, see Savigear (1977); and on Brittany, see Mayo (1974), ch. 4.

16 On this state and its theoretical justifications, see Coulon (1978).

17 Indeed, nationalist movements themselves tend to present essentially social and cultural, or political, demands and problems in largely economic terms, in order to carry conviction; and the latter problems tend to be translated by many analysts into economic language. For an attempt, only partly successful, to allow for so-called 'psychic needs' and costs within an overall economic framework, see H. G. Johnson (1968), ch. 1.

18 On this process, see Bendix (1964).

19 For this thesis, see A. Lijphart: 'Political theories and the explanation of ethnic conflict in the western world: Falsified predictions and plausible postdictions', in Esman (1977). For a similar analysis of the British scene in the 1970s, see Balsom (1976).

20 Plaid Cymru: *Action for Wales*, Denbigh, n.d., 17, cited in Hechter (1975), 304.

21 On Sultan Galiev, see Bennigsen and Lemercier-Quelquejay (1960).

22 For example, Sekou-Touré and Senghor, see Worsley (1964), Markovitz (1977), esp. 132–42 and Goody (1971), ch. 1. On integral nationalism in pre-1914 Europe, see Weiss (1977) and Nolte (1969), Part I.

23 Williams (1977).

24 Payne (1971), 50.

25 Balsom (1976), 26–7; Hechter (1975), ch. 9; Webb (1977), 127–38.

26 Berger, in Esman (1977), esp. 177.

27 Bell (1973).

28 On the repercussions of this 'second' industrial revolution, see Barraclough (1967), ch. 2; and Anderson (1972), 250–68.

29 W. R. Beer: 'The social class of ethnic activists in contemporary France', in Esman (1977), esp. 150–1.

30 *ibid.*, 149, 151.

31 Guindon (1964), for this 'quiet revolution'.

32 M. Rioux: 'Quebec: From a minority complex to majority behaviour', in Tobias and Woodhouse (1969).

33 M. Esman: 'Scottish nationalism, North Sea oil, and the British response', in Esman (1977), esp. 262–3; Begg and Stewart (1971). For a major study of the SNP, see Brand (1978). See also Webb (1977), 133–41.

34 See Pech (1976), esp. 343–7.

35 Rioux, in Tobias and Woodhouse (1969), 39–52.

36 J. Brazeau and E. Cloutier: 'Interethnic relations and the language issue in contemporary Canada: A general appraisal', in Esman (1977); and Spry (1971).

37 Berger, in Esman (1977), esp. 168–70.

38 See Payne (1971); and, for the history of Basque responses, D. Greenwood: 'Continuity in change: Spanish Basque ethnicity as a historical process', in Esman (1977).

39 On the PNV and early Basque nationalism, see Heiberg (1975).
40 Hanham (1969), esp. 175.
41 Esman (1977), 262–4, 268–70; also MacCormick (1970), especially the essay by D. Simpson: 'Independence: the economic issues'.
42 On the Welsh Language Society, see Williams (1977); and on the divisions in Wales, see Thomas and Williams (1978), and Hechter (1975), 270–1; also Morgan (1971), esp. 169–72.
43 For the Belgian case, see A. Zolberg: 'Splitting the difference: Federalisation without federalism in Belgium', in Esman, (1977).
44 Savigear (1977).
45 On the Jura question, see Petersen, in Glazer and Moynihan (1975), 193–5.
46 Berger, in Esman (1977), 165–6.
47 Expressed most forcibly in the thesis and evidence presented by Mayo (1974); see the comments of Nairn (1976) on this fear.
48 Fanon (1961); and for a critique of such revolutionary 'neo-romanticism', see McInnes (1972), chs. 6–8.
49 See Stone (1979) on the 'colonial' link; also McInnes (1972), ch. 6.
50 Mannoni (1956).
51 Frank (1967) and (1969); Wallerstein (1974).
52 See Berger, in Esman (1977), for the Breton case; also Reece (1979).
53 Geiss (1974).

10 Towards the scientific state

1 Seton-Watson (1945), and (1977), chs. 3–4.
2 On the linkage between interstate, state and economic levels, see Spanier (1972); and on the multinationals, see Markovitz (1977), ch. 3.
3 J. Porter: 'Ethnic pluralism in Canadian perspective', in Glazer and Moynihan (1975), esp. 289–98.
4 Examples are the 1974 revolution in Portugal, and the renewal regime of the mid-1960s in Cambodia.
5 Porter, in Glazer and Moynihan (1975), 299.
6 S. Giner and J. Salcedo: 'Migrant workers in European social structures', in Giner and Archer (1978).
7 A. Greeley and W. C. McCready: 'The transmission of cultural heritages: the case of the Irish and the Italians', in Glazer and Moynihan (1975); also Porter, in Glazer and Moynihan (1975), 194–5.
8 E. Kamenka: 'Political nationalism – the evolution of an idea', in Kamenka (1976); and Kohn (1967).
9 As with Tito or Ho Chi Minh or Ben-Gurion.
10 For the West Indian case of mass participation in nationalist movements, see W. Bell (1967).
11 Weber (1947) emphasises both the disenchantment and the role of intellectuals as bearers of cultural values of the community; in the latter context, intellectuals stand opposed to that process of 'rationalisation', which they generally facilitate.

12 See Lefebvre (1947); and Cobban (1965).

13 An example of tension between the bureaucratic state and the sentiments of nationality is provided by mid-nineteenth-century Tsarist Russia, see Rogger (1962).

14 See Mayo (1974); and Berger, in Esman (1977), 168–9.

15 On the European case, see Galtung (1973). In America, the Administration regularly resorts to technical and academic 'advisers'; and in both France and Lebanon, technocrats have formed governments recently.

16 For this dilemma, see Friedmann (1967), chs. 5, 9–10.

17 See Leiden and Schmitt (1968), chs. 7–8, on the Mexican and Turkish revolutions and their ideological consequences.

18 In a sense, this compromise is one aspect of a broader limitation on revolutionary change imposed by enduring traditions of values and institutions; see Smelser (1962) and Rudolph and Rudolph (1967).

19 Examples are mid-nineteenth-century Denmark and Norway, see Elviken (1931).

20 See P. van den Berghe: 'Ethnicity: The African Experience', *International Social Science Journal* 23, 1971, 515, cited in D. Bell: 'Ethnicity and social change', in Glazer and Moynihan (1975).

Bibliography

vwvwvwvwvwvwvwvwvwvwvwvwvwvwvwvwvwvwvwvwvwvwvwvwvwvwvwvwvwvwvwvwvwvwvwvwvwv

Abun-Nasr, J. (1966). 'The Salafiyya movement in Morocco: the religious bases of the Moroccan nationalist movement', in Wallerstein (1966)

Akzin, B. (1964). *State and nation*, Hutchinson, London

Alavi, H. (1972). 'The state in post-colonial societies – Pakistan and Bangladesh', *New Left Review* 74, 59–81

Alworth, E. (ed.) (1967). *Central Asia: a century of Russian rule*, Columbia University Press, New York

Amin, Samir (1973). *Neo-colonialism in West Africa*, Penguin, Harmondsworth

Anchor, R. (1967). *The enlightenment tradition*, Harper and Row, New York, Evanston and London

Anderson, C. W., von der Mehden, F. R. and Young, C. (1967). *Issues of political development*, Prentice-Hall, Englewood Cliffs

Anderson, M. S. (1972). *The ascendancy of Europe, 1815–1914*, Longman, London

Anderson, P. (1974). *Lineages of the absolutist state*, New Left Books, London

Andrewes, A. (1956). *The Greek tyrants*, Hutchinson University Library, London

  (1965). 'The growth of the city state', in Lloyd-Jones (1965)

Antoni, C. (1959). *From history to sociology*, trans. H. V. White, Wayne State University Press, Detroit

Archer, M. and Vaughan, M. (1971). *Social conflict and educational change in England and France, 1789–1848*, Cambridge University Press, Cambridge

Argyle, W. J. (1969). 'European nationalism and African tribalism', in Gulliver (1969)

  (1976). 'Size and scale as factors in the development of nationalist movements', in A. D. Smith (1976)

Armstrong, J. (1963). *Ukrainian nationalism*, 2nd edn, Columbia University Press, New York and London

Aron, R. (1966). *Peace and war*, Weidenfeld and Nicolson, London

  (1957). *The opium of the intellectuals*, Doubleday and Co., New York

Ashworth, G. (1977/78). *World minorities*, vol. I (1977), vol. II (1978), Quartermaine House Ltd, Sunbury, Middlesex

Avineri, S. (ed.) (1969). *Karl Marx on colonialism and modernisation*, Anchor Books, New York

Bacon, H. (1961). *Barbarians in Greek tragedy*, Yale University Press, New Haven

Bibliography

Balsom, D. (1976). 'Nationalism in Britain', *Inter-State* No. 1, 1975–6, 25–28

Barnard, F. M. (1965). *Herder's social and political thought: from enlightenment to nationalism*, Clarendon Press, Oxford

(1969). 'Culture and political development: Herder's suggestive insights', *American Political Science Review* 62, 379–97

Baron, S. W. (1960). *Modern nationalism and religion*, Meridian Books, New York

(1964). *The Russian Jew under Czars and Soviets*, Macmillan, New York

Barraclough, G. (1967). *An introduction to contemporary history*, Penguin, Harmondsworth

Barth, F. (ed.) (1969). *Ethnic groups and boundaries*, Little, Brown and Co., Boston

Barzun, J. (1932). *The French race: Theories of its origins and their social and political implications prior to the Revolution*, Columbia University Studies, New York

Beales, D. (1971). *The Risorgimento and the unification of Italy*, Allen and Unwin, London

Beckett, J. C. (1971). 'Northern Ireland', *Journal of Contemporary History* 6/1, 121–34 (Nationalism and Separatism)

Begg, H. M. and Stewart, J. A. (1971). 'The nationalist movement in Scotland', *Journal of Contemporary History* 6/1, 135–52

Bell, D. (1973). *The coming of post-industrial society*, Basic Books, New York

Bell, W. (1967). *The democratic revolution in the West Indies*, Schenkman, Cambridge, Mass.

Beloff, M. (1954). *The age of absolutism, 1660–1815*, Hutchinson, London

Ben-David, J. (1963/64). *Professions in the class system of present-day societies*, A Trend Report and Bibliography, *Current Sociology* 12/3

Bendix, R. (1964). *Nation-building and citizenship*, Wiley, New York

Bennigsen, A., and Lemercier-Quelquejay, C. (1960). *Les mouvements nationaux chez les musulmans de la Russie*, Mouton, Paris

(1966). *Islam in the Soviet Union*, Pall Mall Press, London

Ben-Sasson, H. H. and Ettinger, S. (1971). *Jewish society through the ages*, Vallentine, Mitchell and Co., London

Berger, S. (1972). 'Bretons, Basques, Scots, and other European nations', *Journal of Interdisciplinary History* 3, 167–75

Berkes, N. (1964). *The development of secularism in Turkey*, McGill University Press, Montreal

Berlin, I. (1976). *Vico and Herder*, The Hogarth Press, London

(1979). *Against the current*, The Hogarth Press, London

Bermant, C. and Weitzman, M. (1979). *Ebla, an archaeological enigma*, Weidenfeld and Nicolson, London

Beteille, A. (ed.) (1969). *Social inequality*, Penguin, Harmondsworth

Binder, L. (1964). *The ideological revolution in the Middle East*, Wiley, New York

Birch, A. (1977). *Political integration and disintegration in the British Isles*, Allen and Unwin, London

Bibliography

Blau, J. L. (1976). *Judaism in America*, University of Chicago Press, Chicago and London

Blau, J. L. *et al.* (eds.) (1959). *Essays in Jewish life and thought*, Columbia University Press, New York

Bloomfield, L. P. and Leiss, A. C. (1969). *Controlling small wars*, Knopf, New York

Bolgar, R. R. (1971). *Classical influences on European culture*, Cambridge University Press, Cambridge

Bond, B. and Roy, R. (eds.) (1975). *War and society*, Croom Helm, London

Bracey, J., Meier, A. and Rudwick, E. (eds.) (1970). *Black nationalism in America*, Bobbs-Merrill, Indianapolis and New York

Braidwood, R. and Willey, G. (eds.) (1962). *Courses towards urban life*, Aldine Publishing Company, New York

Bramson, L. and Goethals, G. L. (eds.) (1964). *War, studies from psychology, sociology, anthropology*, Basic Books, New York and London

Brand, J. (1978). *The national movement in Scotland*, Routledge, London

Brinton, C. (1952). *The anatomy of revolution*, Vintage Books, New York

Brotz, H. (1964). *The black Jews of Harlem*, Schocken Books, New York
  (ed.) (1966). *Negro social and political thought, 1850–1920*, Basic Books, New York and London

Brock, P. (1976). *The Slovak national awakening*, Eastern European Monographs, Toronto

Bruford, W. H. (1965). *Germany in the eighteenth century*, Cambridge University Press, Cambridge

Burgess, E. (1978). 'The resurgence of ethnicity', *Ethnic and Racial Studies* 1/3, 265–85

Cady, J. (1958). *A history of modern Burma*, Cornell University Press, Ithaca

Cahnmann, W. (1944). 'Religion and nationality', *American Journal of Sociology* 49, 524–9

Campbell, J. K. and Sherrard, P. (1968). *Modern Greece*, Benn, London

Carmichael, J. (1967). *The shaping of the Arabs*, Macmillan, New York and London

Carmichael, S. and Hamilton, C. V. (1967). *Black Power*, Vintage Books, New York

Clogg, R. (ed.) (1973). *The struggle for Greek independence*, Macmillan, London

Cobban, A. (1964). *Rousseau and the modern state*, 2nd edn, Allen and Unwin, London
  (1965). *The Social interpretation of the French Revolution*, Cambridge University Press, Cambridge
  (1957–63). *A history of modern France*, 3 vols., Penguin, Harmondsworth

Confino, M. (1972). 'On intellectuals and intellectual traditions in eighteenth- and nineteenth-century Russia', *Daedalus* 101/2, 117–49

Connor, W. (1972). 'Nation-building or nation-destroying?', *World Politics* 24, 319–55
  (1973). ''The politics of ethnonationalism', *Journal of International Affairs* 27, 1–21

(1978). 'A nation is a nation, is a state, is an ethnic group, is a . . .', *Ethnic and Racial Studies* 1/4, 377–400

Cottam, R. (1964). *Nationalism in Iran*, University of Pittsburgh Press, Pittsburgh

Coulborn, R. (1959). *The origin of civilised societies*, Princeton University Press, Princeton

Coulon, C. (1978). 'French political science and regional diversity', *Ethnic and Racial Studies* 1/1, 80–99

Crane, R. I. (1961). 'Problems of divergent developments within Indian nationalism, 1895–1905', in Sakai (1961)

Crowder, M. (1968). *West Africa under colonial rule*, Hutchinson and Co., London

Cruse, H. (1967). *The crisis of the Negro intellectual*, W. H. Allen, London

Cummings, F. J. (1975). 'Painting under Louis XVI, 1774–89', in Detroit (1975)

Davidson, B., Slovo, J. and Wilkinson, A. R. (1976). *Southern Africa, the new politics of revolution*, Penguin, Harmondsworth

Davies, I. (1966). *African trade unions*, Penguin, Harmondsworth

Davis, H. B. (1965). 'Nations, colonies and classes: the position of Marx and Engels', *Science and Society* 29, 26–43

(1967). *Nationalism and socialism: Marxist and labour theories of nationalism*, Monthly Review Press, New York and London

Davison, R. (1963). *Reform in the Ottoman Empire, 1856–76*, Princeton University Press, Princeton

Dawn, C. E. (1961). 'From Ottomanism to Arabism: The origin of an ideology', *Review of Politics* 23, 379–400

Debray, R. (1977). 'Marxism and the national question', *New Left Review* 105, 20–41

De Klerk, W. A. (1975). *The puritans in Africa*, Penguin, Harmondsworth

De Reuck, A. and Knight, J. (eds.) (1967). *Caste and race*, Ciba Foundation, London

Desai, A. R. (1954). *The social background of Indian nationalism*, Bombay Publishing Company, Bombay

Detroit (1975). *French painting 1774–1830: the age of revolution*, Wayne State University Press, Detroit, for the Institute of Arts

Deutsch, K. W. (1961). 'Social mobilisation and political development', *American Political Science Review* 55, 493–514

(1963). 'Nation-building and national development: some issues for political research', in Deutsch and Foltz (1963)

(1966). *Nationalism and social communication*, 2nd edn, MIT Press, New York

(1969). *Nationalism and its alternatives*, Knopf, New York

Deutsch, K. W. and Foltz, W. J. (eds.) (1963). *Nation-Building*, Atherton, New York

Dinur, Ben-Zion (1969). *Israel and the diaspora*, Jewish Publication Society of America, Philadelphia

Doob, L. (1964). *Patriotism and nationalism: their psychological foundations*, Yale University Press, New Haven

Bibliography

Draper, T. (1970). *The rediscovery of black nationalism*, Secker and Warburg, London

Dubnow, S. (1958). *Nationalism and history*, ed. K. S. Pinson, Jewish Publication Society of American, Philadelphia

Easton, D. (1953). *The political system*, Knopf, New York

Edmonds, C. J. (1971). 'Kurdish nationalism', *Journal of Contemporary History* 6/1, 87–107

Eisenstadt, S. N. (1964). 'Social change, differentiation and evolution', *American Journal of Sociology* 29, 375–86

   (1970). *Readings in social evolution and development*, Pergamon Press, Oxford and London

   (1972). 'Intellectuals and tradition', *Daedalus* 101, 1–19

   (1973). *Tradition, change and modernity*, Wiley, New York

Elviken, A. (1931). 'The genesis of Norwegian nationalism', *Journal of Modern History* 3, 365–91

Embree, A. (1972). *India's search for national identity*, Knopf, New York

Emerson, R. (1960a). *From empire to nation*, Harvard University Press, Cambridge, Mass.

   (1960b). 'Nationalism and political development', *Journal of Politics* 22, 3–28

Engels, F. (1859). *Po und Rhein*, in Marx and Engels (1955–63), XIII, 678

Enloe, C. (1980). *Ethnic soldiers*, Penguin, Harmondsworth

Esman, M. J. (ed.) (1977). *Ethnic conflict in the western world*, Cornell University Press, Ithaca and London

Essien-Udom, E. (1962). *Black nationalism*, Chicago University Press, Chicago

Fanon, F. (1961). *Les damnés de la terre*, Maspero, Paris

Feuer, L. S. (1975). *Ideology and the ideologists*, Basil Blackwell, Oxford

Fieldhouse, D. K. (ed.) (1967). *The theory of capitalist imperialism*, Longman, London

Finley, M. I. (ed.) (1960). *Slavery in classical antiquity*, Heffer and Sons, Cambridge

Fondation Hardt (1962). *Grecs et Barbares*, Entretiens sur l'antiquité classique VIII, Fondation Hardt, Geneva

Forrest, W. G. (1966). *The emergence of Greek democracy*, Weidenfeld and Nicolson, London

Francis, E. K. (1968). 'The ethnic factor in nation-building', *Social Forces* 46

   (1976). *Interethnic relations, an essay in sociological theory*, Elsevier Scientific Publishing Co., New York

Frank, A. G. (1967). *Capitalism and underdevelopment in Latin America*, Monthly Review Press, New York

   (1969). *Latin America: underdevelopment or revolution?*, Monthly Review Press, New York

Frankfort, H. (1948). *Kingship and the gods*, Chicago University Press, Chicago

   (1954). *The birth of civilisation in the Near East*, Anchor Books, New York

Bibliography

Frazee, C. A. (1969). *The Orthodox Church and independent Greece, 1821–52,* Cambridge University Press, Cambridge

Frazier, F. (1948). *The Negro in the United States,* Macmillan, New York

Friedmann, G. (1967). *The end of the Jewish people?,* Hutchinson, London

Friedrich, C. J. (1962). *The age of the baroque, 1610–1660,* Harper and Row, New York

Frye, R. N. (1966). *The heritage of Persia,* Mentor Books, New York and Toronto

Furnivall, J. S. (1948). *Colonial policy and practice,* Cambridge University Press, Cambridge

Galtung, J. (1973). *The European community: A superpower in the making,* Allen and Unwin, London

Gans, H. J. (1979). 'Symbolic ethnicity', *Ethnic and Racial Studies* 2/1, 1–20

Gay, P. (1970/1973). *The Enlightenment, An interpretation,* vol. I (1970), vol. II (1973), Wildwood House, London

Geertz, C. (1963). 'The integrative revolution', in C. Geertz (ed.): *Old societies and new states: the quest for modernity in Asia and Africa,* Free Press, New York

Geipel, J. (1970). *The Europeans: The people – today and yesterday – their origins and interrelations,* Pegasus, New York

Geiss, I. (1974). *The pan-African movement,* Methuen and Co., London

Gella, A. (ed.) (1976). *The intelligentsia and the intellectuals,* Sage Publications, Beverley Hills

Gellner, E. (1964). *Thought and change,* Weidenfeld and Nicolson, London
(1973). 'Scale and nation', *Philosophy of the Social Sciences* 3, 1–17

Gellner, E. and Ionescu, G. (eds.) (1970). *Populism, its meanings and national characteristics,* Weidenfeld and Nicolson, London

Gibb, H. A. R. (1947). *Modern trends in Islam,* Chicago University Press, Chicago

Giner, S. and Archer, M. S. (eds.) (1978). *Contemporary Europe, social structures and cultural patterns,* Routledge and Kegan Paul, London

Glazer, N. and Moynihan, D. P. (1964). *Beyond the melting pot,* MIT Press, Cambridge, Mass.
(eds.) (1975). *Ethnicity, theory and experience,* Harvard University Press, Cambridge, Mass. and London

Goldhagen, E. (ed.) (1968). *Ethnic minorities in the Soviet Union,* Praeger, New York

Goody, J. (1971). *Technology, tradition and the state in Africa,* Hutchinson University Library for Africa, London

Gouldner, A. (1952). 'Red Tape as a social problem', in Merton (1952)
(1979). *The future of intellectuals and the rise of the new class,* Macmillan, London

Grant, M. (1973). *The Jews in the Roman world,* Weidenfeld and Nicolson, London

Gray, C. (1971). *The Russian experiment in art, 1863–1922,* Thames and Hudson, London

Bibliography

Gray Cowan, L. (1964). *The dilemmas of African independence*, Walker and Co., New York

Grayzel, S. (1968). *A history of the Jews*, new rev. edn, Mentor Books, New York

Greeley, A. (1974). *Ethnicity in the United States*, John Wiley, New York

Greenberg, L. (1976). *The Jews in Russia*, 2 vols., Schocken Books, New York

Griffin, C. (1964). 'An essay on regionalism and nationalism in Latin American historiography', *Journal of World History* 8, 371–9

Grimal, P. (1968). *Hellenism and the rise of Rome*, Weidenfeld and Nicolson, London

Grunebaum, G. von (1964). *Modern Islam*, Vintage Books, New York

Guindon, H. (1964). 'Social unrest, social class and Quebec's bureaucratic revolution', *Queen's Quarterly* 81, 148–62

Gulliver, P. (ed.) (1969). *Tradition and transition in East Africa*, Pall Mall Press, London

Guthrie, W. K. C. (1968). *The Greeks and their gods*, Methuen, London

Haim, S. (ed.) (1962). *Arab nationalism, an anthology*, University of California Press, Berkeley and Los Angeles

Halpern, M. (1963). *The politics of social change in the Middle East and North Africa*, Princeton University Press, Princeton

Halsey, A. H. (1978). 'Ethnicity: a primordial social bond?', *Ethnic and Racial Studies* 1/1, 124–8

Hamerow, T. (1958). *Restoration, revolution, reaction; Economics and politics in Germany, 1815–71*, Princeton University Press, Princeton

Hanham, H. J. (1969). *Scottish nationalism*, Faber and Faber, London

Harrison, S. S. (1960). *India, the most dangerous decades*, Princeton University Press, Princeton

Harvie, C. (1977). *Scotland and nationalism: Scottish society and politics, 1707–1977*, Allen and Unwin, London

Hechter, M. (1975). *Internal colonialism: The Celtic fringe in British national development, 1536–1966*, Routledge and Kegan Paul, London
   (1978). 'Group formation and the cultural division of labour', *American Journal of Sociology* 84, 293–318

Hechter, M. and Levi, M. (1979). 'The comparative analysis of ethnoregional movements', *Ethnic and Radical Studies* 2/3, 260–74

Heiberg, M. (1975). 'Insiders/outsiders: Basque nationalism', *European Journal of Sociology* XVI, 169–93

Heimsath, C. (1964). *Indian nationalism and Hindu social reform*, Princeton University Press, Princeton

Heraud, G. (1963). *L'Europe des ethnies*, Presses d'Europe, Paris

Herberg, W. (1960). *Protestant–Catholic–Jew*, Doubleday, New York

Herbert, R. (1972). *David, Voltaire, Brutus and the French Revolution*, Allen Lane, London

Hertzberg, A. (ed.) (1960). *The Zionist idea, a reader*, Meridian Books, New York

224

Bibliography

Hobsbawm, E. (1971). 'The attitude of popular classes to national movements of independence', in *Mouvements nationaux d'indépendance et classes populaires au XIX' et XX' siècles en occident et orient*, tome I, Librairie Armand Colin, Paris

(1977). 'Some reflections on *The break-up of Britain*', *New Left Review* 105, 3–23

Hodgkin, T. (1956). *Nationalism in colonial Africa*, Muller, London

(1961). 'A note on the language of African nationalism', *St Antony's Papers* 10, 22–40

(1964). 'The relevance of "Western" ideas in the derivation of African nationalism', in J. R. Pennock (ed.): *Self-government in modernising societies*, Prentice-Hall, Englewood Cliffs

Holborn, H. (1964). *A history of modern Germany, 1648–1840*, Alfred A. Knopf, New York

Honour, H. (1968). *Neo-classicism*, Penguin, Harmondsworth

Hostler, C. (1953). *Turkism and the Soviets*, Praeger, New York

Hourani, A. (1970). *Arabic thought in the liberal age, 1798–1939*, Oxford University Press, London and New York

Howard, M. (1976). *War in European history*, Oxford University Press, London

Humphreys, R. A. and Lynch, J. (eds.) (1965). *The origins of the Latin American revolutions*, Knopf, New York

Huntington, S. P. (1968). *Political order in changing societies*, Yale University Press, New Haven and London

Huszar, G. B. de (ed.) (1960). *The intellectuals*, Free Press, New York

Irwin, D. (1966). *English neo-classical art*, Faber and Faber, London

(ed.) (1972). *Winckelmann*, Phaidon, London

Jacobs, A. (1972). *A short history of music*, Penguin, Harmondsworth

Jacoby, H. (1973). *The bureaucratisation of the world*, trans. E. Kanes, University of California Press, Berkeley and Los Angeles

Janowitz, M. (1964). 'Military elites and the study of war', in Bramson and Goethals

Jelavich, B. and C. (eds.) (1963). *The Balkans in transition; Essays on the development of Balkan life and politics since the eighteenth century*, University of California Press, Berkeley

Johnson, C. (1963). *Peasant nationalism and communist power; the emergence of revolutionary China, 1937–45*, Stanford University Press, Stanford

Johnson, H. G. (ed.) (1968). *Economic nationalism in old and new states*, Allen and Unwin, London

July, R. (1967). *The origins of modern African thought*, Faber and Faber, London

Kamenka, E. (ed.) (1976). *Nationalism, the nature and evolution of an idea*, Edward Arnold, London

Karal, E. Z. (1965). 'Turkey: from oriental empire to modern national state', in G. S. Metraux and F. Crouset (eds.): *The New Asia*, Mentor, New York and Toronto

Bibliography

Katz, J. (1958). 'Jewry and Judaism in the nineteenth century', *Journal of World History* 4, 881–900

Katz, J. (1971). 'The Jewish national movement: a sociological analysis', in Ben-Sasson and Ettinger (1971)

Katzenstein, P. (1977). 'Ethnic political conflict in South Tyrol', in Esman (1977)

Kauffmann, Y. (1961). *The religion of Israel,* Allen and Unwin, London

Kautsky, J. H. (ed.) (1962). *Political change in underdeveloped societies,* Wiley, New York

(1968). *Communism and the politics of development,* Wiley, New York

Keddie, N. (1962). 'Religion and irreligion in early Iranian nationalism', *Comparative Studies in Society and History* 4, 265–95

(1966). *Religion and rebellion in Iran: the tobacco protest of 1892,* Cass, London

Kedourie, E. (1960). *Nationalism,* Hutchinson, London

(1966). *Afghani and Abduh: An essay on religious unbelief and political activism in modern Islam,* Cass, London and New York

(ed.) (1971). *Nationalism in Asia and Africa,* Weidenfeld and Nicolson, London

Keller, S. (1968). *Beyond the ruling class,* Random House, New York

Kemilainen, A. (1964). *Nationalism; Problems concerning the word, concept and classification,* Kustantajat Publishers, Yvaskyla

Kerr, C. *et al.* (1962). *Industrialism and industrial man,* Harvard University Press, Cambridge, Mass.

Kiernan, V. (1964). 'The new nation-states', *New Left Review* 30, 86–95

(1976). 'Nationalist movements and social classes', in A. D. Smith (1976)

Kilson, M. (1958). 'Nationalism and social classes in British West Africa', *Journal of Politics* 20, 368–87

King, P. (1976). 'Tribe: Conflicts in meaning and usage', *The West African Journal of Sociology and Political Science* 1/2, 1976, 186–94

Kitchen, M. (1976). *Fascism,* Macmillan, London

Kohler, A. (1970). *Rousseau and nationalism,* Basic Books, New York and London

Kohn, H. (1940). 'The origins of English nationalism', *Journal of the History of Ideas* I, 69–94

(1944/67). *The idea of nationalism,* Collier-Macmillan, New York

(1957). *Nationalism and liberty, the Swiss example,* Macmillan, New York

(1960). *Pan-Slavism,* 2nd rev. edn, Vintage Books, Random House, New York

(1961a). *Prophets and peoples,* Macmillan, New York

(1961b). *American nationalism; an interpretative essay,* Macmillan, New York

(1965). *The mind of Germany,* Macmillan, London

(1967). *Prelude to nation-states: The French and German experience, 1789–1815,* van Nostrand, Princeton

Koht, H. (1947). 'The dawn of nationalism in Europe', *American Historical Review* 52, 265–80

Bibliography

Kramer, J. and Leventman, S. (1961). *The children of the gilded ghetto*, Yale University Press, New Haven

Kramer, S. N. (1963). *The Sumerians*, Chicago University Press, Chicago

Laclau, E. (1971). 'Imperialism in Latin America', *New Left Review* 67, 19–38

Lartichaux, J-Y. (1977). 'Linguistic politics during the French Revolution', *Diogenes* 97, 65–84

Lefebvre, G. (1947). *The coming of the French Revolution*, Vintage Books, Random House, New York

Legum, C. (1962). *Pan-Africanism: A short political guide*, Pall Mall Press, London and Dunmow

Leiden, C. and Schmitt, K. M. (1968). *The politics of violence: Revolution in the modern world*, Prentice-Hall, Englewood Cliffs

Lenin, V. I. (1916). 'Critical remarks on the national question'
(1948). 'Imperialism, the highest stage of capitalism', both in *Collected works of Lenin*, Foreign Languages Publishing House, Moscow

Lerner, D. (1958). *The passing of traditional society*, Free Press, New York

Levenson, J. (1958). *Confucian China and its modern fate*, Routledge and Kegan Paul, London
(1959). *Liang Ch'i Ch'ao and the mind of modern China*, University of California Press, Berkeley and Los Angeles

Lewis, B. (1968). *The emergence of modern Turkey*, 2nd edn, Oxford University Press, London

Lewis, I. M. (1965). *The modern history of Somaliland: From nation to state*, Weidenfeld and Nicolson, London

Lewis, W. A. (1965). *Politics in West Africa*, Allen and Unwin, London

Lewis, W. H. (ed.) (1965). *French-speaking Africa: The search for identity*, Walker, New York

Lijphart, A. (1969). 'Consociational democracy', *World Politics* 21, 207–25

Lipset, S. M. (1960). *Political man: the social bases of politics*, Doubleday, Garden City, New York

Little, K. (1965). *West African urbanisation*, Cambridge University Press, Cambridge

Lively, J. (ed.) (1966). *The Enlightenment*, Longman, London

Lloyd, P. C. (ed.) (1966). *New elites in tropical Africa*, Oxford University Press, London
(1967). *Africa in social change*, Penguin, Harmondsworth

Lloyd-Jones, H. (ed.) (1965). *The Greek world*, Penguin, Harmondsworth

Lloyd Warner, W. and Srole, L. (1945). *The social systems of American ethnic groups*, Yale University Press, New Haven

Loquin, J. (1912). *La peinture d'histoire en France de 1747 à 1785*, Henri Laurens, Paris

Lynch, H. R. (1967). *Edward Wilmot Blyden, pan-negro patriot, 1832–1912*, Oxford University Press, Oxford, London and New York

Lyon, J. (1980). 'Marxism and ethno-nationalism in Guinea-Bissau, 1956–76', *Ethnic and Racial Studies* 3/2, 156–68

Maccoby, H. (1974). *Revolution in Judea*, Ocean Books, London

Bibliography

MacCormick, N. (ed.) (1970). *The Scottish debate, essays in Scottish nationalism*, Oxford University Press, London

McCulley, B. T. (1966). *English education and the origins of Indian nationalism*, Smith, Gloucester, Mass.

McInnes, N. (1972). *The western Marxists*, Alcove Press, London

McNeill, W. H. (1963). *The rise of the West*, University of Chicago Press, Chicago

McRoberts, K. (1979). 'Internal colonialism: the case of Quebec', *Ethnic and racial studies* 2/3, 293–318

Malinowski, B. (1941). 'An anthropological analysis of war', *American Journal of Sociology* 46, 521–50

Mannheim, K. (1936). *Ideology and utopia*, Routledge and Kegan Paul, London

  (1940). *Man and society in an age of reconstruction*, Routledge and Kegan Paul, London

Mannoni, O. (1956). *Prospero and Caliban*, Methuen, London

Markham, F. (1954). *Napoleon and the awakening of Europe*, Penguin, Harmondsworth

Markovitz, I. L. (1977). *Class and power in Africa*, Prentice-Hall, Englewood Cliffs

Marwick, A. (1974). *War and social change in the twentieth century*, Methuen, London

Marx, K. and Engels, F. (1959). *Basic writings on politics and philosophy*, ed. L. S. Feuer, Anchor Books, New York

  (1955–63). *Werke*, Marx–Engels–Lenin Institute, Moscow

  (1963). *The German ideology*, International Publishers, New York

Masur, G. (1966). *Nationalism in Latin America*, Macmillan, New York

Matossian, M. (1958). 'Ideologies of "delayed industrialisation": some tensions and ambiguities', *Economic development and cultural change* 6, 217–28

Mayo, P. (1974). *The roots of identity: Three national movements in contemporary European politics*, Allen Lane, London

Mazrui, A. (1978). 'Negritude, the talmudic tradition and intellectual performance of Blacks and Jews', *Ethnic and Racial Studies* 1/1, 19–36

Mazrui, A. and Rotberg, R. (eds.) (1970). *Protest and power in black Africa*, Oxford University Press, New York

Mercier, P. (1965). 'On the meaning of "tribalism" in black Africa', in van den Berghe (1965)

Merton, R. K. *et al.* (eds.) (1952). *Reader in bureaucracy*, Free Press, New York

Mill, J. S. (1861). *Considerations on representative government*, Everyman's Library, J. M. Dent and Sons, London 1968

Misra, B. B. (1961). *The Indian middle classes; their growth in modern times*, Oxford University Press, London

Montagne, R. (1952). 'The "modern state" in Africa and Asia', *The Cambridge Journal* 5, 583–602.

Moody, T. W. (ed.) (1968). *The Fenian movement*, The Mercier Press, Cork

Moore, Barrington, Jr (1967). *The social origins of dictatorship and democracy*, Allen Lane, Penguin, London

Bibliography

Mordaunt Crook, J. (1972). *The Greek revival*, John Murray, London

Morgan, K. O. (1971). 'Welsh nationalism: the historical background', *Journal of Contemporary History* 6/1, 153–72

Morner, M. (1967). *Race mixture in the history of Latin America*, Little, Brown and Co., Boston

Moscati, S. (1962). *The face of the ancient Orient*, Anchor Books, New York

Mouzelis, N. (1978). *Modern Greece, facets of underdevelopment*, Macmillan, London

Munger, E. (1967). *Afrikaner and African nationalism: South African parallels and parameters*, Oxford University Press, London

Nadel, S. F. (1956). 'The concept of social elites', *International Social Science Bulletin* VIII, 413–24

Nairn, T. (1976). 'Scotland and Wales: notes on nationalist prehistory', *Planet* 34, 1–11

(1977). *The break-up of Britain: Crisis and neo-nationalism*, New Left Books, London

Nalbandian, L. (1963). *The Armenian revolutionary movement; the development of Armenian political parties through the nineteenth century*, University of California Press, Berkeley

Nettl, J. P. and Robertson, R. (1968). *International systems and the modernisation of societies*, Faber, London

Neuberger, B. (1976a). 'The African concept of Balkanisation', *Journal of Modern African Studies* XIII, 523–29

(1976b). 'The western nation-state in African perceptions of nation-building', *Asian and African Studies* 11, 241–61

(1977). 'State and nation in African thought', *Journal of African Studies* 4, 198–205

Nilsson, M. (1940). *Greek popular religion*, Columbia University Press, New York

Nisbet, R. (1968). *Tradition and revolt*, Random House, New York

(1969). *Social change and history*, Oxford University Press, Oxford, London and New York

Nolte, E. (1969). *Three faces of Fascism*, trans. L. Vennewitz, Mentor Books, New York and Toronto

Norman, E. (1973). *A history of modern Ireland*, Penguin, Harmondsworth

Noth, M. (1960). *The history of Israel*, Adam and Charles Black, London

Obeyesekere, G. (1968). 'Theodicy, sin and salvation in a sociology of Buddhism', in E. R. Leach (ed.): *Dialectic in Practical Religion*, Cambridge Papers in Social Anthropology No. 5, Cambridge

O'Brien, P. J. (1975). 'A critique of Latin American theories of dependency', in Oxaal, Barnett and Booth (1975)

Okun, H. (1967). 'Ossian in painting', *Journal of the Warburg and Courtauld Institutes* 30, 327–56

Olorunsola, V. (ed.) (1972). *The politics of cultural subnationalism in Africa*, Anchor Books, New York

Oxaal, I., Barnett, T. and Booth, D. (eds.) (1975). *Beyond the sociology of de-*

velopment, Routledge and Kegan Paul, London, Boston and Henley

Palloni, A. (1979). 'Internal colonialism or clientelistic politics? the case of Southern Italy', *Ethnic and Racial Studies* 2/3, 360–77

Palmer, R. R. (1940). 'The national idea in France before the Revolution', *Journal of the History of Ideas* I, 95–111

(1959). *The age of the democratic revolution*, Princeton University Press, Princeton

Parsons, T. (1964). 'Evolutionary universals', *American Sociological Review* 29, 339–57

(1966). *Societies, evolutionary and comparative perspectives*, Prentice-Hall, Englewood Cliffs

Payne, S. (1971). 'Catalan and Basque nationalism', *Journal of Contemporary History* 6/1, 15–51

Pech, S. (1976). 'The nationalist movements of the Austrian Slavs in 1848', *Social History* 9, 336–56

Pike, N. (ed.) (1964). *God and evil*, Prentice-Hall, Englewood Cliffs

Pipes, R. (ed.) (1961). *The Russian intelligentsia*, Columbia University Press, New York

Plamenatz, J. (1976). 'Two types of nationalism', in Kamenka (1976)

Plumb, J. H. (1965). *England in the eighteenth century*, Penguin, Harmonds-worth

Pocock, D. (1958). 'Notes on the interaction of English and Indian thought in the nineteenth century', *Journal of World History* 4, 833–48

Poggi, G. (1978). *The development of the modern state*, Hutchinson and Co., London

Popper, K. (1957). *The poverty of historicism*, Routledge and Kegan Paul, London

Porter, J. (1965). *The vertical mosaic*, University of Toronto Press, Toronto

Pritchard, J. B. (ed.) (1958). *The Ancient Near East*, Princeton University Press, Princeton

Reece, J. (1979). 'Internal colonialism: the case of Brittany', *Ethnic and Racial Studies* 2/3, 275–92

Robertson, A. and Stevens, D. (1968). *The pelican history of music*, vol. III, Penguin, Harmondsworth

Robinson, F. (1979). 'Islam and Muslim separatism', in Taylor and Yapp (1979)

Rogger, H. (1962). 'Nationalism and the state: A Russian dilemma', *Comparative Studies in Society and History* 4, 253–64

Ronen, D. (1979). *The quest for self-determination*, Yale University Press, New Haven and London

Rosberg, C. and Nottingham, J. (1966). *The myth of 'Mau Mau': Nationalism in Kenya*, Praeger, New York

Rosdolsky, R. (1964). 'Friedrich Engels und das Problem der "Geschichts-losen Völker" ', *Archiv für Sozialgeschichte* 4, Hanover 87–282

Rosenblum, R. (1967). *Transformations in late eighteenth century art*, Princeton University Press, Princeton

Bibliography

Rosh White, N. (1978). 'Ethnicity, culture and cultural pluralism', *Ethnic and Racial Studies* 1/2, 139–53

Rotberg, R. (1965). *The rise of nationalism in Central Africa,* Harvard University Press, Cambridge, Mass.

(1967). 'African nationalism: concept or confusion?', *Journal of Modern African Studies* 4, 33–46

Roux, J. (1964). *Ancient Iraq,* Penguin, Harmondsworth

Roxborough, I. (1976). 'Dependency theory in the sociology of development: some theoretical problems', *The West African Journal of Sociology and Political Science* 1/2, 116–33

(1979). *Theories of underdevelopment,* Macmillan, London

Rudolph, L. and Rudolph. S. (1967). *The modernity of tradition,* Chicago University Press, Chicago

Said, A. A. (1977) (ed.). *Ethnicity and US foreign policy,* Praeger, New York and London

Said, A. and Simmons, L. (eds.) (1976). *Ethnicity in an international context,* Transaction Books, New Brunswick

Sakai, R. A. (ed.) (1961). *Studies on Asia,* University of Nebraska Press, Lincoln

Sarkiss, H. (1937). 'The Armenian renaissance, 1500–1830', *Journal of Modern History* 9, 433–48

Sarkisyanz, E. (1964). *Buddhist backgrounds of the Burmese Revolution,* Nijhoff, The Hague

Saul, J. (1979). *The state and revolution in East Africa,* Heinemann, London

Savigear, P. (1977). 'Corsicans and the French connection', *New Society,* 10 February, 273–4

Scalapino, R. A. (ed.) (1969). *The communist revolution in Asia,* Prentice-Hall, Englewood Cliffs

Schermerhorn, R. (1970). *Comparative ethnic relations,* Random House, New York

Schlaifer, R. (1960). 'Greek theories of slavery from Homer to Aristotle', in Finley (1960)

Schmitt, C. (1963). *Der Begriff des politischen,* Duncker and Humbolt, Berlin

Schwab, G. (1947). *Gods and heroes,* trans. O. and E. Morwitz, George Routledge and Sons Ltd, London

Seal, A. (1968). *The emergence of Indian nationalism,* Cambridge University Press, Cambridge

Seton-Watson, H. (1945). *Eastern Europe between the Wars,* Cambridge University Press, Cambridge

(1951). 'Twentieth century revolutions', *Political Quarterly* 22, 251–65

(1960). *Neither war, nor peace,* Methuen, London

(1964). *Nationalism and communism,* Methuen, London

(1967). *The Russian Empire, 1801–1917,* Oxford University Press, London

(1971). 'Unsatisfied nationalisms', *Journal of Contemporary History* 6/1, 3–14

(1977). *Nations and states,* Methuen, London

(1978). *The imperialist revolutionaries,* Hoover Institution Press, Stanford

Bibliography

Shafer, B. C. (1938). 'Bourgeois nationalism in the pamphlets on the eve of the French Revolution', *Journal of Modern History* 10, 31–50

   (1955). *Nationalism, myth and reality,* Harcourt, Brace, New York

Shaheen, S. (1956). *The communist theory of self-determination,* Van Hoeve, The Hague

Shapiro, L. B. (1967). *Rationalism and nationalism in Russian nineteenth century political thought,* Yale University Press, New Haven and London

Sharabi, H. B. (1966). *Nationalism and revolution in the Arab world,* van Nostrand, Princeton

   (1970). *Arab intellectuals and the west: the formative years, 1875–1914,* John Hopkins Press, Baltimore and London

Sherwin-White, A. N. (1952). *Racial prejudice in imperial Rome,* Blackwell, Oxford

Shils, E. (1957). 'Primordial, personal, sacred and civil ties', *British Journal of Sociology* 7, 13–145

   (1960). 'The intellectuals in the political development of the new states', *World Politics* 12, 329–68

   (1972a). *The intellectuals and the powers, and other essays,* University of Chicago Press, Chicago

   (1972b). 'Intellectuals, tradition, and the tradition of intellectuals: some preliminary considerations', *Daedalus* 101, 21–34

Sigmund, P. E. (ed.) (1967). *The ideologies of the developing nations,* rev. edn, Praeger, New York

Simmel, G. (1964). *Conflict and the web of group affiliations,* Free Press, New York

Singh, K. (1963). *Prophet of Indian nationalism,* Allen and Unwin, London

Skocpol, T. (1979). *States and social revolutions,* Cambridge University Press, Cambridge

Smelser, N. J. (1962). *A theory of collective behaviour,* Routledge and Kegan Paul, London

   (1968). *Essays in sociological explanation,* Prentice-Hall, Englewood Cliffs

Smith, A. D. (1970). 'Modernity and evil: some sociological reflections on the problem of meaning', *Diogenes* 71, 65–80

   (1971). *Theories of nationalism,* Duckworth, London, and Harper and Row, New York

   (1972). 'Ethnocentrism, nationalism and social change', *International Journal of Comparative Sociology* xiii, 1–20

   (1973). *Nationalism,* A trend report and bibliography, *Current Sociology* 21/3, Mouton, The Hague

   (1973a). 'Nationalism and religion: the role of religious reform in the genesis of Arab and Jewish nationalism', *Archives de Sociologie des Religions* 35, 23–43

   (1973b). *The concept of social change,* Routledge and Kegan Paul, London and Boston

   (1976a). *Social change,* Longman, London and New York

   (ed.) (1976). *Nationalist movements,* Macmillan, London, and St Martin's Press, New York

Bibliography

(1978). 'The diffusion of nationalism', *British Journal of Sociology* 29, 234–48

(1979). *Nationalism in the twentieth century*, Martin Robertson and Co., Oxford

(1979a). 'The "historical revival" in late eighteenth century England and France', *Art History* 2/2, 156–78

(1979b). 'Towards a theory of ethnic separatism', *Ethnic and Racial Studies* 2/1, 21–37

forthcoming. 'War and ethnicity: The role of war in the formation, self-images and cohesion of ethnic communities'

Smith, D. E. (1963). *India as a secular state*, Princeton University Press, Princeton

(1965). *Religion and politics in Burma*, Princeton University Press, Princeton

(ed.) (1974). *Religion and political modernisation*, Yale University Press, New Haven

Snyder, L. (1954). *The meaning of nationalism*, Rutgers University Press, New Brunswick

(1976). *The varieties of nationalism, A comparative view*, The Dryden Press, Hinsdale, Illinois

Spanier, G. (1972). *Games nations play*, Thomas Nelson and Sons Ltd, London

Spry, G. (1971). 'Canada: Notes on two ideas of nation in confrontation', *Journal of Contemporary History* 6/1, 173–96

Stavrianos, L. S. (1957). 'Antecedents of the Balkan revolutions of the nineteenth century', *Journal of Modern History* 29, 333–48

(1961). *The Balkans since 1453*, Holt, New York

Steinberg, J. (1976). *Why Switzerland?*, Cambridge University Press, Cambridge

Stone, J. (1979). 'Introduction: Internal colonialism in comparative perspective', *Ethnic and Racial Studies* 2/3, 255–9

Strayer, J. (1963). 'The historical experience of nation-building in Europe', in Deutsch and Foltz (1963)

Sugar, P. F. and Lederer, I. J. (eds.) (1969). *Nationalism in Eastern Europe*, Far Eastern and Russian Institute, University of Washington, Seattle

Svensson, F. (1978). 'The final crisis of tribalism: comparative ethnic policy on the American and Russian frontiers', *Ethnic and Racial Studies* 1/1, 100–23

Syme, R. (1970). *Colonial elites*, Oxford University Press, Oxford

Szporluk, R. (1973). 'Nationalities and the Russian problem in the USSR: an historical outline', *Journal of International Affairs* 27, 22–40

Talmon, J. (1960). *Political messianism, the romantic phase*, Secker and Warburg, London

Taylor, D. and Yapp, M. (eds.) (1979). *Political identity in South Asia*, Centre of South Asian Studies, SOAS, Curzon Press, London and Dublin, and Humanities Press Inc., Atlantic Highlands, N.J.

Tcherikover, V. (1970). *Hellenistic civilisation and the Jews*, Athenaeum, New York

Bibliography

Thaden, E. C. (1964). *Conservative nationalism in nineteenth century Russia*, University of Washington Press, Seattle

Thomas, C. J. and Williams, C. H. (1978). 'Language and nationalism in Wales: a case study', *Ethnic and Racial Studies* 1/2, 235–58

Thrasher, P. (1972). *Pasquale Paoli*, Constable, London

Thrupp, S. (ed.) (1962). *Millennial dreams in action*, Mouton, The Hague

Thürer, G. (1970). *Free and Swiss*, Oswald Wolff, London

Tibawi, A. L. (1963). 'The American missionaries in Beirut and Butrus al-Bustani', *St Antony's Papers* 16, 137–82

Tillion, G. (1958). *Algeria, the realities*, Eyre and Spottiswoode, London

Tilly, C. (ed.) (1975). *The formation of national states in Western Europe*, Princeton University Press, Princeton

Tipton, L. (ed.) (1972). *Nationalism in the Middle Ages*, Holt, Rinehart and Winston, New York

Tobias, H. J. and Woodhouse, C. E. (eds.) (1969). *Minorities and politics*, University of New Mexico Press, Albuquerque

Van den Berghe, P. (ed.) (1965). *Africa, social problems of change and conflict*, Chandler Publishing Company, San Francisco

(1967). *Race and racism*, Wiley, New York

(1978). 'Race and ethnicity: a sociobiological perspective', *Ethnic and Racial Studies* 1/4, 401–11

Verdery, K. (1979). 'Internal colonialism in Austria-Hungary', *Ethnic and Racial Studies* 2/3, 378–99

Walch, P. (1967). 'Charles Rollin and early neo-classicism', *Art Bulletin* XLIX, 123–7

Wallerstein, I. (1965). 'Elites in French-speaking West Africa', *Journal of Modern African Studies* 3, 1–33

(ed.) (1966). *Social change: The colonial situation*, Wiley, New York

(1974). *The modern world system*, Academic Press, New York

Warburton, T. R. (1976). 'Nationalism and language in Switzerland and Canada', in A. D. Smith (1976)

Wark, R. R. (1954). 'A Note on James Barry and Edmund Burke', *Journal of the Warburg and Courtauld Institutes* 17, 382–5

Webb, K. (1977). *The growth of nationalism in Scotland*, Penguin, Harmondsworth

Weber, E. (1979). *Peasants into Frenchmen, The modernisation of rural France, 1870–1914*, Chatto and Windus, London

Weber, M. (1947). *From Max Weber, essays in sociology*, ed. H. Gerth and C. W. Mills, Routledge and Kegan Paul, London

(1952). *Ancient Judaism*, Free Press, New York

(1964). *The theory of social and economic organisation*, ed. T. Parsons, Free Press, New York

(1965). *The sociology of religion*, trans E. Fischoff, Methuen, London

(1968). 'Ethnic groups', in *Economy and Society*, ed. G. Roth and C. Wittich, Bedminster Press, New York, vol. I, ch. 5

Weiss, J. (1977). *Conservatism in Europe, 1770–1945*, Thames and Hudson, London

Bibliography

Welch, C. (1966). *Dream of unity: Pan-Africanism and political unification in West Africa*, Cornell University Press, Ithaca

Wertheim, W. F. (1958). 'Religious reform movements in South and Southeast Asia', *Archives de Sociologie des Religions* 9, 53–62

Wheeler, G. (1964). *The modern history of Soviet Central Asia*, Weidenfeld and Nicolson, London

Whitaker, A. P. (1962). *Nationalism in Latin America, past and present*, University of Florida Press, Gainsville, Fla.

Whitaker, A. P. and Jordan, D. C. (1966). *Nationalism in contemporary Latin America*, Free Press, New York

Williams, C. H. (1977). 'Non-violence and the development of the Welsh Language Society, 1962–1974', *Welsh History Review* 8, 426–55

Wilson, H. S. (ed.) (1969). *The origins of West African nationalism*, Macmillan, London

Wind, E. (1938). 'The revolution in history painting', *Journal of the Warburg and Courtauld Institutes* 2, 116–27

Wolf, E. R. (1973). *Peasant wars of the twentieth century*, Faber and Faber, London

Woolf, S. (ed.) (1969). *The Italian Risorgimento*, Longman, London and Harlow

Worsley, P. (1964). *The Third World*, Weidenfeld and Nicolson, London

(1970). 'The concept of Populism', in Gellner and Ionescu (1970)

Young, C. M. (1975). *Politics in the Congo*, Princeton University Press, Princeton

Zartmann, W. (1963). *Government and politics in Northern Africa*, Praeger, New York

(1965). 'Characteristics of developing foreign policies', in W. H. Lewis (1965)

Zeine, Z. N. (1958). *Arab–Turkish relations and the emergence of Arab nationalism*, Khayats, Beirut

Zenkovsky, S. (1953). 'A century of Tatar revival', *American Slavic and European Review* 14, 15–41

(1960). *Pan-Turkism and Islam in Russia*, Harvard University Press, Cambridge, Mass.

Zernatto, G. (1944). 'Nation: The history of a word', *Review of Politics* 6, 351–66

Znaniecki, F. (1952). *Modern nationalities*, University of Illinois Press, Urbana, Illinois

Zolberg, A. (1964). *One-party government in the Ivory Coast*, Princeton University Press, Princeton

Index

237

Index